City Spaces – Tourist Places

City Spaces – Tourist Places: Urban Tourism Precincts

Bruce Hayllar, Tony Griffin and Deborah Edwards

ELSEVIER

AMSTERDAM • BOSTON • HEIDELBERG • LONDON •
NEW YORK • OXFORD • PARIS • SAN DIEGO •
SAN FRANCISCO • SYDNEY • TOKYO

Butterworth-Heinemann is an imprint of Elsevier

Butterworth-Heinemann is an imprint of Elsevier
Linacre House, Jordan Hill, Oxford OX2 8DP, UK
30 Corporate Drive, Suite 400, Burlington, MA 01803, USA

First edition 2008

British Library Cataloguing in Publication Data
A catalogue record for this book is available from the British Library

Library of Congress Cataloging-in-Publication Data
A catalog record for this book is available from the Library of Congress

ISBN: 978-0-7506-8195-7

For information on all Butterworth-Heinemann publications
visit our web site at books.elsevier.com

Typeset by Charon Tec Ltd (A Macmillan Company), Chennai, India
www.charontec.com

Printed and bound in Great Britain
08 09 10   10 9 8 7 6 5 4 3 2 1

Contents

Contents

Preface

This book evolved from discussions between the three editors concerning the need to more formally document the research work they were undertaking in precincts. It seemed like a good idea at the time!

However, in thinking through our own work, the rich material that preceded it and that which was happening contemporaneously, we reasoned that it would be more productive to engage with other authors rather than trying to capture the whole field, in an ultimately limited way, ourselves. We were also conscious of the need to make the material 'research driven'.

Each of the contributing authors to this book has attempted to honour the intent of the editors and we thank them for their diligence and timeliness. As editors we also wanted to ensure the overall quality of the manuscripts and therefore subjected all chapters to blind external review in addition to our own editorial processes. The latter has been particularly important to ensure that the book has coherence, and a logical flow in the development of ideas – in our view a limitation of many edited collections.

Bruce Hayllar
Tony Griffin
Deborah Edwards

Sydney 2008

List of Contributors

Gregory J. Ashworth, PhD

Professor of Heritage Management and Urban Tourism
Department of Planning, Rijksuniversiteit Groningen, Netherlands

Gregory is a leading heritage academic and author of numerous books, journal articles and consultancy reports. These include the critically acclaimed Dissonant Heritage: the management of the past as a resource in conflict (with John Tunbridge, 1996). His most recent work is *Senses of Place: Senses of Time* (with Brian Graham, 2005).

Yasminah Beebeejaun, PhD

Lecturer in Spatial Planning
School of Environment and Development, University of Manchester, UK

Yasminah's research focuses on relationships between urban planning and social justice. She is particularly interested in how minority ethnic groups' identities and interests are constructed through participatory processes. Her recent work has focused on the masterplanning of Sheffield and development of Chinatown's in London and Chicago.

Graham Brooks, BArch (Hons), MBEnv, BCons

Chairman
ICOMOS International Cultural Tourism Committee, Australia

Graham Brooks is a specialist in Cultural Heritage and Cultural Tourism Management. He is the Managing Director of an Architectural Heritage Consultancy practice based in Sydney, Australia. His work in cultural tourism has included extensive site investigations, and policy preparation for best practice tourism management at heritage places.

Graham Brown, PhD
Professor of Tourism Management
School of Management, University of South Australia, City West Campus, Adelaide, SA

Graham teaches tourism marketing and is Head of the Tourism and Leisure group at UniSA. He has research interests related to tourist decision-making and behaviour and recent studies have examined these issues in the context of wine tourism, cycle tourism and education tourism.

Simon Darcy, MEnvPl, PhD
Associate Professor
School of Leisure, Sport and Tourism, University of Technology, Sydney

Simon's research and teaching expertise is in the policy, planning and management of sport, tourism and diversity. He currently holds research grants investigating organizational responses to accessible tourism, sports management practices and protected area visitor data systems.

Deborah Edwards, PhD
Sustainable Tourism Co-operative Research Centre: Senior Research Fellow in Urban Tourism
School of Leisure, Sport and Tourism, University of Technology, Sydney

Deborah's interests are in sustainable tourism management, urban attractions, tourism planning, volunteers in tourism attractions and the impacts of events.

Tony Griffin BA(Geog) Grad Dip Urbstud, Grad Dip Tourism Man
Senior Lecturer
School of Leisure, Sport and Tourism, University of Technology, Sydney

Tony's professional background is in urban and environmental planning. In recent years his research has focused on understanding the nature and quality of visitor experiences in cities, national parks and wine tourism.

Bruce Hayllar, PhD
Associate Professor, Head
School of Leisure, Sport and Tourism, University of Technology, Sydney

Bruce has a particular interest in the experience of people in learning and leisure environments and has applied his interest in phenomenology to inform this understanding. His most recent work has been a two-year national project examining the experience of tourists in precincts.

Kirsten Holmes, PhD
Research Fellow
Curtin University of Technology, Perth

Kirsten's research encompasses various aspects of cultural tourism and leisure studies. She is particularly interested in the role of culture within urban regeneration and has recently completed work on notions of sustainable leisure.

Ian Kelly, MA, BEd, MA
Adjunct Senior Lecturer
School of Management, University of South Australia, Adelaide

Ian Kelly is a retired Tourism educator with an academic background in Urban Social Geography. He has maintained involvement with teaching and research, and current responsibilities include coordination of the International Institute for Peace through Tourism Educators Network and production of the annual Australian Regional Tourism Handbook.

Chris Krolikowski, BMgmt, MBus (Tour)
PhD Scholar
School of Management, University of South Australia

Chris is a PhD candidate at the University of South Australia in Adelaide. His research investigates purposefully developed urban tourism precincts in the context of conscious place-making and tourist experiences of place.

Robert Maitland, MA (Cantab.), MA, MBA, MRTPI, FTS

Reader in Tourism and Director
The Centre for Tourism Research, University of Westminster, London, UK

Robert's research focuses on tourism policy and development in major cities, on which he has written extensively and acted as a government adviser. His current research is on local tourism policy, and tourism in national capitals and world cities, particularly London where he is examining visitors' role in the creation of new tourist areas and their perceptions of them.

Peter Newman, PhD

Professor
School of Architecture and the Built Environment, University of Westminster, London, UK

Peter Newman is Professor of Comparative Urban Planning. He has written widely on European cities, governance and planning. Recent research has included studies of urban regeneration through tourism and cultural projects and of the impacts of mega events on city politics.

Munir Morad, PhD

Professor and Head of Department
Department of Urban, Environment and Leisure Studies, London South Bank University, UK

Munir graduated from the University of London in 1986 with a PhD in geography, and has worked in the UK (Wales, Kingston) and New Zealand (Waikato). His teaching and research portfolios span the meeting points between environmental management and planning, research methodology and (more recently) sustainability appraisal of urban forms.

Brent W. Ritchie, PhD

Director
Centre for Tourism Research, University of Canberra, Australia

Brent's research interests are related to urban and capital city tourism: including visitor behaviour, economic impact and school excursion tourism in these settings. He is the co-convenor of a special interest group on capital city tourism hosted by ATLAS (Association for Tourism and Leisure Education).

Glen Searle, PhD

Senior Lecturer
School of the Built Environment, University of Technology, Sydney

Glen is the Chief Editor, for the Urban Policy and Research Journal and is a Member of the NSW Policy Committee, Planning Institute of Australia. His research interests are in institutional analysis and political economy of contemporary urban planning, regional economic development and employment planning and the spatial dynamics of advanced economy services.

Martin Selby, PhD

Senior Lecturer
Centre for Tourism, Consumer and Food Studies, Liverpool John Moores University

Martin has a background in marketing and a PhD focusing on the images and experiences of urban tourism. Martin is a Fellow of the Royal Geographical Society and is a founding member of the Tourism and Leisure Consultancy Group (TLCG).

Jennie Small, PhD

Senior Lecturer
School of Leisure, Sport and Tourism, University of Technology, Sydney

With a background in Environmental Psychology, Jennie moved into the field of tourist behaviour with specific research interest in gender, age, disability, the life-course and embodiment. Her most recent work is the study of the tourist experiences of people with vision impairment, supported by the Co-operative Research Centre in

Sustainable Tourism. She takes a Critical Tourism approach to tourist behaviour.

Costas Spirou, PhD
Professor
College of Arts and Sciences, National-Louis University, Chicago

Costas has focused his research on how cities in the United States utilize cultural policy and tourism to revive themselves following de-industrialization and the economic restructuring of the 1960s and 1970s. He is currently working on a book (with Dennis Judd) on how over the past 20 years Chicago has concentrated its efforts on reimaging itself as a tourist city.

Duncan Tyler, PhD
Head of Tourism, Leisure and Hospitality
Department of Urban, Environment and Leisure Studies, London South Bank University, London, UK

Duncan's research interests are based in both urban tourism, on which he has edited one volume and published several papers, and the politics of tourism policy development. These two aspects come together in his study of the nature and role of tourism in city centre regeneration.

I
Foundations

1

Urban Tourism Precincts: Engaging with the Field

Bruce Hayllar, Tony Griffin and Deborah Edwards

Introduction

Today I traveled 40 kilometres into the city from my home on the outskirts of Sydney, Australia. I came to the city to meet the other editors
of the book and we have chosen a café in *The Rocks*, one of Sydney's
most visited tourist sites, for a working lunch (in reality, probably
more lunch than work).

I came in by train and alighted at Wynyard Station for the short walk
to our meeting place. Turning northward towards Sydney Harbour along
George Street, one of the city's major thoroughfares, I am immediately
surrounded by the clatter and bustle of the city. As I look up, concrete
and glass towers dominate the skyline. At street level, pedestrians compete with buses and cars on what are quite narrow and congested streets.
In addition to the office towers, various retail outlets – boutiques, cafes,
restaurants, travel agents, jewellers, 'designer' outlets and the occasional
bar – are dotted along the street. When I think about this cacophony of
architecture, people and commercial enterprise, what does it tell me
about Sydney? The answer is brief – very little really. It seems to me that

many postmodern cities of the 'New World' are largely distinguished by their lack of distinctiveness. Indeed as Bridge and Watson (2000) observed, these cities typically have more in common with each other than with their surrounding hinterland!

Further down George Street I pass a large five star hotel and observe the signs of morning tourist activity: tour buses disgorging eager patrons; the first of the now ubiquitous 'follow me' flags being waved and post-cards being browsed by interested visitors outside a small fast food outlet. Tourists share this space with city workers, as they do with the uniformed junior school children with their bright red hats who have also arrived by bus. Approximately 8–10 years of age, the children are kept in some semblance of order by their teachers as they head towards the Opera House for a weekday matinee performance. A small group of seniors ambling along the waterfront cast their eyes knowingly towards this gaggle of small and excited faces. This human scene is briefly interrupted by the 'beep-beep' of a delivery truck as it reverses out of a loading bay.

At nearby Circular Quay, the ferry wharves are a hive of activity as suited businesspeople head to their offices after a soporific trip from various points around the harbour. Sightseeing cruise boats compete for space with the workaday ferries, and the departing pleasure seekers jostle with the arriving commuters. Briefly distracted by these scenes, I now move with more purpose towards our meeting place. As I cross underneath the large steel railway overpass at the northern end of George Street, a large banner proclaims *Welcome to The Rocks*. Suitably greeted, I move on.

As I pass under the bridge and enter The Rocks, elements of the scenes just described transform: the road narrows; concrete and glass towers give way to the sandstone and slate of the 19th century buildings that dominate the area; the frenetic goal-directed pace of the city gives way to more relaxed, seemingly aimless activity; visitors browse the shops or take their second coffee; the phalanx that marched off from the tour coach at Circular Quay is now dispersed and engaged in less organized endeavours and commercial and retail activity is dominated by visitor-related services. The collective effect of this change in architecture, scale, tempo and visitor activity, creates a markedly different existential 'feel' to the city experience. This is clearly a different place.

As we sat down for our meeting, my colleagues and I talked of our short urban journeys to The Rocks that morning. Their observations were little different to mine; as were the issues that we raised about our collective experiences. In our discussions, questions such as the following were raised:

- How well do we understand the interactions of tourists and locals in urban settings?
- What aspects of these interactions might be positive or negative?
- What role do places like The Rocks play in the life of the city generally and the tourist experience specifically?
- How might urban design and the built environment impact upon or shape this experience?
- How do tourists use these urban spaces?
- What role do public authorities, planning agencies, commercial investors and attraction managers play in creating, overseeing and monitoring the ongoing management and development of urban tourist spaces?
- What might be the political dynamics of creating and managing public space when it becomes contested by competing interests?
- What benefits – social, economic, cultural and psychological – might accrue as a result of these spaces being developed? What about negative impacts?
- And, in thinking back to my earlier encounter in the city, do tourist spaces provide cities with places where visitors can have distinctive experiences?

It was in thinking through both the positive and problematic responses to these questions that the idea and framework for this book emerged. Overall, we shared a collective belief that it was places like The Rocks that were at the core of the urban tourism experience. Tourism, from both supply and demand perspectives, was not dispersed evenly and seamlessly throughout the city but rather was concentrated into relatively small, quite distinctive geographic areas – precincts – and the tourist's experience was most commonly one of moving between these precincts in search of the city's highlights. Precincts were thus fundamental to understanding the phenomenon of urban tourism, but

5

on reflection we appeared to know little about these places and what made them work, for tourists and other stakeholders within the city.

This book, then, is primarily concerned with making some tentative steps towards filling this gap in our knowledge about a significant, but relatively neglected aspect of tourism. To further establish the book's focus, the remainder of this chapter has three purposes. The first of these is to position the 'tourism precinct' in the context of urban tourism. The second is to briefly examine the precinct from a range of theoretical perspectives. Finally, the chapter concludes by outlining the themes and structure of the book and poses a series of questions that guide its overall direction and intent.

The Urban Tourism Context

Urban environments have for many years been amongst the most significant of all tourist destinations. As Karski (1990) notes:

> People with the means and inclination to do so have been drawn to towns and cities just to visit and experience a multiplicity of things to see and do. Pilgrims in the 14th century were urban tourists visiting cities like Canterbury. The historic Grand Tour of Europe, in the 18th and 19th centuries was essentially an urban experience for the rich, taking in more spectacular towns and cities, usually regional and national capitals. These were the melting pots of national culture, art, music, literature and of course magnificent architecture and urban design. It was the concentration, variety, and quality of these activities and attributes … that created their attraction and put certain towns and cities on the tourism map of the day (Karski, 1990: 15).

The attraction of cities as tourist destinations, so ably described by Karski from an historical perspective, has continued into contemporary times. Law (1996) argues that cities have retained their central focus as a tourist destination because of their inherent scale, locational attributes and opportunities for diverse experiences. For example, they attract friends and relatives as they have naturally large populations and they draw visitors to their attractions because these are often much better developed than in other types of destination areas. As a consequence of their economic significance, cities often have large stocks of accommodation to serve business travellers which is underutilized at weekends and in summer holiday periods. Their related transport services and infrastructure such as airports and rail connections makes the destination accessible for both tourist and commercial purposes. In terms of the tourist experience, the diversity of a city provides opportunities for a range of visitors: older and better educated groups may be attracted by the cultural heritage of a city, while young people may be drawn to the entertainment, nightlife and major sporting events. For many it is not specific attractions but rather the experience of being in a city – the bright lights, the colour and movement, the atmosphere – that represents its fundamental appeal.

Urban areas offer social, cultural, physical and aesthetic stages upon which tourist activity can be played out. However, these are stages shared with others who are the majority – it is the aesthetic and culture of the city and its residents which greet the visitor. This complex urban 'form' shapes experience as visitors interact with: attractions and infrastructure generally developed for non-tourism purposes; local residents (and commuters) who are typically the majority users of these attractions and infrastructure; and the economic activity of the city which is largely unrelated to tourism.

Precincts in the Urban Tourism Context

Ashworth (1989, 2003) was one of the first to identify the city as a significant setting for tourist activity. Prior to this relatively recent recognition, cities, his argument would suggest, were largely ignored by researchers despite their overwhelming importance for tourism. This historic legacy notwithstanding, there is an emerging, more contemporary body of work that has started to redress this imbalance (see Judd & Fainstein, 1999; Hoffman et al., 2003; Page & Hall, 2003). However, as research has started to better understand the phenomenon of urban tourism and the city as a tourist destination, further questions arise about the nature of the urban experience and, in particular, the use of specific spaces in the urban experience of visitors. While the city and its services provide the 'overlay' for urban tourist activity, in most urban destinations tourist visitation tends to be concentrated rather than dispersed. These points of concentration may include iconic sights, shopping areas, landmark cultural institutions or places of historical significance. However, where a number of attractions of similar or differing types aggregate alongside a range of tourism-related services, these areas take on a particular spatial, cultural, social and economic identity – now commonly (but not universally) recognized as a tourist precinct. As Stevenson (2003: 73) observed:

> *Cities divide into geographically discrete precincts which rarely conform to impose administrative or political boundaries. Rather, they form around the activities of commerce, sociability, domesticity, and/or collective identity. The resulting precincts have a vitality and a 'look' that marks each as unique.*

The recognition and debates on nomenclature surrounding these precincts have evolved over a considerable period of time. Stansfield and Rickert (1970) used the term Recreational Business District (RBD) to describe areas 'characterized by a distinctive array of pedestrian, tourist-oriented retail facilities and [which is] separated spatially as well as functionally from the other business districts' (p. 213). As a response to this, and other spatial models, Getz (1993a) proposed the label Tourism Business District to focus more on the functions of these areas. The Tourist-Historic City model suggested by Ashworth (1988), and Ashworth and Tunbridge (1990) provided significant insight into the development and management of the tourist-historic city but its application to urban tourism more generally is limited. Other terms used include: Consumption Compounds (Mullins, 1991); Specialized Tourism Zones (Weaver, 1993); Tourist Districts (Pearce, 1998) or 'tourist areas'Maitland and Newman (2004). McDonnell and Darcy (1998) in their comparative study of Fiji and Bali, appear to have been amongst the first researchers in tourism to formally use the term *tourism precinct* but not exclusively within an urban context.

Debates around terminology and what each encapsulates have been ongoing. However, for our purposes we have adopted the term 'urban tourism precinct' and used a definition that has spatial, functional and embedded psycho-social dimensions. The latter dimension is suggestive of the view that one 'psychologically' engages with a precinct. This 'movement' is also recognition of how space, people, activity and architecture dialectically interact and shape the experience of the precinct visitor – an experience that may be qualitatively different for each of them. This theme is developed further by Selby, Hayllar and Griffin (see Chapter 9 in this volume). For our purposes a precinct has been defined as:

> *A distinctive geographic area within a larger urban area, characterised by a concentration of tourist-related land uses, activities and visitation, with fairly definable boundaries. Such precincts generally possess a distinctive character by virtue of their mixture of activities and land uses, such as restaurants, attractions and nightlife, their physical or architectural fabric, especially the dominance of historic buildings, or their connection to a particular cultural or ethnic group within the city. Such characteristics also exist in combination. Hayllar and Griffin, 2005: 517*

Studying Precincts

The study of urban tourism precincts has traditionally been approached from a geographic or urban planning perspective (Stansfield & Rickert, 1970; Wall & Sinnott, 1980; Ashworth & de Haan, 1985; Law, 1985; Jansen-Verbeke, 1986; Meyer-Arendt, 1990). During the 1990s, while a major emphasis on a planning and geographic approach was evident (Burtenshaw et al., 1991; Getz, 1993a, b; Getz et al., 1994; Fagence, 1995; Pearce, 1998) other disciplinary perspectives began to emerge. An analysis of tourism precincts and their role in the lives of both locals and tourists from a sociological perspective was included in work by Mullins (1991), Conforti (1996) and Chang et al. (1996). McDonnell and Darcy (1998) raised the notion of tourism precincts functioning as part of the overall marketing strategy of destinations, while Judd (1995) developed ideas around the economic development role of precincts.

In respect of economic development there have also been studies of what Judd and Fainstein (1999: 36) described as 'pure tourist spaces' which have been carved out of urban decay. The festival marketplace (Rowe & Stevenson, 1994) or the revitalized waterfront development (Craig-Smith, 1995) such as Harborplace (Baltimore) and Darling Harbour (Sydney) are typical of the genre. In the case of Baltimore, Judd and Fainstein (1999) argue that Harborplace is an enclave that separates and 'protects' visitors from the crime, poverty and urban decay of the 'other' Baltimore – the physical manifestation of the 'tourist bubble' (Urry, 1990). Other critical perspectives include those examining the politics of precinct development (Hall & Selwood, 1995), Searle (see Chapter 10 in this volume) and those offering cultural critiques (Huxley, 1991).

The extant research has also examined the activity of the tourist within the precinct such as their 'pathways' through precincts, expenditure patterns and a range of socio-demographic characteristics (e.g. Masberg & Silverman, 1996; Beeho & Prentice, 1997; McIntosh & Prentice, 1999; Wickens, 2002).

More recent approaches to understanding tourist experience have focused on examining the key attributes of a place and how these contribute to the quality of experience. Maitland and Newman (2004: 339), for example, sought to understand the desired experiences of those who are 'tempted to leave the well-worn paths and 'discover' new areas'. Drawing on Canter's Metaphor for Place (Canter, 1977), Montgomery (2004) argued that a 'cultural quarter' (a specific type of precinct) must possess an appropriate combination of activity, built form and meaning, and within this framework discusses specific attributes, for example, a strong night-time economy, active street frontages and legibility, that contribute most to their success.

Hayllar and Griffin (2005) employed a phenomenological approach to exploring tourist experiences in The Rocks precinct of Sydney and subsequently in the nearby Darling Harbour (Hayllar & Griffin, 2006). The same authors later employed a modified, semi-structured interview approach, still based on phenomenology but somewhat simplified and more focused, in precincts in a number of other Australian cities (Griffin & Hayllar, 2006). All these related studies concluded that a distinctive sense of place was fundamental to the tourist experience, but this was derived from different specific attributes in different precincts. In a similarly conducted study of two precincts in London, Maitland (2006) reinforced the importance of distinctiveness of place, and indeed argued that the serial production of standardized tourism zones would lead to placeless and inherently unappealing environments for tourists.

City Spaces and Tourist Places

The study of tourist precincts is a study of particular space(s) in the city. Some of these spaces, particularly in large cities, form part of the everyday urban fabric where tourists and locals share communal space for purposes embedded into the urban lexicon of experience, such as a hub for transport, a location for shopping or a venue for dining. Other precincts purposively stand apart from the everyday experience of the city with the potential to create *Fordist* type reproductions of space (Judd, 1995). It is likely that most 'tourism' precincts locate themselves somewhere between the two and each have the potential to 'create' experience for their visitors – what we have called elsewhere, the existential 'feel' of the space (Hayllar & Griffin, 2005).

Given the title of this book, some consideration of the notions of space and place is appropriate at this point. The notion of what constitutes 'space' (and 'place') is contested (see Relph, 1976; Lefebvre, 1991; Suvantola, 2002; Creswell, 2004). Couclelis (1992) in Suvantola (2002) identified five different types of spaces: mathematical, physical, socio-economic, behavioural and experiential. Mathematical space reflects ideas relating to the precise measurement of relations in space – size, distance, scale and the like. Physical space is more labile and considers the entire universe as 'space'. However, physical space has a relation to mathematical space as its conceptualization is both our common sense understanding of space (the 'space' around us), and it is positional or relativist – we are located in a particular space relative to other spaces. Socio-economic space is concerned with the spatial analysis of regions and the socio-economic phenomena embedded within them. Here, too, space is quantifiable by the comparative value of space according to, (e.g., its utility, position and location). Behavioural space focuses on the ways in which we perceive and use space. In understanding this type of space, the concern is with investigating the ways behaviour is affected, through our perceptions, when the space changes. For example, a reconfiguration in the aspect of a precinct may lead to changes in behaviour. Here the emphasis is on measuring or analysing the impact of such change – a potentially problematic construct.

Finally, experiential space is the use of space as lived and experienced. Of the five different types of space, it is perhaps the least quantifiable yet arguably the most important in respect of the tourist experience. It is within the experiential realm that meaning is applied to space through our experiencing of it. Theoretically, space imbued with meaning becomes place. As Tuan (1977: 6) elegantly notes:

> *What begins as undifferentiated space becomes place as we get to know it better and endow it with value .... The ideas 'space' and 'place' require each other for definition. From the security and stability of place we are aware of the openness, freedom, and threat of space, and vice versa. Furthermore, if we think of space as that which allows movement, then place is pause; each pause in movement makes it possible for location to be turned into place.*

City spaces are a pastiche of conflicting and complementary forms. They are modern and ageing. They are a part of, and apart from, the city. They are confined and open, colourful and plain, commonplace and unique. They are organic and highly structured. They serve different purposes and perform a range of functional roles. However, underpinning these diverse expressions of a distinctly organized city space, is their fundamental human dimension. They are human spaces, where visitors and locals 'create' places for civil interaction – to meet, eat, amble, spectate, shop, view or to simply pass time.

Clearly, however, some precincts are more 'successful' than others in fulfilling the roles and functions ascribed to them. Likewise they differ in their effectiveness to create meaningful experiences or to be financially sustainable. Why do some precincts 'work' and others fall into a state of disrepair? Why are some abandoned at night while others are 24-hour places of human activity? Why do some precinct architects choose serial reproduction over unique local designs? Why do governance structures fail in some places yet are highly effective in others? The remainder of this book seeks to shed some light on these and other questions surrounding the evolution, development and management of the urban tourism precinct.

Looking Forward: Organizing Themes and Structure

The book is organized around three themes. The first theme we have labeled *Foundations*. This section comprises four chapters that provide the reader with some organizing frameworks – descriptive, theoretical and analytical – for their initial consideration of the urban tourism precinct. Some of the key questions that these foundational chapters set out to answer include:

- How have city spaces evolved into tourism precincts over time?
- How and why have some city spaces been deliberately developed into precincts?
- How might we categorize precincts into some form of workable typology?
- What functions or roles do precincts perform, particularly in relation to the tourist's experience of a city?
- What contribution do differing disciplinary perspectives bring to our understanding of urban tourism precincts?
- Does a disciplinary perspective limit our understanding or are there more meta-theoretical positions that would aid our understanding?

The second theme, *Key Themes and Issues*, is the focal point of the book. These seven chapters 'unpack' existing knowledge of urban tourism precincts and provide substantial insight into their development, structure and form. Some of the key questions these chapters set out to answer include:

- What are the critical design elements of an effective precinct?
- Does precinct form and structure shape behaviour?

13

- What is the impact of distinctive architectural forms on the precinct experience?
- How important is ongoing regeneration and renewal?
- What are the significant economic impacts of precinct development?
- What costs and benefits accrue to both visitors and the local community?
- How might we understand the experience of the precinct from the perspective of the visitor and local?
- Are there any common attributes of a precinct experience?
- Are visitor–host relationships contested, mutually beneficial or benign?
- Do different political approaches to development deliver similar outcomes?
- How are potentially diverse stakeholder relationships effectively managed?

The final section of the book focuses on the theme of *Precincts in Practice*. Essentially this theme is concerned with how we can effectively plan, design, manage and market urban tourism precincts. After an introductory chapter that outlines the nature and key challenges associated with these tasks, this section comprises a series of case studies drawn from the United Kingdom, The Netherlands, Australia, Vietnam and Portugal. The purpose of these case studies is to illustrate how these practical challenges can be addressed in a range of different cultural and political contexts.

References

Ashworth, G.J., & de Haan, T.Z. (1985). *The Tourist-Historic City: A Model and Initial Application in Norwich. U.K.* Groningen University, The Netherlands: Field Studies Series, No. 8, Geographical Institute, University of Groningen.

Ashworth, G.J. (1988). Marketing the historic city for tourism. In B. Goodall, & G.J. Ashworth (Eds.), *Marketing in the Tourism Industry: The Promotion of Destination Regions* (pp. 162–175). London: Croon Helm.

Ashworth, G.J. (1989). Urban tourism: an imbalance in attention. In C.P. Cooper (Ed.), *Progress in Tourism, Recreation and Hospitality Management: Volume 1* (pp. 33–54), London: Belhaven.

Ashworth, G.J. (2003). Urban tourism: still an imbalance in attention?. In C. Cooper (Ed.), *Classic Reviews in Tourism* (pp. 143–163). Clevedon: Channel View Publications.

Ashworth, G.J., & Tunbridge, J.E. (2000). *The Tourist-Historic City: Retrospect and Prospect of Managing the Heritage City* (2nd edn.). Amsterdam: Pergamon.

Beeho, A.J., & Prentice, R.C. (1997). Conceptualizing the experiences of heritage tourists: a case study of New Lanark World Heritage Village. *Tourism Management*, 18(2), 75–87.

Bridge, G., & Watson, S. (2000). City economies. In G. Bridge, & S. Watson (Eds.), *A Companion to the City*. Oxford: Blackwell.

Burtenshaw, D., Bateman, M., & Ashworth, G. (1991). *The European City*. London: David Fulton Publishers.

Canter, D. (1977). *The Psychology of Place*. London: Architectural Press.

Chang, C., Milne, T.S., Fallon, D., & Pohlmann, C. (1996). Urban heritage tourism: the global-local nexus. *Annals of Tourism Research*, 23(2), 284–305.

Conforti, J.M. (1996). Ghettos as tourism attractions. *Annals of Tourism Research*, 23(4), 830–842.

Craig-Smith, S.J. (1995). The role of tourism in inner-harbor redevelopment: a multinational perspective. In S.J. Craig-Smith, & M. Fagence (Eds.), *Recreation and Tourism as a Catalyst for Urban Waterfront Redevelopment: An International Survey* (pp. 15–35). Westport CT: Praeger.

Creswell, T. (2004). *Place: A Short Introduction*. Carlton: Blackwell Publishing.

Fagence, M. (1995). Episodic progress toward a grand design: waterside redevelopment of Brisbane's South Bank. In S.J. Craig-Smith, & M. Fagence (Eds.), *Recreation and Tourism as a Catalyst for Urban Waterfront Redevelopment: An International Survey* (pp. 71–90). Westport CT: Praeger.

Getz, D. (1993a). Planning for tourism business districts. *Annals of Tourism Research*, 20(1), 58–60.

Getz, D. (1993b). Tourist shopping villages: development and planning strategies. *Tourism Management*, 14(1), 15–26.

Getz, D., Joncas, D., & Kelly, M. (1994). Tourist shopping villages in the Calgary region. *Journal of Tourism Studies*, 5(1), 2–15.

Griffin, T., & Hayllar, B. (2006). Historic waterfronts as tourism precincts: an experiential perspective. *Tourism and Hospitality Research*, 7(1), 3–16.

Hall, C.M., & Selwood, J.H. (1995). Event tourism and the creation of a postindustrial portscape: the case of Fremantle and the 1987 America's Cup. In S.J. Craig-Smith, & M. Fagence (Eds.), *Recreation and Tourism as a Catalyst for Urban Waterfront Redevelopment: An International Survey* (pp. 105–114). Westport CT: Praeger.

Hayllar, B., & Griffin, T. (2005). The precinct experience: a phenomenological approach. *Tourism Management*, 26(4), 517–528.

Hayllar, B., & Griffin, T. (2006). A tale of two precincts: a phenomenological analysis. Presented at *Cutting Edge Research in Tourism – New Directions, Challenges and Applications* (CD-ROM). University of Surrey, UK, 6–9 June.

Hoffman, L.M., Fainstein, S.S., & Judd, D.R. (2003). *Cities and Visitors: Regulating People, Markets, and City Space*. Malden MA: Blackwell Publishing.

Huxley, M. (1991). Darling Harbour and the immobilisation of the spectacle. In P. Carroll, K. Donohue, M. McGovern, & J. McMillen (Eds.), *Tourism in Australia* (pp. 141–152). Sydney: Harcourt Brace Jovanovich.

Jansen-Verbeke, M. (1986). Inner city tourism: resources, tourists, promoters. *Annals of Tourism Research*, 13(1), 79–100.

Judd, D.R. (1995). Promoting tourism in US cities. *Tourism Management*, 16(3), 175–187.

Judd, D.R., & Fainstein, S.S. (1999). *The Tourist City*. New Haven: Yale University Press.

Karski, A. (1990). Urban tourism: a key to urban regeneration? *The Planner*, 76(13), 15–17.

Law, C.M. (1996). *Tourism in Major Cities*. London: International Thomson Business Press.

Law, C.-M. (1985). *Urban Tourism: Selected British Case Studies.* Salford, UK: Urban Tourism Project Working Paper No. 1, Department of Geography, University of Salford.

Lefebvre, H. (1991). *The Production of Space.* Oxford: Blackwell Publishing.

Maitland, R. (2006). Tourists, conviviality and distinctive tourism areas in London. Presented at *Cutting Edge Research in Tourism – New Directions, Challenges and Applications* (CD-ROM). University of Surrey, UK, 6–9 June.

Maitland, R., & Newman, P. (2004). Developing tourism on the fringe of central London. *International Journal of Tourism Research*, 6(5), 339–348.

Masberg, B.A., & Silverman, L.-H. (1996). Visitor experiences at heritage sites. *Journal of Travel Research*, Spring, 20–25.

McDonnell, I., & Darcy, S. (1998). Tourism precincts: a factor in Fiji's fall from favour and the rise of Bali. *Journal of Vacation Marketing*, 4(4), 353–367.

McIntosh, A.J., & Prentice, R.C. (1999). Affirming authenticity: consuming cultural heritage. *Annals of Tourism Research*, 26(3), 589–612.

Meyer-Arendt, K. (1990). Recreational business districts in the Gulf of Mexico seaside resorts. *Journal of Cultural Geography*, 11, 39–55.

Montgomery, J. (2004). Cultural quarters as mechanisms for urban regeneration. Part 2: a review of four cultural quarters in the UK, Ireland and Australia. *Planning, Practice & Research*, 19(1), 3–31.

Mullins, P. (1991). Tourism urbanization. *International Journal of Urban and Regional Research*, 15(3), 326–342.

Page, S., & Hall, C.M. (2003). *Managing Urban Tourism.* Harlow: Pearson Education.

Pearce, D. (1998). Tourist districts in Paris: structure and functions. *Tourism Management*, 19(1), 49–66.

Relph, E. (1976). *Place and Placelessness.* London: Pion.

Rowe, D., & Stevenson, D. (1994). 'Provincial Paradise': urban tourism and city imaging outside the metropolis. *Australian and New Zealand Journal of Sociology*, 30(2), 178–193.

Stansfield, C., & Rickert, J. (1970). The recreational business district. *Journal of Leisure Research*, 2(2), 209–225.

Stevenson, D. (2003). *Cities and Urban Cultures.* Maidenhead: Open University Press.

Suvantola, J. (2002). *Tourist's Experience of Place.* Aldershot: Ashgate.

Tuan, Y.F. (1977). *Space and Place: The Perspective of Experience.* Minneapolis: University of Minnesota Press.

Urry, J. (1990). *The Tourist Gaze.* London: Sage.

Wall, G., & Sinnott, J. (1980). Urban recreational and cultural facilities as tourist attractions. *Canadian Geographer*, 24(1), 50–59.

Weaver, D.B. (1993). A model of urban tourism space in small Caribbean islands. *Geographical Review*, 83(2), 134–140.

Wickens, E. (2002). The sacred and the profane: a tourist typology. *Annals of Tourism Research*, 29(3), 834–851.

2

The Evolution of the Tourism Precinct

Costas Spirou

Introduction

Urban tourism precincts have evolved or been developed in a variety of ways and contexts. In many instances, tourism precincts have been created and maintained as structured responses to maximize economic development outcomes within rapidly emerging consumption settings. The construction of these precincts can be viewed as a focused reaction to the enhancement of place, contributing to the conversion of sites into significant tourism destinations. This chapter focuses on three key ideas: the political economy that gives rise to tourism precincts; the role and function of tourism precincts within the broader urban landscape; and an analysis of the dynamic nature and developmental complexities of precincts, including internal and external issues of authenticity and sustainability. By utilizing notions of continuity and change, this chapter assists in uncovering the evolving characteristics of tourism precincts and contributes to discussions on their future direction.

To provide a basis for this discussion, three tourism precincts that fall into two general contexts will be examined. One context relates to the role that tourism precincts play as an agent of urban revival in formerly industrial cities. These are unique spaces, typically controlled by government authorities but often involving public–private partnerships as a means of assisting a city to recast its image. Thus, the re-emergence of places in these cities as locales of entertainment and leisure within a post-industrial economy becomes of primary concern. Albert Dock in Liverpool (UK) and Navy Pier in Chicago (USA) are two such places that have been converted into popular visitor destinations within their respective cities. Yet, their extraordinary success has proven to be a double-edged sword. While both played a pioneering role in the urban redevelopment process and stimulated further growth in their surrounding areas, they have also faced the complexities of differentiated consumption demands. This has inadvertently applied pressure on these precincts as surrounding developments have grown and competed for the interest of visitors and locals alike. Such changes have necessitated an evolution of each precinct's presentation to maintain their uniqueness and appeal to consumers.

The other context explores the evolution of tourist precincts in light of issues of authenticity and sustainability. Plaka in Athens, Greece, is a neighbourhood adjacent to the Acropolis that typifies old Athens and is visited by millions every year. While it has evolved considerably during the past 30 years and has gained a strong tourist element, the area has also retained its strong residential heritage within rich archaeological grounds. At the same time, this district is facing the consequences of commercialism and, although it has attempted to maintain an indigenous identity unspoiled by the ever intensified pressures of a needed tourist economy, signs of 'disneyfication' abound.

Within complex urban settings, tourism precincts emerge as distinct forms of economic (re)development. It is the evolving character of these spaces that provide us with unique insights that point to the intricacies, fluidity and fragile identities of these locales. In the end, tourism precincts are situated either within a set of sophisticated policies of urban resurgence and fiscal growth, or subjected to management challenges aimed at balancing the natural and human environments.

The Context of Development: The Political Economy of Tourism Precincts

In recent years, we can observe the emergence of a developing trend in urban policy, concerned with the use of cultural capital in redefining the post-industrial city as a place of tourism and play. Cultural policy has increasingly become an integral part of economic and physical redevelopment strategies for many urban centres as public officials have employed this approach to develop new areas or regenerate ailing ones. Driven by the negative consequences of deindustrialization, decentralization and globalization, many cities have utilized these culturally based planning initiatives as a means to reposition themselves in a rapidly changing economic environment and/or to reaffirm their standing in an evolving metropolitan hierarchy. The formation of these precincts, though closely connected and shaped by pertinent local policies, also spatially necessitates reformulating their public presentation. This becomes reflected in the extensive reorganization of the geography of the cities in which they are located, marked by the emergence of these newly born districts.

It is critical to understand that urban tourism precincts are part of the production process of a city and their investigation should not be simply reduced to consumption-oriented analytic frameworks. The shifting nature of post-industrial economies in recent decades has often obfuscated key elements of flexible accumulation, inherent in capitalism and has reduced needed focus on the production side of spatial representation. Additionally, other forces, including civic elites, business and corporate interests, have increasingly played key roles in the creation of precincts. These forces have remained generally under-researched.

The longstanding and ongoing general debate as to whether tourism is an industry, and whether it should be examined as such, is pertinent here. Smith (1995) provides a comprehensive overview of this discourse, pointing to its critical importance. Tucker and Sundberg (1988) indicate that the lack of both a specified production process and a single product of tourism makes it difficult to examine tourism as an industry. Leiper (1990, 1993) argues that tourism is a mix of industries and cannot be examined independently. Finally, Smith (1991, 1993,

21

1994) asserts the existence of a tourism industry by utilizing a supply side approach, offering in the process a definition of the industry for further analysis.

These exchanges primarily centre on economic rationales and classifications in order to better understand aspects of tourism. However, a coherent integration of political and sociological rationales can also greatly contribute to this discussion. Specifically, how do social institutions actively aid in the creation and evolution process of tourism precincts? What role does the public sector, private–public partnerships, image building campaigns, and broader debates about the role and function of the city play in the rationale for the creation of these spaces and places? These are important issues, especially when we examine the foundational aspects and forces that fuel the development and growth of these spatial settings. As Judd (2004: 1) appropriately urges: '[tourism spaces have] to be viewed as an industry, a system of production, as opposed to a consumption activity and the tourist product as part of the commodity chain process'.

This notion of spatial production within tourism can be extracted by observing the extraordinary building boom aimed at supporting new and existing localities. Recent tourism-related infrastructural development activities can be found across the world in cities of all sizes. Waterfront districts, museum campuses, sport complexes, large outdoor festival venues and elaborate entertainment locales have come to be significant forms of urban development. Such projects generally require extensive financial investments, but substantial political capital must additionally be expended to ensure their realization. Judd (2003: 3) refers to this as a 'global phenomenon' and a recent study of Chicago revealed that, as a result of a planned multi-billion dollar construction programme, the city has made a deliberate effort to physically reorganize the lakefront and embrace the advancement of urban tourism as an economic development tool (Spirou, 2006).

It is evident that tourism precincts have evolved into significant and common policy instruments for pursuing urban growth and/or promoting urban change. Attention to creating, promoting and maintaining these locales has intensified in recent years, which is an outcome of complex forces embedded in the rapidly evolving political economy of cities and framed within the dynamic nature and interplay between structure and agency. A close examination of this policy development reveals that tourism precincts are now capable of constructing distinctive urban identities. Specifically, the infusion of marketing and related destination planning strategies creates powerful landscapes furthering municipal advancement, while re-imaging the urban core. This broad direction has encouraged competition between cities as they seek to differentiate themselves based on the 'entertainment' possibilities they offer to visitors and residents.

These observations suggest a deliberate plan of action on the part of local government, civic elites and business interests within a city to create spaces and places that can draw larger numbers of visitors and generate considerable profits. These investments are also designed to make cities more attractive, often resulting in highly structured visitor experiences. It is within this framework that the concept of the 'tourist bubble' may be perceived as a defining descriptor of these precincts. The 'tourist bubble', Judd (1999: 39) suggests, 'is like a theme park ... [with] standardized venues ... mass produced, almost as if they are made in a tourism infrastructure factory'. These spaces may also ensure a sense of security as the visitor is mass transported in and out, often without observing or experiencing the everyday life of nearby residents. However, as the cases discussed in this chapter reveal, tourism precincts are not always so monolithic nor as easily conceptualized. While they may possess many of the attributes found in the 'tourist bubble' they can also operate within distinctive and varying settings. Having evolved from a multitude of developmental scenarios, they are often subjected to idiosyncratic forces and shaped by unexpected circumstances.

Tourism Precincts: Economic Redevelopment and Cultural Authenticity

Albert Dock in Liverpool and Navy Pier in Chicago both involved major regeneration projects in their respective cities. They thus represent examples of a particular urban tourism precinct type and share similar elements of development, allowing us the opportunity to compare and contrast their evolving characteristics. As a counterpoint to these two projects, Plaka in Athens provides an opportunity to view an evolving tourism precinct where economic development has not been the sole or even dominant imperative. In Plaka, the evolution of the precinct has been guided by an attempt to strike a delicate balance between economic growth, authenticity and sustainability.

Albert Dock as an Agent of Liverpool's Urban Revival

While Liverpool was a well-known seaport in the 17th and 18th centuries, it emerged as a major commercial force in the 19th century through the combined impact of a burgeoning industrial economy and the importance of England as supplier of manufactured goods and trader of natural resources to the world. Liverpool developed an active trade function primarily through its complex of docks located along the River Mersey, trading goods to Asia, Africa, and North and South America.

Albert Dock was opened in 1846 by Prince Albert and in 1848 it possessed the world's first hydraulic hoist, a key advantage in the shipping business. The dock and warehouse complex encompassed 1.25 million square feet of space and included a variety of structures. Increasingly, though, the introduction of large steam ships placed pressure on the functionality of the dock, which was originally designed to accommodate sailing ships. By the latter part of the 19th century, sailing ships constituted only a small proportion of the vessels using the port. The goods to and from Albert Dock's storage buildings were transferred by barges or rail to nearby boats berthed at more modern facilities elsewhere in the port. By 1920, the commercial shipping activity from Albert Dock was non-existent and its structures served largely as storage for cargo waiting to be released following payment of duties and taxes (Hartley, 1988).

Albert Dock, like Liverpool as a whole, was subjected to the effects of the broader decline in British manufacturing. Once bustling with waterfront activity, the area's docks, factories and related industrial units were progressively shut down and slowly deteriorated: many of the buildings were eventually razed. In 1972, the area closed to shipping altogether and discussion ensued about demolishing the remaining structures. In the early 1980s, Parliament created the Merseyside Development Corporation which, in partnership with the Arrowcroft Group, embarked on the redevelopment of Albert Dock. In September 1983 an agreement between these organizations, led by the newly created Albert Dock Company and the Liverpool City Council, paved the way to bring the abandoned and derelict building complex back to life. This project was viewed as part of an activist agenda by government, which was engaged in partnership with the private sector for the improvement of local conditions (Bailey, 1993).

When the Prince of Wales officially opened the redeveloped Albert Dock in 1988, it had been converted to serve a very different function. The precinct now incorporated numerous attractions, including the Merseyside Maritime Museum, the Granada TV News Centre, the HM Customs and Excise National Museum, the Tate Gallery and The Beatles Story Museum. The area also included many small shops, bars, restaurants and other businesses. The restoration of the dock buildings and warehouses was very impressive, and Albert Dock stood out as being distinctly different from the vast areas of dilapidated dock structures that otherwise dominated Liverpool's waterfront.

The £100 million refurbishment proved extraordinarily successful, slowly helping transform the place into a centrepiece of Liverpool and a sign of the city's economic rebirth and waterfront revival. Albert Dock was now a major heritage attraction. Moreover, with its multitude of entertainment opportunities it became the most popular attraction in Liverpool and one of the most visited tourist sites in the UK (Loney et al., 2004).

By the early part of the 1990s, the redeveloped dock was the topic of conversation amongst travellers, as well as local authorities across the country and abroad. Its status was quickly elevated to a major, successful regeneration project and to a tourist locale that offered unique entertainment opportunities within its spatially enclosed delta district. Visitation grew rapidly from about 3 million in 1989 to 5 million in 1993 and 5.7 million in 1995. Eventually, though, the popularity of the precinct started to decline, with visitation falling to 4.2 million in 2002. It still maintained its pre-eminent position as Liverpool's major attraction, however, well ahead of its nearest rival, Southport Pleasureland, which had attracted 2.2 million visitors that same year (The Mersey Partnership, 2005).

Attendance at Albert Dock continued to decline in 2003 (4 million visitors), and a trend that was documented in many local reports, especially as the city was preparing a bid to serve as the 2008 European Capital of Culture. For example, the *Destination Benchmarking 2002, Liverpool Report* (North West Tourist Board, 2003) included the following negative comments from visitors to the precinct: 'I feel that the Albert Dock has deteriorated ...' (p. 57); 'There is not enough seating indoors at the Albert Dock for the elderly and disabled ...' (p. 60) and 'We thought there would be lots of shops and things to see and do at the Albert Dock ... It used to be such a tourist attraction, but now it looks really run down' (p. 59). Another key report by The Mersey Partnership (2003), which aimed to develop a vision and a strategy for tourism in Liverpool to 2015, concluded that there was a 'need to improve the retail offer in Albert Dock' (p. 28) and 'despite anchor attractions, [Albert Dock] requires better supporting facilities to retain its appeal to visitors' (p. 60).

It is clear from these recent appraisals that as a tourism precinct Albert Dock is entering a second stage of internal development, necessitating its upgrading to meet varied demands. But, as it evolves, its function within this new era also begins to slowly change. More than 20 years after its redevelopment, Albert Dock is now externally viewed as part of a wider waterfront development effort that has helped anchor and fuel Liverpool's renaissance. According to The Mersey Partnership (2003: 22), 'a re-energized Albert Dock [is] a fundamental element of the wider sub-regional Mersey Waterfront Regional Park project and a vital element of improving the city's waterfront appeal which will have spin off benefits for all visitor segments'. Similarly, a city centre residential development study acknowledged the positive impact of the precinct on the further development of the area, noting that 'there is recognition that improving the physical environment of the region will bring important and tangible benefits ... The restoration of Liverpool's once derelict Albert Dock has proved to be a major tourist asset, and it has attracted new investment in housing, offices and leisure facilities' (Jones Lang LaSalle, 2002: 22).

This tourism precinct is at the core of Liverpool's revival, as its presence has stimulated many millions of pounds in investment within the general area. At the same time, beyond its economic contributions, its effect has also proven to be psychological. There have been numerous instances of its spillover effect. For example, the Leo Casino opened in December 2002 on the Queen's Dock (adjacent to Albert Dock), and with live entertainment, a restaurant, two bars and more than 20 gaming tables has become one of the city's most popular night-spots.

As part of the Waterfront District, one of the city's most important assets, Albert Dock can be credited for the broader residential and commercial revival of the city. The addition of a new cruise liner structure at the recently revitalized Pier Head will bring tourists directly to the city from the sea. The impressive gardens in that facility serve as a centre of civic pride and a greeting station for visitors. Nearby Mariners Wharf, South Ferry Quay and Navigation Wharf, all part of the Liverpool Marina, have experienced substantial residential growth with newly constructed or converted apartment units and townhouses. Homes are selling at high prices, attracting predominantly affluent residents who are rediscovering the area and taking advantage of the nearby cultural amenities. In 2003, Kings Waterfront, on Kings Dock, saw the development of 200 residential units that included luxury penthouses. An additional ambitious mixed-use project is forthcoming and the nearby yacht club offers many leisure opportunities.

There have been numerous other developments in the revitalized Waterfront District in recent years. The Crowne Plaza Hotel was erected in 1998 as part of a £150 million redevelopment of Princess Dock, and other hotels have been constructed in the adjacent area. The commercial office sector has also grown substantially in the last few years, and new office buildings on the redeveloped docks have lured major tenants, including PriceWaterhouseCoopers, KMPG and the Criminal Records Bureau. These successes have not been accidental, with a recent City Council report commenting that 'the seeds of Liverpool's renaissance were actually planted as long ago as the early

1980s ... by [the] transformation of the Albert Dock into one of the city's major tourist attractions' (Liverpool City, 2004: 2).

Navy Pier: Evolving Planning of a Tourist Themed Environment

Chicago's history has always been powerfully linked to its waterfront. It emerged as a major city in the 19th century largely due to the Great Lakes waterway system which, via the Chicago River and the Illinois and Michigan Canal, provided merchants with easy access to the Mississippi River. Thus, coupled with Chicago's rapidly developed and far-reaching railroad system, afforded direct access to the interior of the country, making the city the 'Gateway to the West'.

Navy Pier, located on Chicago's waterfront, has a long history of being connected to the city. The Pier opened for the first time to the public in 1916 and it primarily served as a centre of business and recreation. The public increasingly visited the area, especially after its accessibility improved with the introduction of a streetcar. Theatres and restaurants made the place a popular destination, and in the 1920s it is estimated that visitation reached 3.2 million annually. The Pier declined during the Great Depression, though even during that period it continued to be a Chicago favourite. During World War II, the city leased the structure to the Navy. Its public use was restricted, as it was utilized as a training facility for pilots and other military personnel. After the war, the University of Illinois employed gradually it as one of its branch campuses, but it slowly fell into disrepair throughout the 1970s and 1980s. Efforts to revitalize the Pier were unsuccessful and the area became a symbol of urban decay. A 1986 report urged its redevelopment into a cultural and recreational facility at an estimated cost of US$100 million (Ziemba, 1986).

The redevelopment of Navy Pier was part of a broader urban development agenda. Since the 1990s, Chicago has embarked on a very aggressive public works revitalization programme along its lakefront, aimed at creating amenities that would attract visitors and help to generate additional revenues. In addition to Navy Pier, other major construction projects have included Millennium Park, Soldier Field, Meigs Field, the Museum Campus and numerous expansion projects at McCormick Convention Centre. These have been in addition to extensive municipal expenditures on urban beautification, as well as a continuously growing array of outdoors festivals, shows, parades and related events that have brought millions of visitors to the downtown area.

In 1989, ownership of Navy Pier was transferred to a government agency, the Metropolitan Pier and Exposition Authority (MPEA), which initiated and oversaw a major restructuring process. MPEA have subsequently maintained control over the ongoing development and operations of the facility. At a cost of over US$200 million, the redevelopment was completed and Navy Pier was once again opened to the public in 1995. Since then it has become a major entertainment precinct along the mouth of the Chicago River, drawing millions of visitors to the city and its lakefront. Its original attractions included the Chicago Children's Museum, a 32,000 square foot indoor botanical garden, a 15-storey Ferris wheel, street entertainment areas with outdoor stages, an IMAX theatre, retail concessions, restaurants, food courts, a skyline stage, a festival hall, a huge ballroom, and 50 acres of parks and promenades. Over the years, the Pier has become the most popular attraction in the city. According to the Chicago Office of Tourism and the Chicago Convention and Visitors Bureau (2006), 3.5 million visited the site in 1995, its first year of operation. Annual visitation rose quickly to more than 7 million in 1997 and continued to rise until 2000, when it peaked at 9 million. Subsequently, it declined to 8.7 million in 2005, although this represented an increase on the visitor numbers achieved in 2002 (8.5 million). It was estimated in 2003 that the 8.7 million visitors to the Pier in that year generated a total of $45.8 million in revenue.

Like Albert Dock, Navy Pier is primarily serving as a centre of tourism for the local region. Data from MPEA in June 2005 reveal that over 70 per cent of the visitors to Navy Pier are local. Specifically, 39 per cent come from the city of Chicago and 32 per cent from nearby suburbs. A further quarter of visitors originate from other US cities, with the remaining 4 per cent being international tourists. The Pier has also proved to be a comprehensive entertainment centre, capable of keeping visitors occupied for long periods of time. According to the

MPEA (2005), 44 per cent of visitors spent 5 hours or more at the site, with 52 per cent averaging visits of 3–4 hours duration.

The success of this precinct has been simply extraordinary, and most tourists visiting the city for business or pleasure spend some time at Navy Pier. However, it could be argued that this success has come at a cost. The renovations at Navy Pier have been so extensive that it is no longer on the National Register of Historic Places. Redevelopment activities in 1991 compromised the historical integrity of the Pier, resulting in the loss of this distinction (Reardon, 1992). In contrast, Albert Dock maintained its Grade 1 listed building status (1952) and conservation area status (1976) after its rejuvenation.

A key ingredient to Navy Pier's sustained popularity has been the management authority's commitment to keep it 'fresh' by continuously introducing new attractions and activities. In 1997, along with the first ever Tall Ships Festival, a new six-storey parking garage was constructed, increasing the total number of parking spaces to 1800. The following year saw the opening of the 525-seat Chicago Shakespeare Theatre, modelled after London's Swan Theatre. An English style pub, a Teachers' Resource Centre and an English Garden were also added, significantly diversifying the overall use of the pier. In 2000, the Smith Museum of Stained Glass Windows debuted on the site, the first museum of its type in the USA (Weiss, 1999; Wilk, 2000).

Early in 2006, MPEA unveiled plans for additional changes. A major renovation was mooted, fundamentally reorienting the precinct, the goal being to boost attendance and revenues. According to Leticia Peralta Davis, CEO of MPEA, 'Navy Pier is a great success today, but we need to make sure that success continues ... We hope to see a framework of what Navy Pier might look like in the next 10 years. We want to keep things very fresh. An entertainment venue like Navy Pier needs to keep things fresh' (Ryan, 2006). Plans include: additional parking structures, bringing the total available spaces to 3300; a new 900-seat venue for the Chicago Shakespeare Theatre; a new hotel; a monorail system that will aid visitors' experience of the Pier; and a larger Ferris wheel that could be used year round, equipped with access to food and drinks during the rides. The most ambitious portion of the plan includes an 80,000 square foot, Great Lakes – themed water park, the second largest of its type in the world. In addition, an indoor park with rides, and a new marina with 250 boat slips will be added to the complex.

Public response to this proposed massive facelift of Navy Pier has been mixed. Critics have described the plan as an 'aesthetic planning lapse', a 'cheesy makeover', a 'shopping mall' and 'a bunch of junk thrown together' (Kamin, 2006). The city government is currently exploring economic aspects and is attempting to identify sources of finance to initiate the plans.

In spite of some opposition to the current proposals, Navy Pier appears to have generated some significant benefits. Like Albert Dock in Liverpool, the Pier has had a considerable impact on the nearby communities, including stimulating the revitalization of housing in the adjacent neighbourhood of Streeterville (Kaiser, 1997; McCarron, 1997; Bernstein, 2004).

The Neighbourhood of the Gods: Representation and Identity in Plaka Athens

Located at the base of the hill of the Acropolis, Plaka is the oldest district in Athens. A quaint and picturesque neighbourhood, for many years Plaka has served as a gateway to the millions who annually visit the impressive Temple of Athina. In recent decades, the precinct has developed in a variety of ways, maintaining a vibrant commercial, cultural, residential, intellectual and tourist identity. Indeed, tourism has profoundly influenced Plaka, making it synonymous with Athens and a necessary place to visit prior to heading to the islands of the Aegean (Loukaki, 1997).

While the urban character of the area projects a bygone era of Greek society and culture, a feature that has helped to define its appeal, there has also been widespread commercialization. This latter aspect raises questions of authenticity and threatens the very core of the qualities which have been responsible for the precinct's success. Its fluid composition and representation, as well as the coexistence of contradictory and conflicting identities within its boundaries, make this a distinctive tourism precinct environment. Plaka combines the traditional and the contemporary, the ancient and the modern; it promotes local culture, yet it also expresses a strong desire to embrace its newly bestowed European identity. Religious institutions and secular practices coexist and cheap souvenir shops are located adjacent to expensive art galleries. There is a strong sense of neo-Bohemia, yet upon closer examination this gives way to structured and mass-produced consumption environments.

At its highest point, just under the Acropolis, Plaka contains a 19th century recreated island village settlement. The steep, charming, white-washed structures of the Anafiotika (migrants from the island of Anafi built the small enclave) and intimate tavernas reflect the architecture of the Aegean. With its picturesque, narrow streets Plaka served over the centuries as part of the centre of Athens and maintained a strong residential character. Historically the area was a working-class district, but the socioeconomic background of its residents has changed in recent decades. Housing options now include single-storey structures of neoclassical architecture, impressive villas and apartment quarters, alongside lively settings in winding alleys. Automobile traffic has been restricted in most parts of the precinct, encouraging pedestrianism and giving the area an atmosphere of energy and dynamism (Economou et al., 1997).

During the 1970s, Plaka maintained an active music scene and a vibrant nightlife environment. Night clubs and discos spread rapidly, attracting young people who poured into the area in search of various entertainment opportunities. The neighbourhood slowly developed an unpleasant reputation largely caused by increasing incidents of violence and drug use. Fearing the reduction of tourism so close to the Acropolis, local authorities introduced a noise ordinance, elim-inating most of the existing music establishments and thereby chan-ging the tone of the district. The government has also protected the historical nature of the area by approving a 1982 Presidential Decree. In the 1990s, this law was employed to enable the demolition of more than 30 buildings that had been constructed without building permits. According to the Greek Minister of Environment, Town Planning and Public Works, '[the decree will be followed] to the letter ... a climate of terror cannot be allowed to prevail in the neighbourhood of the gods' (*Athens News Agency Bulletin*, 1996: 28).

All this helped propel Plaka into a powerful tourist destination. Because of its geographical location, small souvenir and gift shops lined the pedestrian route to the Acropolis. Antique sellers, boutiques and jewellery stores specializing in mass-produced and handmade icons were added to older leather stores and textile establishments that had operated in the neighbourhood for decades. Tavernas and restaurants, small inns and larger hotels, as well as the implementation of long shopping hours further contributed to the commercial vibrancy of this precinct (Deffner, 2005).

But this tourist/residential mix only partially reflects the many urban functions that the area performs. For example, Plaka has had a long history as the leading retail district of Athens. Before the introduction of large, multi-storey department stores, nearby Ermou Street possessed a string of clothing and shoe stores that attracted thousands from the city as well as those visiting Athens during the government endorsed 'shopping sales' of the 1970s and 1980s. During the mid-1990s some of these shops moved upmarket, to match in form and presentation those found in other cosmopolitan cities of Europe.

Plaka is also a religious centre as it contains a number of churches, including Kapnikarea Church, built in the 11th century, the Metropolitan Cathedral and its adjacent Little Cathedral. The distinct Byzantine style of these places of worship has become an attraction for locals and wandering tourists. In addition, the first University of Athens in the late 1830s was housed here and today the Museum of the University of Athens, the Children's Museum, the Museum of Greek Folk Art, the Frissiras Museum and the Jewish Museum are all located in Plaka. Numerous art galleries also add a cultural aura to the neighbourhood.

The composition of Plaka proves to be even more diverse and complex given the infusion of archaeological attractions. At the western part of the precinct, close to Monastiraki Square, the Tower of the Winds impressively depicts and names the various directions winds blow. Dating back to the 1st century BC, the tower was later used as a Christian church and as a mosque under the reign of the Ottomans. Adjacent to that structure, the Roman Agora was built between 19th and 11th century BC during the era of Julius Caesar. Over the centuries, like the Tower of the Winds, the Roman Agora also served both Christian and Moslem religious needs. Other attractions include the Lysikrates Monument, constructed during the 4th century BC, and the ancient Street of the Tripods. Archaeologically, this area is still under scientific investigation and at the forefront of research. For example, recent scholarly work suggests that the Athenian Prytaneion was purportedly located beneath an existing square (Schmalz, 2006).

Plaka is unique when compared to other urban precincts. Its complex and diverse compositional functions allow for the formation of its distinctive characteristics. It is through these contrasting images (residential, presentation of historical epochs, commercial, artistic, religious and archaeological) that the community comes to construct its tourist identity.

Projecting traditional culture through what might be seen as hyper-commercialization raises questions about the neighbourhood's authenticity. The consequence of commercialization arising from tourism may mean that Plaka is losing its edge as a paradigmatic 'traditional village' within the city, where visitors can easily access indigenous Greek folk culture. This in turn may make Plaka predictable, threatening its future viability as a preferred tourist destination. Within these dynamics, central Athens (including Plaka) is currently undergoing a re-urbanization process driven by gentrification. A possible spatial reorganization may also prove influential in converting this tourist locale back to its past status as a predominantly residential district (Leontidou et al., 2002).

Conclusion

As the three cases outlined above point out, tourism precincts have evolved in various ways. Moreover, they have developed from a diverse range of fundamentally different bases and with a variety of processes and influences driving them. The origins of urban tourism precincts vary, as do the outcomes of the development processes that underlie them – their ultimate structure, functions and relationships to their surrounding environments. The deliberate focus and sustained composition of Albert Dock over time thus make it distinctly different from Plaka, where the precinct evolved in a more organic fashion.

Furthermore, while tourism precincts in old European cities such as Athens, Rome, London and Paris maintain themselves by drawing from their powerful historical heritage and world famous attractions, the situation is different elsewhere. Cities like Sydney (Darling Harbour), Chicago (Navy Pier), Liverpool (Albert Dock) and Baltimore (Inner Harbor) have constructed precincts to complement existing attractions or to create new ones. In addition, they have employed these projects as means of reviving their image, reversing chronic physical deterioration and/or generating increased revenue capabilities. Yet, there are other modes of urban tourism precincts, often unpredictable in their birth and highly specialized in their function. For example, there are enclaves like the International Drive (I-Drive) in Orlando, Florida, where within a 4-mile stretch, thousands of tourists mingle in 226 eateries, 102 hotels and motels, and 41 movie screens. Interestingly, the I-Drive emerged to complement the needs of another nearby precinct, Disney World.

There are a number of issues facing urban tourism precincts given that local authorities and investors attempt to ensure their continued success. Overall concerns regarding authenticity abound due to the intense commodification of these structured locales. For instance, Albert Dock inspired the remodelling of Buenos Aires's own dock, Puerto Madero. However, replicating visitor experiences in other locales creates competition, which may prove potentially threatening to the future viability of investments in tourism precinct infrastructure. The intense competition between cities as tourist destinations can also obfuscate the economic development effectiveness of these, often public, investments.

Discussion Questions and Exercises

(1) Does the 'tourist bubble' epitomize the notion of the tourism precinct? Is it possible for tourism precincts to evolve without attaining the spatial arrangements and elements that define that structure? What could other alternatives be?

(2) How can an authentic culture or environment be maintained as a tourism precinct emerges and develops? What internal and/or

external factors can be employed to promote sustainability in tourism precincts?

(3) The creation of tourism precincts has emerged as a distinct redevelopment strategy that has been utilized by local governments to induce urban growth. Can tourism precincts be created to serve alternative purposes? What would those purposes be and how can these be formed?

(4) How can urban tourism precincts maintain their competitiveness as a continuously attractive entertainment option to consumers? For example, how should precinct managers respond to current trends found in super-resorts which have been able to effectively reproduce outdoor experiences in indoor settings (e.g. *Tropical Islands* in Germany, a massive dome that includes a swimming lagoon, a beach, a water park, a rainforest and an island with 500 species of exotic plants and trees).

References

Athens News Agency Bulletin (1996). Stiff Measures to Protect Historical Character of Plaka. Athens: Greek Press and Information Office (No. 1064). December 12

Bailey, C. (1993). The politics of work in an enterprise culture: technology networks and the revival of the inner cities. *Journal of Design History*, 6(3), 185–197.

Bernstein, D. (2004) Just a quite night at home. *Crains Chicago Business*, 3 May, p. 7.

Chicago Convention and Visitors Bureau (2006). *Home Page*. Available at www.choosechicago.com (accessed 20 August 2006).

Deffner, A. (2005). The combination of cultural and time planning: a new direction for the future of European cities. *City*, 9(1), 125–141.

Economou, D., Betoura, D., & Loukissas, P. (1997). The impact of the pedestrianisation of the Plaka district. *Technica Chronica: Scientific Journal of the TCG*, 17(2), 33–49.

Hartley, J. (1988). Liverpool's dockland heritage. *History Today*, 38(2), 6.

Jones Lang LaSalle (2002). *Liverpool City Centre, Residential Capacity Study*. Final Report for Liverpool Vision (December).

Judd, D.R. (1999). Constructing the tourist bubble. In D.R. Judd, & S.S. Fainstein (Eds.), *The Tourist City* (pp. 35–53). New Haven: Yale University Press.

Judd, D.R. (2003). *The Infrastructure of Play: Building the Tourist City* Armonk, NY: M.E. Sharpe.

Judd, D.R. (2004). The spatial ecology of the city. In L.M. Hoffman, S.S. Fainstein, & D.R. Judd (Eds.), *Cities and Visitors: Regulating Cities, Market, and City Space*. New York: Blackwell.

Kaiser, R. (1997). Blazing a trail through lost Chicago. *Chicago Tribune*, 5 August, p. 11.

Kamin, B. (2006). Navy Pier's cheesy makeover plan is full of holes. *Chicago Tribune*, 22 January, 12.

Leiper, N. (1990). Partial industrialization of tourist systems. *Annals of Tourism Research*, 17, 600–605.

Leiper, N. (1993). Industrial entropy in tourism systems. *Annals of Tourism Research*, 20(2), 221–225.

Leontidou, L, Afouxenidis, A., & Kourliouros, E. (2002). *Causes of Urban Sprawl in Athens and East Attica, 1981–2001*. Report by the Hellenic Open University, Unit of Geography and European Culture (September).

Liverpool City Council (2004). *Council Regeneration and Development in Liverpool City Centre, 1995–2004*, July, UK: Liverpool City Council.

Loney, N., Carpenter, J., & Dutton, C. (2004). Risks in regeneration. *Regeneration and Renewal*, 30 July, 18–25.

Loukaki, A. (1997). Whose genius loci? Contrasting interpretations of the 'sacred rock' of the Athenian Acropolis. *Annals of the Association of American Geographers*, 87(2), 306–329.

McCarron, J. (1997). Downtown Unchained? The building boom is back. *Chicago Tribune*, 11 August, p. 18.

MPEA (2005). *Navy Pier Survey*, Chicago Office of Tourism, Chicago, June.

North West Tourist Board (2003). *Destination Benchmarking 2002*. Liverpool Report, March.

Reardon, P. (1992). Navy Pier off US historic list. *Chicago Tribune*, 18 February, 2.

Ryan, K. (2006). Navy Pier unveils plans for sweeping makeover. *Crain's Chicago Business*, 13 January, 32.

Schmalz, G. (2006). The Athenian Prytaneion discovered? *Hesperia*, 75(1), 33–81.

Smith, S.L.J. (1991). The supply side definition of tourism: reply to Leiper. *Annals of Tourism Research*, 18, 312–318.

Smith, S.L.J. (1993). Return to the supply-side. *Annals of Tourism Research*, 20(2), 226–229.

Smith, S.L.J. (1994). The tourism product. *Annals of Tourism Research*, 21(3), 582–598.

Smith, S.L.J. (1995). Tourism Analysis: A Handbook. New York: Longman.

Spirou, C. (2006). Infrastructure development and the tourism industry in Chicago. In M.J. Bouman, D. Grammenos, & R. Greene (Eds.), *Chicago's Geographies: A 21st Century Metropolis* (pp. 113–128). Washington, DC: Association of American Geographers Press.

The Mersey Partnership (2003). *The Liverpool City Region Winning Tourism for England's North West: A Vision and Strategy for Tourism to 2015*, Liverpool, UK: Tourism Solutions (1st edn. June).

The Mersey Partnership (2005). *Digest of Liverpool and Merseyside Tourism* (p. 23). Liverpool, UK: The Northwest Regional Research Service, February.

Tucker, K., & Sundberg, M. (1988). *International Trade in Services*, London: Routledge.

Weiss, H. (1999). Building for the millennium: theater companies playing bigger role in the community. *Chicago Tribune*, 12 September, 14.

Wilk, D. (2000). At the top of the glass: museum of stained glass windows is making its debut at Navy Pier. *Chicago Tribune*, 11 February, 56.

Ziemba, S. (1986). Pier project dealt funding setback. *Chicago Tribune*, 22 January, 1.

3

Places and People: A Precinct Typology

Tony Griffin, Bruce Hayllar and
Deborah Edwards

Introduction

In most cities that attract tourists in significant numbers precincts
are clearly observable phenomena. They are observable because they
tend to possess distinctive characteristics that mark them out as places
for tourists, even if the bulk of users are local residents. These characteristics may be predominantly physical, relating to green space or
architectural scale and style, or cultural, reflecting the dominance and
influence of a particular ethnic community. Alternatively, distinctiveness may arise from the concentration of certain land use activities,
such as restaurants and nightlife, shopping, museums and other cultural attractions, entertainment or sporting venues, or from the juxtaposition of the precinct to an attractive physical environment such
as beach, harbour or riverfront. These all represent fairly superficial characteristics of precincts, but this is typically the way in which
precincts have been described and categorized in the literature. The

question that arises is whether this constitutes a useful way of categorizing urban tourism precincts from the perspective of understanding how they work and what might need to be done make them work better.

This chapter is founded on the view that it is more useful to understand what precincts do for visitors rather than merely being able to recognize them by their distinctive characteristics, although the latter at least provides a basis for describing precincts in ways that can be readily appreciated. Most people can easily comprehend the meaning of a historic precinct, theatre district or cultural quarter, although the concept of a festival marketplace may not be quite so readily understood. A description of a place as a 'Chinatown' or 'Little Italy' similarly evokes a clear mental picture. However, such descriptions provide few precise clues as to why tourists are drawn to such places, what specific features of these places contribute to the quality of the tourist experience and how such experiences contribute to the overall experience of being a tourist in a city. Neither does it explain why some of a city's ethnic precincts, for example, attract tourists while others do not. Moreover, it may be that precincts with ostensibly different characteristics may actually be performing the same or similar functions for the tourists. From the perspective of developing appropriate approaches to the planning, management or marketing of a precinct, we would argue that it is far more useful to understand the functions that precincts perform, and how to facilitate the performance of these functions, than it is to be able to describe a precinct using a superficial label.

This chapter thus commences by discussing how urban tourism precincts have been categorized or described in the literature in the past, before presenting an alternative typology of precincts based on the functions that they perform for the tourist.

A Descriptive Typology of Precincts

A broad range of terms has been used to describe different types of urban tourism precincts. The various types of precincts identified and discussed in the literature as having some significance or relevance for tourism have included:

- recreational or tourism business districts;
- tourist shopping villages;
- historic or heritage precincts;
- ethnic precincts or quarters;
- cultural precincts or quarters;
- entertainment precincts;
- red-light districts or bohemian quarters;
- waterfront precincts;
- festival marketplaces.

Most of the above categories of precinct rely on a concentration of a particular set of land uses within the area. One of the earliest characterizations of areas that could now be described as tourism precincts was 'recreational business districts' (Stansfield & Rickerts, 1970; Taylor, 1975), which emphasized a concentration of business activities intended to serve the particular needs of tourists and other recreationalists. Getz (1993a) later used the term 'tourism business district' to describe places characterized by fairly eclectic mixes of commercial activities, but all primarily geared to serving the needs of visitors to a city rather than its residents. More narrowly, precincts which featured concentrations of tourist-oriented retail outlets have been described as 'tourist shopping villages' (Getz, 1993b; Getz et al., 1994). Other studies have implicitly acknowledged that tourists are drawn to precincts which offer particular types of activities, whether or not these were originally intentionally provided to serve the needs of tourists. Pearce (1998), for example, discussed the touristic functions of entertainment districts in Paris, as did Hannigan (1998) in the context of London. Ashworth et al. (1988), in their study of red-light districts in Western Europe, recognized the appeal that such places possessed for tourists, although such an appeal may not be without its contradictions and tensions. In exploring tourists' perceptions of the King's Cross district of London, for example, Maitland and Newman (2004) discovered that the area's association with prostitution was one of the features that visitors least liked about it, but also recognized that this 'urban "grit" continues to contribute to the distinctive qualities of the area' (p. 346).

Other types of precinct rely more on a particular physical or socio-cultural characteristic as a basis for their development into, and utility as, a tourism precinct. Such characteristics make these places inherently appealing to tourists, and tourist-related economic activities may subsequently concentrate here in acknowledgement of that appeal. Often, these characteristics represent what is most distinctive, interesting or aesthetically appealing about the city in which the precinct is located. Most notably, much attention has been devoted to historic or heritage precincts since the seminal work on the tourist-historic city by Ashworth and Tunbridge (1990). A well-preserved physical fabric, which sets the precinct apart from the more contemporary, mundane surrounding city, is most often the basis for the place's attractiveness, and a broad range of touristic uses may be accommodated within this fabric (Nasser, 2003). On the other hand, the sociocultural character of the place may provide the basis for its appeal, as Conforti (1996) recognized in discussing the tourist attraction role of ethnic quarters in American cities.

Some specific types of tourism precincts have been particularly associated with attempts to redevelop, revitalize or regenerate urban areas. In such instances there is an element of the precinct being 'manufactured' rather than evolving 'naturally' based on some inherent characteristics of the place. The redevelopment of redundant commercial waterfront areas for tourism and recreation purposes has become a common and much studied feature of cities (Craig-Smith & Fagence, 1995). The waterfront location is often an attribute that makes such areas highly suited to tourism uses (Griffin & Hayllar, 2006a). The 'festival marketplace' is one such precinct type. The term was originally applied to the redevelopment of Faneuil Hall and surrounding harbourside land in Boston and is characterized by a concentration of specialty shopping, restaurants and a variety of entertainment venues. It has subsequently been applied to similarly motivated major redevelopment schemes such as Harborplace in Baltimore and Darling

Harbour in Sydney (Rowe & Stevenson, 1994). On a less grand scale, the role of 'cultural quarters' as agents for urban regeneration has also been recognized (Montgomery, 2003, 2004). Cultural quarters represent areas of both cultural production and consumption, characterized by a variety of cultural venues and events, a strong nighttime economy and public spaces that allow for people watching. Rather than relying on the wholesale transformation of an area, as occurs with the festival marketplace, the creation of cultural quarters involves a more organic and subtle facilitation of these activities, combined with an appropriate built form (Montgomery, 2003).

A Functional Perspective

The precinct types described above appear to be quite different. It would be hard to imagine places more ostensibly different in character than the Latin Quarter in Paris and Darling Harbour in Sydney. The one obvious uniting feature of these precincts is the presence of large numbers of tourists. They are thus clearly meeting some needs or performing some functions for tourists that other places in the city cannot satisfy to the same degree. Indeed it could be argued that precincts with superficially contrasting characteristics may be performing a similar range of functions for the tourists. The key to understanding precincts would thus become an appreciation of the functions they perform for the tourists, and the qualities or features that they possess that enable them to perform those functions. The planning and subsequent management of urban tourism precincts would then focus on firstly recognizing and subsequently developing, enhancing or maintaining these functional attributes.

Research on the tourist experience of urban tourism precincts has been fairly limited, and consequently there is a relatively poor understanding of the range of functions that such places perform. The functional typology presented in this chapter is based primarily on a series of recent studies undertaken in a number of precincts in major Australian cities.

What Tourist Experiences Tell Us about Precinct Functions

The initial study in this series was of The Rocks precinct in Sydney (Hayllar & Griffin, 2005). The Rocks is the site of the first European settlement in Australia and is effectively Sydney's historic quarter. It adjoins the central business district (CBD) but a large part of its historic built fabric has been maintained (see Fig. 3.1). Since the mid-1970s it has been actively developed, managed and marketed for tourism. It is one of the most visited sites in Australia, particularly by international tourists. This study sought to break new ground by focusing on developing an understanding of how tourists actually experience the precinct, and to this end it was based on a series of in-depth interviews with both international and domestic visitors. It employed the particular approach of phenomenology to both conduct the interviews and to analyse the qualitative data that emerged. The aim of phenomenology has been described as being 'to transform lived experience into a textual expression of its essence' (Van Manen,

Figure 3.1 Historic terraces, souvenirs and fast food in The Rocks

1990: 36). The interviews revealed that The Rocks was performing a range of significant functions for visitors, including: offering contrast and respite from the bustle of the CBD; allowing the tourist to make a connection to Sydney's people and history; and providing a more distinctive sense of place than was afforded by most other parts of the city.

The second study in this series involved Darling Harbour (see Chapter 14 in this volume), another precinct in Sydney but one which, in a physical sense, contrasted quite markedly with The Rocks. Darling Harbour represents the archetypal festival marketplace, developed in the mid-1980s out of an industrial wasteland of redundant docks, warehouses and railway goods yards (see Fig. 3.2). Unlike The Rocks, the redevelopment of Darling Harbour involved the wholesale clearing away of the pre-existing built fabric and the creation of a precinct containing a range of major attractions, cultural institutions, tourist shopping, eating, drinking and entertainment venues, convention and

Figure 3.2 Darling Harbour: from industrial wasteland to global playground

exhibition facilities, hotels, and significant areas of public open space, including performance spaces. A somewhat surprising outcome of this study was that, in spite of its apparent differences to The Rocks, it was actually performing some similar important functions for tourists (Hayllar & Griffin, 2006). Like The Rocks, it was a place of contrast and respite. It was also a place where the tourists were comfortable and felt some connection to Sydney people because here, unlike in the streets of the CBD, both the tourist and the local were in a similar, playful state of mind. The perceptions that Darling Harbour catered to a diverse range of people, and moreover that everyone was welcome and had equal licence to 'play' were prominent positive components of the experience. Most unexpectedly, Darling Harbour was seen as conveying a strong sense of place, with some tourists reporting that this was where they headed on return visits to Sydney in order to experience the feeling of having truly arrived. This latter finding certainly went against the conventional wisdom that Darling Harbour in particular and festival marketplaces in general were bland, characterless and actually fostered feelings of placelessness (Huxley, 1991; Rowe & Stevenson, 1994).

The remaining studies in this series took place in two other Australian cities. In Melbourne, tourists were interviewed in relation to three locations: Federation Square, the Southbank promenade and Williamstown. The final study was based in Fremantle in the city of Perth. Both Federation Square and Southbank (see Figs 3.3 and 3.4) were the outcomes of major redevelopment projects in the 1990s and are adjacent to the CBD, although the latter precinct is on the opposite bank of the Yarra River (Griffin et al., 2006). Williamstown is located on Port Phillip Bay, some considerable distance from the CBD. The site of the original port for Melbourne, it possesses a considerable historical legacy. It emerged as a leisure and tourism precinct as the surrounding suburb became gentrified and a café and specialty shopping strip developed along the waterfront area. The tourist experiences in Williamstown were particularly compared and contrasted with those in Fremantle (Griffin & Hayllar, 2006b), a place that possesses a similar character and history, although it has maintained its role as Perth's major port.

Figure 3.3 Federation Square: a dynamic space, but what is it all about?

Figure 3.4 The riverside promenade at Melbourne's Southbank

Generally, these latter studies reinforced many of the findings of the initial Sydney-based research. Most of the functions that had been identified in the earlier studies emerged as being important in relation to at least some of the later precincts. Additional functions also emerged. For example, Federation Square appeared to be performing functions that were not apparent in the other precincts: as a meeting place for tourists, and as a place of orientation, where visitors could get their bearings and subsequently explore the city. Overall, while there was some similarity in the functions that all precincts performed, a number of other significant findings emerged:

- The differences in the functions were not necessarily related to the different physical or sociocultural characteristics that they possessed. There were strong similarities between contrasting precincts like The Rocks and Darling Harbour, and substantial differences between such ostensibly similar precincts as Williamstown and Fremantle.
- Some precincts performed those functions better than others. In some cases it was possible to discern reasons why a precinct was not performing a particular function well. For example, the physical form and layout of Federation Square made it unduly difficult for visitors to understand and explore it. Few reported that they were able to discover all that it offered because most could not comprehend how to access the internal spaces from the external public space. The configuration of the Square, moreover, neither invited exploration nor suggested that there was more to discover than met the eye. In contrast, the narrow, cobbled lanes of The Rocks enticed visitors to find out what was around the next corner and generally led to a sense that the visitor was discovering something worthwhile about both the precinct and the city within which it was located.
- Generally, there appeared to be a relationship between the functions that the precinct performed and the tourists' perceptions of the quality of experience. Where a precinct was not performing a function particularly well, or was only performing a narrow range of functions, it was more likely that tourists would express some disappointment with their experience. Southbank, for example, was perceived to be a pleasant place to be, but it offered a fairly narrow range of

experiences and few opportunities to explore aspects of Melbourne in depth, and it was not particularly distinctive as a place. Darling Harbour, on the other hand, was described in quite euphoric terms by many visitors, and seen as a place where each repeat visit offered the opportunity to discover and experience something new and different. Furthermore, it was seen as quintessentially Sydney, or how the visitors had imagined contemporary Sydney to be.

- Just as there may be different types of precincts, there may be different types of tourist who visit and use precincts. A precinct may actually be simultaneously performing different functions for these different types of visitors. Hence a deficiency in a precinct's performance of a particular function may only be a deficiency in the sense that it affects the experience of a particular type of tourist. For other types of tourist it may meet their expectations and provide a thoroughly satisfying experience. In the original study of The Rocks (Hayllar & Griffin, 2005), three types of tourist emerged based on how visitors described their experiences of the precinct – Explorers, Browsers and Samplers. This typology was reinforced in the subsequent studies, although it was observable that some precincts served the needs of some of these types worse than others. The confusing configuration of Federation Square and the linear, one-dimensional layout of Southbank frustrated the Explorer (Griffin et al., 2006), while the lack of specific things to see and do offered little to the Sampler in the case of Williamstown. The defining characteristics of these three types of tourist, and some of the implications for precinct planning and management, are presented later in this chapter.

The Principal Functions of Precincts

Generally, the studies described above identified a broad range of functions that urban tourism precincts appeared to be performing. On close examination these functions seemed to fall into three broad categories, which could be classified as:

- facilitating functions;
- external or place-connecting functions;
- internal or state-of-mind functions.

The *facilitating* functions reflect some basic needs that tourists have when they are in an unfamiliar environment. Precincts tend to be relatively well known and recognizable parts of a city. They therefore can act as relatively familiar, easily negotiated places to meet up with other tourists, or even with locals, before embarking upon other activities such as sightseeing or socializing. A central location or good transport connections can facilitate this function. In spite of its shortcomings with respect to some other functions, Federation Square performs this function very effectively, by virtue of its striking physical appearance and location adjacent to Melbourne's CBD and main public transport hub; Piccadilly Circus performs a similar function in London. The landmark characteristics and central location of some precincts may also assist the tourist to become oriented to the geography of a city by providing a strong reference point, thereby facilitating its broader exploration by the tourist. Finally, precincts may provide efficient opportunities, in terms of time and expenditure, for tourists to have relatively short but enjoyable and satisfying experiences of a destination – a phenomenon that could be described as 'experience compression'. The clustering of desirable activities in precincts, described elsewhere in this volume, facilitates this compression and economy of tourists' time and effort.

The *external or place-connecting* functions are fundamentally about helping the tourist relate to, appreciate or comprehend the place they are visiting. In this context 'the place' is the broader destination of the city, or even country, rather than just the precinct *per se*. The contention here is that the tourist does not visit the city to experience the precinct but rather, that visiting the precinct is an important part of experiencing the city. In a sense, the precinct acts as an intermediary, which enhances the tourist's feelings of connection to or experience of the place, in particular its people, history, way of life and spirit (see Fig. 3.5). Much has been written about the tourist's desire for authenticity, and this desire was prominent in the interviews with precinct visitors discussed above, although what represented 'authenticity' was variously interpreted or expressed. Ironically, the tourists did not perceive the everyday business areas of cities to offer them this authenticity or sense of connection. Downtown Sydney or Melbourne was seen as indistinguishable from the downtown area of any modern city; it was not regarded as even

Figure 3.5 People watching on the Cappuccino Strip in Fremantle – connecting with the precinct's southern European heritage

being distinctly Australian. A city's tourism precincts, however, would appear to be important markers of place distinctiveness. They thereby provide the tourist with strong memories of the city and may validate pre-conceived notions of the city's character and special qualities.

Precincts may make a city more legible or comprehensible, especially in a situation where the tourist does not have a lot of time to develop a comprehensive understanding of the place. It may be that, from a tourist's perspective, a successful precinct is effectively a caricature which captures and then conveys the essence of the city. The portrayal may not even have to be accurate, just convincing. Based on the evidence reported above, however, tourists are sensitive and respond positively to signifiers of 'real' life within a precinct: local children at play in Darling Harbour; washing on clotheslines in The Rocks; students congregating after school in Federation Square; and the earthy smells of live sheep transporter ships on the Fremantle foreshore. There are parallels, too, with the value of 'urban grit' as observed by Maitland and Newman (2004) and alluded to previously. In a more recent study based on the emerging tourism precincts of Bankside and Islington in London, Maitland (2006) found that observing local people doing everyday things served a significant purpose within the urban tourist's experience. He noted that even

> *the humdrum occurrence of seeing an office worker at their keyboard became a point of interest, a pleasurable and convivial experience …. Getting to know the city was a convivial experience – local people and local places to drink coffee and shop were important. The emphasis is on the everyday and the conviviality of the ordinary (p. 10).*

The *internal or state-of-mind* functions relate to how precincts make the tourist within the city feel. Generally, precincts allow the individual tourist to obtain or maintain the sense or feeling of being a tourist in a setting, i.e., a city, which was not really created for that purpose. In travelling, tourists hope to achieve a desired changed state of mind through the experience of tourism. Tourists who visit a resort find themselves in a place which was built for the primary purpose of satisfying leisure and pleasure needs and where the majority of the people they encounter will either be tourists pursuing similar ends or service workers whose primary function is to satisfy the tourists' needs and desires. However, urban tourists find themselves in settings where the normal routines of everyday work and commerce predominate, and the prime current objective of most people they encounter or observe is unlikely to be similar to that of tourists. Urban tourists still generally need to be satisfying some psychological needs associated with tourism, such as freedom, novelty, escape from routine and the everyday, and social interaction or being at play, with both local people and with other tourists. The precinct offers labile space within the city where these desired feelings can be achieved. A recurrent theme within the studies referred to above was that precincts represented places of contrast to the normal city, where the tourist could escape, take refuge, relax or just take time out from the hustle and bustle of the city. The tourist here is not seeking to connect to the physical place they are in, but rather arrive at the mental place where they desire to be! The physical place, the precinct, needs to facilitate that by generating an appropriate atmosphere or providing certain opportunities for the tourist. Of the Australian precincts studied, Federation Square seemed to perform poorly in this regard because of its lack of legibility and obvious activities, and hence seemed to engender a feeling of being slightly lost, or at a loss. Moreover, visitors seemed to sense this in others within the precinct, and that in turn made the place less interesting for people watching. In contrast, the most satisfying and appealing precincts generated feelings such as a sense of exploration, where the tourist felt the freedom to wander without purpose and without fear of getting lost. Tourists also referred to the mental 'slowing down' they experienced in the precinct, and feelings of having the licence to be playful in a place that was focused on play. This, in turn, engendered a sense of belonging, whereas in normal business areas of the city tourists felt as though they were intruding on the serious lives of the locals. In tourism precincts, on the other hand, tourists felt comfortable with being a tourist.

To some extent, the state-of-mind functions may complement and help fulfil certain place-connecting functions. An aspect of the city that tourists wish to connect to and understand is its people. Precincts may facilitate this in a number of ways. Firstly, tourists seem to place considerable value on there being a local presence within the precinct, but more importantly that locals within the precinct are generally at leisure and thus in a similar state of mind to the tourists. This in turn makes them more accessible to the tourist and there is a sense of sharing the space rather than intruding on someone else's territory. Within the city, precincts represent places of intimacy, where people have the opportunity to get know one another. Secondly, there was a feeling amongst the tourists interviewed in the aforementioned precinct studies that people are at their most genuine when they are relaxed and at leisure. Hence precincts provide an opportunity to observe or encounter the locals as they really are.

Not all urban precincts can or will perform all of the above functions. However to be successful, tourism precincts need to effectively perform at least some of them. Most will perform a significant number of these functions. To be sustainable as places that attract and provide rewarding experiences for tourists, the features or qualities of a precinct that enable it to perform a certain function must be identified and maintained.

A Functional Typology of Precincts

The above discussion suggests that an understanding of how urban tourism precincts need to be planned and managed relies on an appreciation of the functions they should be performing for the tourists. A typology that relies on describing their essentially superficial characteristics, e.g. historic precinct or cultural quarter, fails to serve that purpose. A more meaningful typology may then be one that is based on functional considerations. For example, precincts could be classified as:

- meeting places,
- places of orientation,
- comfort zones,
- places of respite or refuge,
- play spaces,
- encounter zones,
- zones of intimacy,
- zones of authenticity,
- zones of distinctiveness and contrast.

Based on the evidence and arguments presented above, most precincts will perform multiple functions and consequently represent hybrids of these types.

A Typology of Urban Precinct Visitors

An additional outcome of the precinct studies conducted in Australian cities was the emergence of a number of visitor types, based on the ways in which different visitors experienced the precincts. These types were initially defined in the first study of The Rocks (Hayllar & Griffin, 2005), but still appeared to hold true in subsequent studies.

Three basic visitor types were identified:

- *Explorers* are those visitors who want to move beyond the façade of a precinct, to find their own way and discover its inner complexities and qualities. They are looking for the unexpected discovery or the chance encounter. The visit is not tightly planned but rather serendipitous, wandering aimlessly but with hope. For the Explorer, the precinct needs to have a variety of textures and not be laid out too simply or obviously. It must offer the opportunity to 'get lost,' although it must achieve this without creating the feeling that there is a significant risk in doing so. The Explorer is interested in finding out what is around the next corner, but to satisfy the Explorer the precinct must possess these 'bends' and reward the process of exploration.
- *Browsers* also move throughout the precinct, but are more content to stay within the confines of the main precinct area and to follow the well-demarcated tourist routes (see Fig. 3.6). Compared to the Explorer, theirs is a more superficial engagement with the precinct, focusing primarily on its most obvious charms.
- *Samplers* visit precincts as just another stop on their schedule of moving through a city's attractions, and are often concerned purely with visiting a specific attraction rather than experiencing the precinct in a comprehensive way or for its own sake. The Sampler may also use the precinct as a place of brief respite or refuge but will not move beyond the fringe or specified 'refuge point', a café for example.

Although there are three basic types of tourist individual tourists may vary in the way they experience different precincts, due to both circumstances surrounding a visit and personal preferences: different people can simultaneously experience a precinct in quite different ways. An individual tourist may be a Sampler in some instances where their time may be constrained or the precinct fails to stimulate their

Figure 3.6 Catering to the 'Browser' in Williamstown, Melbourne

curiosity, and an Explorer in others. Behaving as a Sampler, Browser or Explorer may also be contingent on the amount of previous experience that the visitor has had with the precinct. Consequently precincts will need to offer opportunities for different 'layers' of experience. For the Explorer it is about depth and offering the prospect of worthwhile experiences beyond the obvious. For the Browser it is about providing a visually stimulating environment and well-defined paths to follow. For the Sampler it is about providing a range of specific activities, including attractions and cafes that will provide something to do and thereby stimulate an interest in visiting initially and then possibly a desire to return to sample something else.

Conclusion

This chapter has considered and reviewed the different types of places within a city that may develop, or be developed, as tourism precincts.

Typically such places have been classified and described according to certain superficial characteristics. It has been argued, however, that while this may allow us to recognize the general types of places that tourists will visit within a city, it does not reveal much about what attracts and provides tourists with rewarding experiences. Clearly it is not enough to possess historic buildings or the iconography of a particular ethnic community. While there are numerous instances of these sorts of places developing into tourism precincts within cities, there are many more instances of them not. Hence the possession of these characteristics is an insufficient basis, in and of itself, for becoming a tourism precinct. Consequently this chapter has focused on discussing the range of functions that precincts may perform from the perspective of the tourist.

In this regard, three main sets of functions have been identified: facilitating, place-connecting and state-of-mind functions. Within these broad categories, specific functions that precincts perform include:

- providing places for tourists to meet, orient themselves and begin the process of exploring a city;
- providing places that assist the tourist to compress their experience of the city and economize on their time and effort;
- providing respite or refuge from the everyday life of the city being visited;
- putting the tourist into a state of mind that reflects their desires as a tourist (at leisure) within a setting (the city) that is not normally associated with being a tourist;
- enabling the visitor to connect with the people of the city in a setting where the needs and mind-states of both tourists and residents are compatible;
- enabling the tourist to develop a better understanding of the city, its people and its history;
- providing opportunities for convivial encounters, with other tourists, with locals and with aspects of local life;
- enabling the tourist to experience a more distinctive sense of place than is afforded by an 'internationalized' city centre; and

- providing an environment where the tourist has more freedom to wander and explore.

This list of functions is far from exhaustive, and more research is needed in a wider range of tourism precincts to both confirm the validity and significance of these functions and to identify additional functions that precincts may perform. Research is also needed to develop a better understanding of the features and qualities of precincts that enable them to effectively and appropriately perform each of these functions.

Discussion Questions and Exercises

(1) Consider the descriptive typology of precincts outlined above. What would you see as the key experiences being provided by each of these precinct types? What differences might there be between the experiences of tourists and locals in each? Would there be differing experiential needs being satisfied?

(2) Using your responses to Question 1 as a guide, can you identify any common functions that might be performed across the different precinct types? Again, thinking of tourists and locals, how might the precincts perform different functions?

(3) Consider a precinct that you have used as a tourist. Using the three principal categories of functions described in this chapter – facilitating, place connecting and state of mind – undertake an analysis of your selected tourism precinct and identify the specific functions it performs for the tourist.

(4) Either by yourself or with a small group, identify six to eight precincts that you have visited. Next, using the typology of precinct visitors – Explorer, Browser and Sampler – rate each precinct on a five-point scale from *very satisfied* to *very dissatisfied* as to how each group of visitors might rate their experience. For example, you might consider an *Explorer* would be very satisfied, a *Browser* satisfied and a *Sampler* very dissatisfied by their experience at your selected precinct.

(5) Taking into account your responses above, what particular functions of the individual precincts led to your rating of each?

(6) Using one precinct that you have discussed or considered, what recommendations would you make to the precinct manager for improving the overall quality of the precinct experience for both locals and tourists.

References

Ashworth, G.J., & Tunbridge, J.E. (1990). *The Tourist-Historic City*. London: Belhaven.

Ashworth, G.J., White, P., & Winchester, H. (1988). The red light district in the West European city. *Geoforum*, 19(2), 201–212.

Conforti, J.M. (1996). Ghettos as tourism attractions. *Annals of Tourism Research*, 23(4), 830–842.

Getz, D. (1993a). Planning for tourism business districts. *Annals of Tourism Research*, 20(3), 583–600.

Getz, D. (1993b). Tourist shopping villages: development and planning strategies. *Tourism Management*, 14(1), 15–26.

Getz, D., Joncas, D., & Kelly, M. (1994). Tourist shopping villages in the Calgary region. *Journal of Tourism Studies*, 5(1), 2–15.

Griffin, T., & Hayllar, B. (2006a). The tourist experience of historic waterfront precincts. Presented at *Cutting Edge Research in Tourism – New Directions, Challenges and Applications* (CD-ROM). University of Surrey, UK, 6–9 June.

Griffin, T., & Hayllar, B. (2006b). Historic waterfronts as tourism precincts: an experiential perspective. *Tourism and Hospitality Research*, 7(1), 3–16.

Griffin, T., Hayllar, B., & King, B. (2006). City spaces, tourist places? An examination of tourist experiences in Melbourne's riverside precincts. In G.B. O'Mahony, & P.A. Whitelaw (Eds.), *CAUTHE: Proceedings of 16th Annual Conference: To the City and Beyond* (pp. 1036–1050) (CD-ROM). Victoria University, Melbourne, 6–9 February.

Hannigan, J. (1998). *Fantasy City: Pleasure and Profit in the Post-modern Metropolis.* London: Routledge.

Hayllar, B., & Griffin, T. (2005). The precinct experience: a phenom-enological approach. *Tourism Management*, 26(4), 517–528.

Hayllar, B., & Griffin, T. (2006). A tale of two precincts: a phenomeno-logical analysis. Presented at *Cutting Edge Research in Tourism – New Directions, Challenges and Applications* (CD-ROM). University of Surrey, UK, 6–9 June.

Huxley, M. (1991). Darling Harbour and the immobilisation of the spectacle. In P. Carroll, K. Donohue, M. McGovern, & J. McMillen (Eds.), *Tourism in Australia* (pp. 141–152). Sydney: Harcourt Brace Jovanovich.

Maitland, R. (2006). Tourists, conviviality and distinctive tourism areas in London. Presented at *Cutting Edge Research in Tourism – New Directions, Challenges and Applications* (CD-ROM). University of Surrey, UK, 6–9 June.

Maitland, R., & Newman, P. (2004). Developing metropolitan tourism on the fringe of central London. *International Journal of Tourism Research*, 6(5), 339–348.

Montgomery, J. (2003). Cultural quarters as mechanisms for urban regeneration. Part 1: Conceptualising cultural quarters. *Planning, Practice and Research*, 18(4), 293–306.

Montgomery, J. (2004). Cultural quarters as mechanisms for urban regeneration. Part 2: A review of four cultural quarters in the UK, Ireland and Australia. *Planning, Practice and Research*, 19(1), 3–31.

Nasser, N. (2003). Planning for urban heritage places: reconciling conservation, tourism, and sustainable development. *Journal of Planning Literature*, 17(4), 467–479.

Pearce, D.G. (1998). Tourist districts in Paris: structure and functions. *Tourism Management*, 19(1), 49–66.

Rowe, D., & Stevenson, D. (1994). 'Provincial Paradise': urban tour-ism and city imaging outside the metropolis. *Australian and New Zealand Journal of Sociology*, 30(2), 178–193.

Stansfield, C., & Rickerts, J. (1970). The recreational business district. *Journal of Leisure Research*, 2(2), 209–225.

Taylor, V. (1975). The recreational business district: a component of the East London urban morphology. *South African Geographer*, 2, 139–144.

Van Manen, M. (1990). *Researching Lived Experience.* London, Ontario: State University of New York Press.

4

Theorizing Precincts: Disciplinary Perspectives

Simon Darcy and Jennie Small

Introduction

This chapter presents a background to the disciplinary perspectives that have informed research, policy and practice in urban tourism in general and urban precincts in particular.

Prior to the 1980s, there was a dearth of interest in the subject. The limited research on urban tourism was dominated by the traditional discipline of geography (Pearce, 2001). Post-1980s, urban tourism has increasingly been regarded as an important part of tourism with a developing literature (Ashworth & Tunbridge, 1990, 2000; Law, 1993, 1996, 2002; Berg et al., 1995; Page, 1995; Tyler et al., 1998; Hall & Page, 2002; Russo & van der Borg, 2002; Shaw & Williams, 2002; Selby, 2004b). The increased interest in urban tourism can be attributed primarily to two powerful sources: the reactive need to regulate or coordinate the adverse effects of high visitation to predominantly historic cities; and the urgency to restructure post-industrial areas within cities. City planners have moved from ad hoc approaches to urban tourism to adopt more strategic engagement through urban political economic agendas. Urban tourism is now regarded by the mayors of major cities around the globe to be an important dynamic to consider in all aspects of city planning (City Mayors, 2007).

The chapter presents an overview of urban tourism from the traditional disciplines of geography, economics, politics, psychology and sociology. From this 'traditional' background, the more recent post-structural theorizing on urban tourism, which has taken direction from cultural studies approaches (Aitchison et al., 2000), is examined. Consideration is also given to the 'new urbanism' literature that places cities in the context of globalization and the conceptualizing of community (Smith, 2002).

Disciplinary Approaches

Geographic Approaches

The geographic dimension has been the most commonly utilized of the approaches. The study of urban tourism precincts has directly come from geography where the concept of *tourism precincts* has been developed from a literature that has used a variety of terms to describe 'areas' over a number of decades. As McDonnell and Darcy (1998) summarized, the terminology used to describe these areas included:

- Tourist-Historic Cities (Ashworth & Tunbridge, 1990)
- Tourism Shopping Villages (Getz, 1993b)
- Tourism Business Districts (TBDs) (Getz et al., 1994)
- Recreational Business Districts (RBDs) (Stansfield & Rickert, 1970; Meyer-Arendt, 1990)
- Tourism Destination Area Development (Travis, 1994)
- Enclaves (Brohman, 1996; Rutheiser, 1997; Davis & Morais, 2004; Brenner, 2005)
- Integrated Beach Resort Development (Smith, 1992; Pearce, 1995)

With the exception of enclaves and integrated beach resort developments (which are closed areas) all of the above have contributed towards a definition of tourism precincts. A review of the literature led McDonnell and Darcy to define a tourism precinct as:

> *an area in which various attractions such as bars, restaurants, places of entertainment or education, accommodation, amenities and other facilities are clustered in freely accessible public spaces. Tourism precincts by their nature enhance certain aspects of the touristic experience and facilitate social interaction between tourists, and between tourists and locals (1998: 354).*

In tracing the development of this definition, McDonnell and Darcy (1998) examined a number of essential components. As Gunn (1994: 125) notes, '... for many reasons, attraction features function best not in isolation but when clustered together'(Gunn, 1988: 275). The combination of the clustering of facilities around freely accessible public spaces facilitates social interaction.

Similarly, Getz (1993a: 258) refers to TBD as, 'concentrations of visitor orientated attractions and services located in conjunction with urban central business district (CBD) functions'. Getz's argument is developed by contrasting TBDs to Stansfield and Rickert's (1970) RBDs that are based on 'a linear aggregation of restaurants, various food stands, candy stores and a varied array of novelty and souvenir shops which cater to visitors leisurely shopping' (p. 215). Getz clearly delineates the differences between TBDs and RBDs as being the sprawl associated with a linear environmental focus, lack of CBD functions, seasonality and exclusion of residents' needs. After reviewing the tourism planning of Niagara Falls, New York (USA) and Niagara Falls, Ontario (Canada), Getz suggested that, while TBD planning ingredients will vary, there are some essential requirements. From a tourism precinct perspective the essential elements are:

- Core Attractions: natural, heritage, cultural, events, shopping and conventions.
- CBD Functions: retail, government and meetings.

- Services: transport to, access within, catering, accommodation and information.

(Adapted from Getz [1993b: 597]).

Travis (1994: 37) labels tourism precincts as tourism destination zones and states they should be of very limited physical extent and contain:

- One or more attractions, treated thematically for marketing, so as to give one or more products with appeal to specific sectoral markets.
- A set of services and facilities, including accommodation, catering, shopping, information and publicity – for residents and visitors.
- Transport and communications, high accessibility, spare capacity, and possible treatment in relation to tourism, e.g. via landscaping, signposting, stopping and service points.

All mass tourism destinations have tourism precincts whether they are major metropolitan city gateways or regional destinations. Sydney's Darling Harbour, Hawaii's Waikiki, Athens' Plaka and San Francisco's Fishermen's Wharf are all examples of planned or unplanned tourism precincts which adhere to Travis's model. The geographic approach is largely functional and this is extended to the government planning, regulation and coordination roles implemented through urban political economy processes. These processes are discussed in the next section.

Urban Political Economy Approaches

There are clear interrelationships between the economic, political and planning approaches to urban tourism precincts. Better conceptualized as the urban political economy of tourism, it should be recognized that this has overlaps with geographic approaches. Seminal urban tourism texts invariably portray this overlap context (Law, 1993; Page, 1995; Tyler et al., 1998). The importance of the economic, political and planning theme is demonstrated by the number of research articles that document the economic regeneration of cities and redevelopment of post-industrial/post-fordist urban places.

Rogerson (2002), Coles (2003) and Paddison (2003) suggest that the importance of the economics of urban tourism is partly attributed to how cities are marketed to promote economic redevelopment. It becomes almost a circular logic where cities make policy decisions to carry out redevelopment for economic purposes that require significant marketing campaigns that focus on the attractiveness of destinations before economic success can be generated. Interestingly, few studies present a critical analysis of the economics or the economic impact of urban tourism redevelopment. This may not be surprising given the complications of separating urban tourism from the economics of the city (Kurtzman, 2005; Gratton et al., 2006). A good example is the way that mega-events like the Olympics are used for both urban regeneration and economic impact (Evangelia, 2003).

Economic development as a rationale for the establishment of tourism precincts has been extensively explored in the literature (Judd, 1995). Judd's exploration of the approaches used by US cities to take advantage of the economic development value of tourism included framing destination brand image, revitalizing post-industrial areas, establishing specialist units to attract conferences and using retail, leisure and entertainment to create 'carousal' zones. McDonnell and Darcy (1998) recognized the importance of these 'carousal' zones and linked the presence of tourism precincts to the relative success and marketing strategy of the island destination, Bali. Their argument suggested that the success of Bali as a destination for Australians was due to its (urban) tourism precincts that brought together conglomerations of hotels, bars, nightclubs and marketplaces with a beach focus. In this sense, Bali was very similar to Australia's Gold Coast, Hawaii's Waikiki or France's Riviera where the precinct itself was also an attraction.

Governments have long used public policy initiatives to create precincts to ensure economic development opportunities for cities (Veal, 2002). Veal (2002) suggests that in the Australian context economic development has been characterized by *hallmark decision-making* where a government would politically expedite opportunities for economic development potential. The most celebrated case was the decision to bid for the Sydney 2000 Olympic and Paralympic Games. It appears that a small group of politicians, who regarded the Olympics as an economic development opportunity, met over lunch and set in train the political processes for establishing a bid through what became known as the *Baird Report* (Sydney Organising Committee for the Olympic Games, 2001). The Baird Report was soon supported by an independent economic impact assessment that estimated the 2000 Games would have a $7.3 billion economic impact from 1993 to 2004 (CSAES & KPMG Marwick, 1993). The main precinct of the Sydney 2000 Olympic and Paralympic Games, Homebush Bay, was essentially a post-industrial wasteland where the Olympics offered an opportunity to reinvent the area as a sport, commercial and residential precinct. The Homebush Bay site was regarded as one of the most industrially contaminated sites in the southern hemisphere and one which could be rehabilitated by the Olympics (Cashman, 2006). However, at no stage was there any broader social debate about the merits of hosting the Games. A preliminary cost–benefits analysis of staging the Games was terminated (Mules & Dwyer, 2005).

More recently, this style of government initiative has been more closely linked with tendering opportunities for the private sector which have become known as public–private partnerships (PPPs). PPPs can be defined as:

> ... *partnerships between the public sector and the private sector for the purposes of designing, planning, financing, constructing and/or operating projects which would be regarded traditionally as part of the public sector (Webb & Pulle, 2002).*

The development of PPPs has been advocated as a strategy for efficient use of government resources and as a way to avoid budget deficits. Governments, the private sector and the public have, to some degree, accepted PPPs as an instrument of economic management. Tourism is a logical partner of PPPs because the public recognizes that the supply side, market-driven nature of tourism businesses should be undertaken by the private sector.

An illustration of a PPP is the Honeysuckle redevelopment on the Newcastle (NSW, Australia) waterfront. This involves the Honeysuckle Redevelopment Authority, a government statutory authority, working in conjunction with private sector developers to reinvigorate the harbour promenade (Rofe, 2003). Honeysuckle is a mix of residential, commercial, retail and tourism-based activities on a multiple precinct site – seven precincts have been planned for specific purposes (Honeysuckle Redevelopment Corporation, 2000). Central to the economic development opportunities are strategies to encourage tourism from outside the region and, most importantly, from high yielding tourists. One strategy adopted was the *Cruise Hunter Project* which sought to attract cruise ships back to berth at Newcastle (Honeysuckle Redevelopment Corporation, 2004). This has proved a successful strategy with regular cruise and naval vessels using the berths in this precinct.

The success of the Honeysuckle development notwithstanding, the 'substantial shift towards both private sector involvement and the privatizing of state-owned goods and services require a comprehensive debate and the development of guidelines about the appropriateness of implementing PPPs in any given context' (King & Pitchford, 1998: 313).

From an economic and tourism perspective, urban policies which offer mixed-use development to create a sense of place and space provide the tourist with a richer environment (Stevenson, 1998). The importance of creating a sense of place for tourists within urban tourism precincts has been examined more recently through sociocultural approaches as follows.

Sociocultural Approaches

Sociocultural approaches to urban tourism draw heavily on the disciplines of sociology, anthropology and history with sociology being the guiding discipline. The sociology of tourism has been well served both theoretically and empirically (Dann & Cohen, 1991; Boniface & Robinson, 1999; Dann, 2002; Cohen, 2004). As Cohen (2004) suggests, the sociology of tourism can be divided into four 'issue areas':

(1) the tourist;
(2) relations between tourists and locals;
(3) the structure and functioning of the tourist system;
(4) the social and environmental consequences of tourism.

Yet, the social and cultural dimensions of urban tourism have predominantly focused on host–guest relationships (Chang, 2000). Within urban precincts this has included the impact that tourism urbanization has on host communities (Mullins, 1991), the implications of conserving ethnic 'ghettos' for the purpose of tourism (Conforti, 1996) and the call for an integrated approach to urban heritage tourism that brings together macro level planning with local communities (Chang et al., 1996). A number of more recent studies provide newer directions for the study of tourism in urban precincts through recognizing the value of the ethnic heritage of areas.

Ethnic representation has become a significant area of study within multicultural settler nations like the USA, Canada, Australia and the UK. A number of studies of ethnic representation within cities provide a valuable contribution to urban precincts research (Rath, 2002; Collins, 2003). These studies developed arguments for the role of migrant groups in entrepreneurialism, the identity of the community, and broader immigration and social policy concerns. In particular, there seems to be a commonality of experience with Chinatowns in the settler nations of the USA (Boston and San Francisco), Australia (Sydney and Melbourne), Canada (Vancouver and Toronto) and the UK (Birmingham and London). All to some extent have become part of the tourism fabric of their cities and consciously or unconsciously appropriated by tourism marketing authorities. The cultural heritage upon which these appropriations are based include architecture, migration history and the celebration of the importance of the Chinese to the contemporary fabric of the city.

Within the Australian context, Collins (2003) has examined the spatial settlement of ethnic entrepreneurs and the nexus to the development of ethnic precincts. As new waves of migrants come to Australia, their settlement patterns determine the newer areas of ethnic concentration, for example, the Vietnamese in Sydney's Cabramatta and Melbourne's Springvale, and the Middle Eastern and Muslim representation in Sydney's Bankstown. Importantly, Collins (2003) suggests that as time progresses and the relative wealth of each group grows, the precincts become more a representation of the cultural group than a living dynamic as more people from the ethnic groups move to more affluent areas of a city. Collins suggests that while the entrepreneurs break out to all areas of the city, ethnic precinct identities become appropriated within tourism marketing strategies. More recently, cities have co-opted their ethnic communities as important parts of bidding strategies for major conferences, events and sporting events (Garcia, 2001; Cashman, 2006; Chalip, 2006).

Halter (2003) has noted similar marketing appropriations in Boston's Irish, Italian, Armenian, Latino and Caribbean precincts through ethnic festivals, walking tours of ethnic neighbourhoods and the celebration of ethnic cuisine. These newer offerings are set alongside Boston's traditional tourism marketing emphasis as an historic heritage destination.

Lastly, the complexity of the social and cultural dynamics within urban tourism precincts is duly noted in Chang's (2000) study of Little India in Singapore. Chang (2000) adopts Relph's (1976) notion of 'insideness' and 'outsideness' to analyse the Little India historic district in terms of the perspectives of the relationship between guest and hosts, the ongoing ethnic tensions between the Indian and Chinese commu-nities in Singapore, and the relationship of the planning regulators and users of the area. Chang (2000) argues that the relative positions of the insider and outsider are negotiable but the degree of identification with place determines the relative attachment of those involved. It is only through an examination of these multiple precinct perspectives that a broader understanding of the struggle over place can be appreciated.

Psychological/Behavioural Approaches

Psychologists have long acknowledged that behaviour occurs in a social environment but it was not until the 1960s that the field of "environmental psychology" emerged investigating the interactions people had with their physical (built and natural) environments. In addition to studying people's experience of specific urban building types, a number of environmental psychologists took a more macro perspective to cities, with particular interest in images of cities, orientation and distance estimation. Cognitive mapping became a useful research method to understand these psychological concepts. The city was often perceived as an 'unnatural habitat' (Ittelson, 1974). Studies of personal space, privacy, crowding, territoriality and crime highlighted the stresses of urban life. The changing face of cities and neighbourhoods was examined.

Amongst those studying user behaviour in the urban context, the focus has been on the urban dweller and his/her experiences of living in a city, rather than tourists visiting the city. However, it is only more recently that tourism scholars have focused on the tourist urban environment. Pearce (1977) examined the role of landmarks, paths and districts in the cognitive maps of tourists to Oxford while Walmsley and Jenkins (1992) studied the cognitive maps of tourists to Coffs Harbour in New South Wales. Tourists' orientation, way-finding and maps in urban environments are also discussed by Pearce (Pearce, 1982, 1988) as are historic sites and the concept of place (Pearce, 1988). Shaw and Williams (2002) have discussed studies on tourist motivation to urban centres. Page (1995) listed a range of cited motives for visiting urban areas while Jansen-Verbeke (1986) highlighted the methodological problem of identifying tourists as users of the city. Studies on the activity spaces of urban tourists are cited by Shaw and Williams (2002). Tourist satisfaction with the urban experience has been investigated by Haywood and Muller (cited in Page, 1995). A popular topic in tourism research has been the study of destination images. However, a review of research papers from 1973 to 2000 (Pike, 2002) found that only 26 of the 143 papers focused on cities. Fortunately, a change is now occurring in destination image analysis where the city is starting to feature more prominently together with an understanding of the future tourist consumer (Aram, 2005; Yeoman et al., 2006).

One of the key criticisms of behavioural research in urban tourism is its positivist origins. As Selby (2004b: 83) claimed:

> *The focus is the individual rather than social groups, conceptualising images as the result of psychologically determined processes of perception and cognition. Mental images were thus considered to be natural, non-political distortions of an objective reality.*

It is this experiential dimension of space that was acknowledged by Canter (1977). For him the notion of *place* is considered as the result of the interaction of activities, physical attributes and conceptions. Tuan (1977) argued that place did not exist independently of the person. He distinguished place from space when he noted that 'what begins as undifferentiated space becomes place as we get to know it better and endow it with meaning' (p. 6).

A criticism of the urban tourism literature is that the tourist *experience* (including the embodied and emotional experience) of urban places has not been fully explored. Research in urban tourism undertaken from a phenomenological perspective has stressed that 'knowledge of places does not exist independently of the knower. Knowledge is produced through experiencing the world, and can only be analysed on that basis' (Selby, 2004b: 141). Recently, Hayllar and Griffin (2005) have taken a phenomenological approach to study the *essence* of international and domestic tourists' experience of an historic precinct the Rocks, Sydney. Their findings suggested that 'intimacy, authenticity and the general notion of place are the essential characteristics (or essences) of their [tourists'] experiences' (Hayllar & Griffin, 2005: 526).

Knowledge of urban places and precincts from the user's perspective is fundamental to an understanding of place but the argument remains that humanistic and phenomenological approaches 'focus upon individuals and essences, rather than social groups and variety' (Selby, 2004b: 142).

Disciplinary Summary

The disciplinary approaches to urban tourism and precincts have been largely functional in their nature. They have focused on the key components, the spatial and functional forms, the role in economic development, the likely economic impact, the potential for urban regeneration or gentrification, and the urban political economy. Surprisingly, there has been limited examination of tourist behaviour and experiences within these areas given that tourism is a social activity and has its foundation in leisure experience.

Poststructuralist Approach

In contemporary social sciences there has been a move to more critical, alternative approaches to mainstream disciplinary analyses. As a consequence, disciplinary lines have blurred and moved towards a shared epistemology, ontology and, to some extent, methodology, through poststructuralism. Cultural geography has been a key force in this paradigm shift. A poststructuralist approach to tourism places, spaces and landscapes considers their representation, production and consumption as a sociocultural process. Place is not something 'out there' but is socially constructed and thus unstable, fluid, not fixed (Blunt & Rose, 1994). There is a shifting struggle of dominance and resistance among the stakeholders.

A poststructuralist position on tourist places claims that there is nothing random or haphazard about how places are presented and how we, as tourists, experience places. Urry (2002), for example, stresses the role of tourist professionals in regulating and systematizing how a tourist experiences a place.

Tourist places, such as precincts, are consumed differently according to gender, sexual orientation, age, ethnicity, social class, dis/ability and other dimensions of identity with their associated power relations. A full understanding of tourists' experiences of place requires an understanding of spatial differences along many social dimensions. Places may be sites for resistance or sites for the maintenance and reinforcement of existing power relations (Scraton & Watson, 1998). Places are also consumed differently at different historical times as Hayllar and Griffin (2005) found in their examination of the contemporary tourist precinct which was once a working-class suburb for dock workers.

Contemporary tourism landscapes are seen as landscapes of consumption with conflict and social tensions between different user groups. Cartier (2005: 11) claims that, 'The city is the vortex for the concentration of things and affords the most extreme views of consumption.' The shopping mall 'has been read as a new representation of the spatial and as the ultimate postmodern consumption site' (Selby, 2004b: 101). As Selby (2004b: 101) states, 'the attention lavished upon the shopping mall is partly due to its apparent appropriation of representations of distant places, and the sense in which they replace 'real' places.'

Recently, there has been a move away from the sole focus on the visual experience of tourism to recognize that the tourist experience is multi-sensual rather than locked in a tourist gaze (Dann & Cohen, 1991). Dann and Jacobsen (2003) discuss *smellscapes* and the distinct odours of urban places. Foggin (1999) uses the example of a blind person to exemplify that any person experiencing a space or place uses the totality of their senses to delight in multidimensional experiences whether they be the sounds, the smells or the culinary tastes on offer (Foggin, 1999). A focus on the embodied tourist experience 'implies a more active engagement with space and place' (Selby, 2004b: 112). 'Non-representational' geographies have shifted attention from representation and text, from the production to the consumption of texts. This approach sees tourists as 'doing' tourism, where 'space is considered as a complex conduit through which the individual may participate in these processes of producing the world: that is of making sense of it, of making tourism' (Crouch, 2007: 45).

City spaces are negotiated, contested, subverted and transgressed (Aitchison et al., 2000) by different groups of tourists and residents who share that space. They can be sites where power relations will affect which tourists can and cannot use the space, and who feels comfortable or uncomfortable in the space. Gender, sexual orientation, social class, age, race and dis/ability are social dimensions of embodiment which can be included or excluded in certain spaces.

Tourism generally has been more concerned with participation than non-participation (Darcy, 2006) although certain groups have not only been marginalized but also have clearly been omitted from the yield-driven agenda of the market and government tourism policy (e.g. Commonwealth Department of Tourism, 1995; Dwyer et al., 2006). Tourism studies and the mainstream tourism industry have embraced seniors as a market group (Ruys & Wei, 1998; Pearce, 1999; Shoemaker, 2000; Small, 2003) and while tourism studies are beginning to recognize groups of tourists based on sexual orientation and disability they are doing so in a segregated sense. There is little in the tourism literature that examines the intersections of these subjectivities.

A brief discussion of the relationship of sexual orientation and disability to urban space and place follows before an in-depth examination of poststructuralist approaches to gender concludes the chapter.

Urban landscapes and urban places are sexualized with heterosexuality normalized within the landscape. '[D]ominant and repeated performances of sexuality inscribe and repeat particular forms of spatial identity from a corporeal scale right through to the scale of the city itself' (Aitchison et al., 2000: 161). Social exclusion from destinations and places based on sexual orientation is well documented for gay and lesbian tourists. As a consequence of exclusion, gay and lesbian tourists have sought other gay spaces where their sexual preference has been welcomed rather than derided (Holcomb & Luongo, 1996; Clift & Forrest, 1999; Pritchard & Morgan, 2000; Pritchard & Kendrick, 2001; Markwell, 2002). In an urban tourism context, cities with a high-profile gay and lesbian community (San Francisco, Sydney and Rio de Janeiro) or gay and lesbian events/parades (Johnston, 2005) have become key destinations for the growing 'pink market' (Hughes, 2006). Yet, even in these cities, it is often only in particular precincts (San Francisco's Castro District and Sydney's Oxford Street) where gay and lesbian tourists experience fully inclusive tourism experiences. While the mainstream city environments and tourism industry might remain hostile to the groups, opportunities have arisen for specialist gay and lesbian tourism operators (Pritchard & Kendrick, 2001). The contestation and transgression of urban spaces is apparent where gay space has replaced heterosexual tourist space and, in turn, where heterosexual tourists, through their visitation, have reappropriated gay space. Straight tourists:

> *may 'degay' spaces and events and erase their essentially gay identities. Such developments run the risk of undermining the 'sanctity' of gay spaces and places, threatening these hard won oases in a largely heterosexual world, a threat which has implications for gay people and their place in heterosexual societies (Pritchard et al., 1998: 274).*

That the creation of tourist spaces can impact on local spaces is apparent in Visser's (2003) study of Cape Town as a gay space. Visser (2003: 186) found that while Cape Town is today recognized as a gay space, it is a gay space for the wealthy, 'empowered gay play boy' which marginalizes 'the already disempowered of Cape Town'.

Similarly, there has been an increasing body of work in the USA, UK, Australia and Hong Kong that documents the exclusion of people with disabilities and others with access needs from tourism environments. These studies identified urban destination accessibility as a significant constraint to these tourists' travel experiences (Murray & Sproats, 1990; Darcy, 1998, 2002a, b; Burnett & Bender-Baker, 2001; Market and Communication Research, 2002; Ray & Ryder, 2003; Yau et al., 2004). The accessibility of destination areas is a complex issue that requires greater attention (Israeli, 2002). Only preliminary work on destination models for accessibility and access precincts has been undertaken (Darcy, 1997, 2003a; Ernawati, 2003). There are many examples of the inaccessibility of destination areas that are conceptualized by a continuous pathway of travel (steps, no lifts or ramps, etc.) (Sport and Recreation Victoria, 1997; Preiser & Ostroff, 2001; Standards Australia, 2001).

These constraints mean that people with disabilities do not enjoy the same destination experiences that other tourists enjoy and are forced to make accessibility a prime determinant of destination choice (Darcy, 2002a; Market and Communication Research, 2002). As Shaw (2007) notes, in an urban context accessibility is also about notions of relative power or powerlessness where mechanisms need to be delivered to allow people to influence the environments that challenge their independence. The UK, USA and Australia have developed legislation to empower people with disabilities to challenge the disabling environmental practices. There have been a number of significant changes to urban tourism environments to make them more enabling for these groups (Darcy, 2002b; Goodall, 2002). Yet, the majority of these changes have focused on physical accessibility for people with mobility disabilities. Other dimensions of disability (vision, hearing or cognitive) have been shown to have lower levels of tourism participation (Darcy, 2003b). Recent research on people who are blind or with vision impairment has documented the auditory, and tactile experience of the urban tourism environment (Small et al., 2007). This study reinforces Urry's (2002) thinking that the tourist experience is one of interconnected senses.

With this preliminary understanding of the multiplicity of experience, the remainder of the chapter will examine gendered landscape, space and place for the implications of gender for urban tourism precincts.

Gender: Tourist Places and Spaces

Tourism places, including tourism precincts, can be understood as gendered in terms of construction (planning and design), representation (marketing and promotion) and consumption (interpretation and use). Deem (1996) and Aitchison and Jordan (1998) have argued for a consideration of gender in postmodern approaches to the tourist experience of the physical environment:

> *For when gender is introduced [into the tourist experience], it appears to threaten to disrupt some of the taken-for-granted assumptions in malestream theory about de-industrialized, post-industrialized and restructured cities, space, place and time, tourist gazes and flâneurs, post-tourism, and risk societies. Places, both familiar and unfamiliar, are indeed part of consumption but they are not consumed in the same way regardless of gender. Nor are time and space ungendered (Deem, 1996: 117).*

An understanding of the gendered tourist requires knowledge of the socially constructed gendered space in which tourism occurs. Aitchison and Jordan (1998) argue that the gendered nature of space within leisure and tourism can be considered around four themes:

> *the gendered construction and organisation of public and private leisure space; gendered power and control in leisure and tourism practices and consumption; the use of leisure and tourism spaces, places and practices to reinforce gendered identities or create new identities; and sexual identity and urban space in the form of lesbian space, gay space, queer space (p. v).*

Researchers have examined the gendered representation, production and consumption of tourism landscapes, highlighting the social construction and thus cultural and historical specificity of space (Blunt & Rose, 1994; Aitchison et al., 2000).

The male tourist gaze, according to Craik (1997: 130) 'is conceived as being structured by voyeurism'. Berger (1972: 64) previously expressed it thus: 'the "ideal" spectator is always assumed to be male and the image of the woman is designed to flatter him'. Craik (1997: 130) agrees that 'images of women, in particular, but not exclusively, function as the passive object of the gaze from a masculine point of view. The dominant position of spectatorship is thus *as if* through male eyes, irrespective of the actual gender of the spectator'.

The orthodox feminist position is summarized by Rojek and Urry (1997: 17): 'Travel and tourism can be thought of as a search for difference. From a male perspective, women are the embodiment of difference'. Pritchard and Morgan (2000) explain the privileging of the male gaze in terms of tourism destination promotion. Landscapes are gendered as masculine adventure, corresponding to the powerful north and west, and as feminine seduction, associated with the less privileged south and east. The tourism discourse remains not only gendered but also colonial and racial.

The embodiment of the 'male gaze', and the precursor to the tourist in postmodern feminist discourse, is the 19th century 'flâneur' who has 'voyeuristic mastery over women' and whose freedom to wander the city at will is 'essentially a masculine freedom' (Wilson, 1992: 98). Wolff (1990) argues that the life of the 'flâneur', solitary and independent, was not open to women.

Women have been associated with private/domestic spaces and men with public/economic, political and cultural spaces. Men and women have experienced different types of sociality linked to these spaces. Burden (2001: 14) says, 'Confinement to private space limits the extent to which women can take part in the social construction of meaning'. Traditionally public space has been seen as unsafe for women and, in the past, respectable women did not venture into the public world unchaperoned. Escape from the private realm has been a motive for women travellers of the past and their counterparts today (Riley, 1988). Much has been made of the division between women/private space and men/public space; however, it is argued that such a separation is not necessarily relevant to groups who are not white and middle class (Rose, 1993). Shifting subject positions do not always place women at the margin. As Ardener (1993: 120) states:

> *because individuals of both sexes are constituted in multiple personhoods ... worlds may correspond in certain contexts of relevance and differ in others. On the other hand it can be argued, of course, that even if there are elements in two discrepant constructs which look superficially the same they cannot be, because differences in other elements will cause a 'shadow' effect or exert 'pull' and thus will affect their meanings or values ... 'objects are affected by the place in space of other objects'.*

The gendered consumption of space and time was investigated by Deem (1996) in her study of holidaymakers in Lancaster, England. She found that visitors experienced the city differently than residents who were holidaying 'at home', for example, risk-taking was more prevalent amongst the visitors than the residents. Safety can be a gendered issue for tourists. Women as tourists have not developed the complex methods of avoidance of certain spaces, at certain times, under certain conditions, that women develop in their familiar home region (Valentine, 1989). In a study of young tourists' perception of danger within London, Carr (2001) found that women perceived London at night as more dangerous than did men, but that there were still a number of young women out by themselves at night who perceived low levels of danger. He claimed that one explanation 'could be related to the increasingly hedonistic and risk oriented behaviour linked to young people, irrespective of gender' (Wilkinson 1994 cited in Carr, 2001: 569). Carr (2001: 569) also proposed that 'a rising determination amongst women not to be controlled by men or their perceived fears' could be an explanation for women going out in single-sex groups, as opposed to mixed-sex groups.

Scholars have also taken a gendered approach to attractions observing that museums, galleries, statues and other attractions reflect 'masculinist myth making' (Aitchison et al., 2000: 34) rather than women's history or current activities. The masculine tourist gaze is stimulated while women are constructed as the other (Aitchison, 1996). As long as there is a his/story and not a her/story this is inevitable. As Aitchison et al. (2000: 135) conclude, 'Our engendered heritage has been identified as a complex cultural product that is continually negotiated and contested'.

Summary

In the past 40 years, there has been increasing interest in urban tourism and a shift in disciplinary focus. Despite the developing interest, implications for tourism precincts have often been assumed, as specific focus on 'the precinct' has been scant. A problem in researching urban places, including tourism precincts, has been the difficulty in isolating the activities ascribed to tourism from the activities ascribed to other urban precinct functions. This chapter has shown that research into urban tourism generally, has crossed over into a number of disciplines. Today, radical cultural geographies appear to be dominating the tourism literature on urban space and place. Recognition that the urban environment is socially constructed and that there are multiple versions of this space has expanded the study of this territory. However, as Selby (2004a: 186) warns, 'many cultural studies still fail to engage with landscapes, representations and encounters which are salient to place consumers'. The focus is too often on the production rather than the consumption of the text.

The challenge for future research is to examine how urban tourists *practice* cultural texts. What is also required are studies of different urban tourists' practices and the changing nature of these. To enable such study, research methods are required which, not only enable tourists to speak for themselves but also allow for the intersubjective tourist experience to be produced. The 'consensus repertory grid' employed by Selby (2004b) and 'memory-work' (Haug et al., 1987; Small, 2004) are research approaches which can permit the interface of the subjective and intersubjective experience of urban tourism precincts.

> ### Discussion Questions and Exercises
>
> (1) In what ways can specific disciplinary approaches colour our understanding of the urban tourism experience?
>
> (2) What do you see as the gaps in contemporary urban tourism knowledge? Can you identify other gaps that are not discussed in this chapter?
>
> (3) In what ways might urban tourism precincts be considered 'gendered'?
>
> (4) What affect might the reappropriation of gay space to heterosexual space have on the gay tourist?
>
> (5) What can tourism managers and marketers do to be more inclusive of certain tourist groups in tourism precincts?

References

Aitchison, C., & Jordan, F. (1998). Gender, space and identity: introduction. In C. Aitchison, & F. Jordan (Eds.), *Gender, Space and Identity: Leisure, Culture and Commerce* (pp. v–ix). Eastbourne: Leisure Studies Association.

Aitchison, C., MacLeod, N.E., & Shaw, S.J. (2000). *Leisure and Tourism Landscapes: Social and Cultural Geographies.* London: Routledge.

Aram, S. (2005). The measurement of tourist destination image: applying a sketch map technique. *International Journal of Tourism Research*, 7(4–5), 279–294.

Ardener, S. (1993). Ground rules and social maps for women: an introduction. In S. Ardener (Ed.), *Women and Space: Ground Rules and Social Maps* (pp. 1–30). Providence, RI: Berg Publishers.

Ashworth, G.J., & Tunbridge, J.E. (1990). *The Tourist-Historic City.* London: Belhaven.

Ashworth, G.J., & Tunbridge, J.E. (2000). *The Tourist-Historic City: Retrospect and Prospect of Managing the Heritage City.* London: Pergamon.

Berg, L.V.d., Borg, J.V.d., & Meer, J.V.d. (1995). *Urban Tourism.* Aldershot: Avebury.

Berger, J. (1972). *Ways of Seeing.* London: BBC & Penguin Books.

Blunt, A., & Rose, G. (1994). Introduction: women's colonial and post-colonial geographies. In A. Blunt, & G. Rose (Eds.), *Writing Women and Space: Colonial and Postcolonial Geographies* (pp. 1–25). New York: The Guilford Press.

Boniface, P., & Robinson, M. (1999). *Tourism and Cultural Conflicts.* New York: CABI Publishing.

Brenner, L. (2005). State-planned tourism destinations: the case of Huatulco, Mexico. *Tourism Geographies*, 7(2), 138–164.

Brohman, J. (1996). New directions in tourism for third world development. *Annals of Tourism Research*, 23(1), 48–70.

Burden, J. (2001). Women and leisure. In I. Patterson, & T. Taylor (Eds.), *Celebrating Inclusion and Diversity in Leisure* (pp. 7–21). Williamstown, Victoria: HM Leisure Planning.

Burnett, J.J., & Bender-Baker, H. (2001). Assessing the travel – related behaviors of the mobility – disabled consumer. *Journal of Travel Research*, 40(1), 4–11.

Canter, D. (1977). *The Psychology of Place.* London: The Architectural Press.

Carr, N. (2001). An exploratory study of gendered differences in young tourists perception of danger within London. *Tourism Management*, 22(5), 565–570.

Cartier, C. (2005). Introductions: touristed landscapes/seductions of place. In C. Cartier, & A. Lew (Eds.), *Seductions of Place: Geographical Perspectives on Globalization and Touristed Landscapes* (pp. 1–20). Abingdon, Oxon: Routledge.

Cashman, R. (2006). *The Bitter-Sweet Awakening: The Legacy of the Sydney 2000 Olympic Games.* University of Technology, Sydney: Walla Walla Press in conjunction with the Australian Centre for Olympic Studies.

Chalip, L. (2006). Towards social leverage of sport events. *Journal of Sport & Tourism*, 11(2), 109–127.

Chang, T.C. (2000). Singapore's little India: a tourist attraction as a contested landscape. *Urban Studies*, 37(2), 343–366.

Chang, T.C., Milne, S., Fallon, D., & Pohlmann, C. (1996). Urban heritage tourism: the global–local nexus. *Annals of Tourism Research*, 23(2), 284–305.

City Mayors (2007). *City Mayors: Urban Tourism*. Retrieved 28 April 2007, from http://www.citymayors.com/sections/tourism_content. html

Clift, S., & Forrest, S. (1999). Gay men and tourism: destinations and holiday motivations. *Tourism Management*, 20(5), 615–625.

Cohen, E. (2004). *Contemporary Tourism: Diversity and Change* (1st edn). London: Elsevier.

Coles, T. (2003). Urban tourism, place promotion and economic restructuring: the case of post-socialist Leipzig. *Tourism Geographies*, 5(2), 190–219.

Collins, J. (2003). Cultural diversity and entrepreneurship: policy responses to immigrant entrepreneurs in Australia. *Entrepreneurship and Regional Development*, 15(2), 137–149.

Commonwealth Department of Tourism (1995). *The Yield from Inbound Tourism*. Canberra: Department of Tourism.

Conforti, J.M. (1996). Ghettos as tourism attractions. *Annals of Tourism Research*, 23(4), 830–842.

Craik, J. (1997). The culture of tourism. In C. Rojek, & J. Urry (Eds.), *Touring Cultures: Transformations of Travel and Theory* (pp. 113–136). London: Routledge.

Crouch, D. (2007). The power of the tourist encounter. In A. Church, & T. Coles (Eds.), *Tourism, Power and Space* (pp. 45–62). Abingdon, Oxon: Routledge.

CSAES, & KPMG Marwick (1993). *Sydney Olympics 2000: Economic Impact Study*. Adelaide: KPMG. Peat Marwick in association with Centre for South Australian Economic Studies.

Dann, G. (2002). *The Tourist as a Metaphor of the Social World*. New York: CABI Publishing.

Dann, G., & Cohen, E. (1991). Sociology and tourism. *Annals of Tourism Research*, 18, 155–169.

Dann, G., & Jacobsen, J.K.S. (2003). Tourism smellscapes. *Tourism Geographies*, 5(1), 3–25.

Darcy, S. (1997). Developing access precincts – disability and tourism. Paper presented at the *Tourism Research: Building a Better Industry*, 7 February, Manly.

Darcy, S. (1998). *Anxiety to Access: Tourism Patterns and Experiences of New South Wales People with a Physical Disability.* Sydney: Tourism New South Wales.

Darcy, S. (2002a). Marginalised participation: physical disability, high support needs and tourism. *Journal of Hospitality and Tourism Management*, 9(1), 61–72.

Darcy, S. (2002b). People with disabilities and tourism in Australia: a human rights analysis. Paper presented at the *Tourism and Well Being – 2nd Tourism Industry and Education Symposium*, 16–18 May, Jyvaskyla, Finland.

Darcy, S. (2003a). Access precincts: understanding spaces and places for people with disabilities. Paper presented at the *6th Australia and New Zealand Association of Leisure Studies Biennial Conference – Leisure, Change and Diversity*, 9–12 July, University of Technology, Sydney.

Darcy, S. (2003b). Disabling journeys: the tourism patterns of people with impairments in Australia. Paper presented at the *Riding the Wave of Tourism and Hospitality Research*, 5–8 February, CAUTHE – Southern Cross University, Lismore.

Darcy, S. (2006). *Setting a Research Agenda for Accessible Tourism.* Gold Coast: Sustainable Tourism for Cooperative Research Centre.

Davis, J.S., & Morais, D.B. (2004). Factions and enclaves: small towns and socially unsustainable tourism development. *Journal of Travel Research*, 43(1), 3.

Deem, R. (1996). Women, the city and holidays. *Leisure Studies*, 15(2), 105–119.

Dwyer, L., Forsyth, P., Fredline, L., Jago, L., Deery, M., & Lundie, S. (2006). *Concepts of Tourism Yield and Their Measurement.* Gold Coast: Sustainable Tourism Cooperative Research Centre.

Ernawati, D.B. (2003). Stakeholders' views on higher tourism education. *Annals of Tourism Research*, 30(1), 255–258.

Evangelia, K. (2003). Economic aspects and the Summer Olympics: a review of related research. *International Journal of Tourism Research*, 5(6), 433–444.

Foggin, S.E.A. (1999). Delighting the senses: a sense-ational prescription for life. Paper presented at the *Ninth Australian Tourism and Hospitality Research Conference Delighting the Senses*, University of South Australia, University of Adelaide and the Flinders University of South Australia.

Garcia, B. (2001). Enhancing sport marketing through cultural and arts programs: lessons from the Sydney 2000 Olympic Arts Festivals. *Sport Management Review*, 4(2), 193–220.

Getz, D. (1993a). Planning for tourism business districts. *Annals of Tourism Research*, 20(3), 583–600.

Getz, D. (1993b). Tourist shopping villages: development and planning strategies. *Tourism Management*, 14(1), 15–26.

Getz, D., Joncas, D., & Kelly, M. (1994). Tourist shopping villages in the Calgary region. *Journal of Tourism Studies*, 5(1), 2–15.

Goodall, B. (2002). Disability discrimination legislation and tourism: the case of the United Kingdom. Paper presented at the *Tourism and Well Being – 2nd Tourism Industry and Education Symposium*, 16–18 May, Jyvaskyla, Finland.

Gratton, C., Shibli, S., & Coleman, R. (2006). The economic impact of major sports events: a review of ten events in the UK. *The Sociological Review*, 54(s2), 41–58.

Gunn, C.A. (1988). *Tourism Planning*. New York: Taylor & Francis.

Gunn, C.A. (1994). *Tourism Planning*. New York: Taylor & Francis.

Hall, C.M., & Page, S. (2002). *The Geography of Tourism and Recreation: Environment, Place and Space*. New York: Routledge.

Halter, M. (2003). Immigrants, tourism, and the marketing of metropolitan Boston. Paper presented at the Draft paper prepared for *New Immigrants in Urban New England: A Workshop*, 25 April 2003, Center for the Study of Race and Ethnicity, Brown University, Providence, Rhode Island.

Haug, F., et al. (1987). *Female Sexualization: A Collective Work of Memory*, trans. E. Carter. London: Verso.

Hayllar, B., & Griffin, T. (2005). The precinct experience: a phenomenological approach. *Tourism Management*, 26, 517–528.

Holcomb, B., & Luongo, M. (1996). Gay tourism in the United States. *Annals of Tourism Research*, 23(3), 711–713.

Honeysuckle Redevelopment Corporation (2000). *Honeysuckle Public Domain Strategy.* Newcastle: Honeysuckle Redevelopment Corporation.

Honeysuckle Redevelopment Corporation (2004). *Annual Report.* Newcastle: Honeysuckle Redevelopment Corporation.

Hughes, H.L. (2006). *Pink Tourism: Holidays of Gay Men and Lesbians.* Wallingford, Oxfordshire CABI Publishing.

Israeli, A. (2002). A preliminary investigation of the importance of site accessibility factor for disabled tourists. *Journal of Travel Research,* 41(1), 101–104.

Ittelson, W.H. (1974). *An Introduction to Environmental Psychology.* New York: Holt, Rinehart and Winston.

Jansen-Verbeke, M. (1986). Inner city tourism: resources, tourists, promoters. *Annals of Tourism Research,* 13(1), 79–100.

Johnston, L. (2005). *Queering Tourism: Paradoxical Performances at Gay Pride Parades.* London: Routledge.

Judd, D.R. (1995). Promoting tourism in US cities. *Tourism Management,* 16(3), 175–187.

King, S., & Pitchford, R. (1998). Privatisation in Australia: understanding the incentives in public and private firms. *The Australian Economic Review,* 31(4), 313–328.

Kurtzman, J. (2005). Economic impact: sport tourism and the city. *Journal of Sport & Tourism,* 10(1), 47–71.

Law, C.M. (1993). *Urban Tourism: Attracting Visitors to Large Cities.* London: Mansell.

Law, C.M. (1996). *Tourism in Major Cities.* London: Thomson Business Press.

Law, C.M. (2002). *Urban Tourism: The Visitor Economy and the Growth of Large Cities.* London: Continuum International Publishing Group.

Market and Communication Research (2002). *People with Disabilities: A Market Research Report.* Brisbane: Tourism Queensland – Special Interest Tourism Unit.

Markwell, K. (2002). *Mardi Gras Tourism and the Construction of Sydney as an International Gay and Lesbian City.* Retrieved 6 May 2005, from http://muse.jhu.edu/journals/journal_of_lesbian_and_gay_studies/v008/8.1markwell.pdf

McDonnell, I., & Darcy, S. (1998). Tourism precincts: a factor in Bali's rise in fortune and Fiji's fall from our – an Australian perspective. *Journal of Vacation Marketing*, 4(4), 353–367.

Meyer-Arendt, K. (1990). Recreational business districts in Gulf of Mexico seaside resorts. *Journal of Cultural Geography*, 11(1), 39–56.

Mules, T., & Dwyer, L. (2005). Public sector support for sport tourism events: the role of cost–benefit analysis. *Sport in Society*, 8(2), 338–355.

Mullins, P. (1991). Tourism urbanization. *International Journal of Urban and Regional Research*, 15(3), 326–342.

Murray, M., & Sproats, J. (1990). The disabled traveller: tourism and disability in Australia. *Journal of Tourism Studies*, 1(1), 9–14.

Paddison, R. (1993). City Marketing, Image Reconstruction and Urban Regeneration. *Urban Studies*, 30(2), 339–349.

Page, S. (1995). *Urban Tourism*. London: Routledge.

Pearce, D.G. (1995). *Tourism Today: A Geographical Analysis*. Harlow, Essex Longman.

Pearce, D.G. (2001). An integrative framework for urban tourism research. *Annals of Tourism Research*, 28(4), 926–946.

Pearce, P.L. (1977). Mental souvenirs: a study of tourists and their city maps. *Australian Journal of Psychology*, 29(3), 203–210.

Pearce, P.L. (1982). *The Social Psychology of Tourist Behaviour*. London: Pergamon.

Pearce, P.L. (1988). *The Ulysses Factor: Evaluating Visitors in Tourist Settings*. New York: Springer-Verlag.

Pearce, P.L. (1999). Touring for pleasure: studies of the senior self-drive travel market. *Tourism Recreation Research*, 24(1), 35–42.

Pike, S. (2002). Destination image analysis – a review of 142 papers from 1973 to 2000. *Tourism Management*, 23, 541–549.

Preiser, W.F.E., & Ostroff, E. (2001). *Universal Design Handbook*. New York: McGraw-Hill.

Pritchard, A., & Kendrick, D. (2001). Practice nurse and health visitor management of acute minor illness in a general practice. *Journal of Advanced Nursing*, 36(4), 556–562.

Pritchard, A., & Morgan, N. (2000). Privileging the male gaze: gendered tourism landscapes. *Annals of Tourism Research*, 27(4), 884–905.

Pritchard, A., Morgan, N., Sedgely, D., & Jenkins, A. (1998). Reaching out to the gay tourist: opportunities and threats in an emerging market segment. *Tourism Management*, 19(3), 273–282.

Rath, J. (2002). Immigrants and the tourist industry: the commodification of cultural resources. Paper presented at the *XVth World Congress of Sociology*, 7–13 July, Brisbane, Queensland Australia.

Ray, N.M., & Ryder, M.E. (2003). 'Ebilities' tourism: an exploratory discussion of the travel needs and motivations of the mobility-disabled. *Tourism Management*, 24(1), 57–72.

Relph, E. (1976). *Place and Placelessness*. London: Pion Ltd.

Riley, P. (1988). Road culture of international long-term budget travelers. *Annals of Tourism Research*, 15(3), 313–328.

Rofe, M.W. (2003). 'I want to be global': theorising the gentrifying class as an emergent élite global community. *Urban Studies*, 40(12), 2511–2526.

Rogerson, C.M. (2002). Urban tourism in the developing world: the case of Johannesburg. *Development Southern Africa*, 19(1), 169–190.

Rojek, C., & Urry, J. (1997). Transformations of travel and theory. In C. Rojek, & J. Urry (Eds.), *Touring Cultures: Transformations of Travel and Theory* (pp. 1–19). London: Routledge.

Rose, G. (1993). *Feminism and Geography: The Limits of Geographical Knowledge*. Oxford: Polity Press.

Russo, A.P., & van der Borg, J. (2002). Planning considerations for cultural tourism: a case study of four European cities. *Tourism Management*, 23(6), 631–637.

Rutheiser, C. (1997). Making place in the nonplace urban realm: notes on the revitalisation of downtown Atlanta. *Urban Anthropology*, 26(1), 9–42.

Ruys, H., & Wei, S. (1998). Accommodation needs of mature Australia travellers. *Australian Journal of Hospitality Management*, 5(1), 51–59.

Scraton, S., & Watson, B. (1998). Gendered cities: women and public leisure space in the 'postmodern city'. *Leisure Studies*, 17(2), 123–137.

Selby, M. (2004a). Consuming the city: conceptualizing and researching urban tourist knowledge. *Tourism Geographies*, 6(2), 186–207.

Selby, M. (2004b). *Understanding Urban Tourism: Image, Culture and Experience.* London: IB Tauris.

Shaw, G. (2007). Disability legislation and empowerment of tourists with disability in the United Kingdom. In A. Church, & T. Coles (Eds.), *Tourism, Power and Space* (pp. 83–100). London: Routledge.

Shaw, G., & Williams, A.M. (2002). *Critical Issues in Tourism: A Geographical Perspective.* Oxford: Blackwell Publishing.

Shoemaker, S. (2000). Segmenting the mature market: 10 years later. *Journal of Travel Research*, 39(1), 11–26.

Small, J. (2003). The voices of older women tourists. *Tourism Recreation Research*, 28(2), 31–39.

Small, J. (2004). Memory-work. In J. Phillimore, & L. Goodson (Eds.), *Qualitative Research in Tourism: Ontologies, Epistemologies and Methodologies* (pp. 255–272). London: Routledge.

Small, J., Darcy, S., & Packer, P.T.L. (2007). Beyond the visual gaze: tourist experiences of individuals with vision impairment. Paper presented at the *Council of Australian Tourism and Hospitality Education Conference Tourism – Past Achievements, Future Challenges*, 11–14 February, Manly – Sydney Australia.

Smith, N. (2002). New globalism, new urbanism: gentrification as global urban strategy. *Antipode*, 34(3), 427–450.

Smith, R.A. (1992). Review of integrated beach resort development in Southeast Asia. *Land Use Policy*, 9(3), 209–217.

Sport and Recreation Victoria (1997). *Access for All: A Guide to the Design of Accessible Indoor and Outdoor Recreation and Sporting Facilities.* Melbourne: Sport and Recreation Victoria.

Standards Australia (2001). *AS 1428.1 Design for Access and Mobility – General Requirements for Access – New Building Work.* Homebush, NSW: Standards Australia.

Stansfield, C.A., & Rickert, J.E. (1970). The recreational business district. *Journal of Leisure Research*, 2(4), 213–225.

Stevenson, D. (1998). *Agendas in Place: Urban and Cultural Planning for Cities and Regions.* Rural Social and Economic Research Centre, Rockhampton Central Queensland University.

Sydney Organising Committee for the Olympic Games (2001). *Official Report of the XXVII Olympiad.* Sydney: SOCOG.

Travis, A. (1994). Tourism destination area development. In S. Witt, & L. Moutinho (Eds.), *Tourism Marketing and Management Handbook*. (2nd edn). New York: Prentice Hall International.

Tuan, Y. (1977). *Space and Place: The Perspective of Experience*. Minneapolis: University of Minnesota Press.

Tyler, D., Guerrier, Y., & Robertson, M. (eds) (1998). *Managing Tourism in Cities: Policy, Process, and Practice*. New York: J. Wiley.

Urry, J. (2002). *The Tourist Gaze* (2nd edn). London: Sage.

Valentine, G. (1989). The geography of women's fear. *Area*, 21(4), 385–390.

Veal, A.J. (2002). *Leisure and Tourism Policy and Planning*. Wallingford, Oxon: CABI Publishing.

Visser, G. (2003). Gay men, tourism and urban space: reflections on Africa's 'gay capital'. *Tourism Geographies*, 5(2), 168–189.

Walmsley, D.J., & Jenkins, J.M. (1992). Tourism cognitive mapping of unfamiliar environments. *Annals of Tourism Research*, 19(2), 268–286.

Webb, R., & Pulle, B. (2002). Research Paper No 1 2002-03 – Public Private Partnerships: an Introduction. Retrieved 12 March, 2006, from: http://www.aph.gov.au/library/pubs/rp/2002-03/03RPO1.htm

Wilson, E. (1992). The invisible flâneur. *New Left Review*, 191, 90–110.

Wolff, J. (1990). *Feminine Sentences: Essays on Women and Culture*. Berkeley, CA: University of California Press.

Yau, M.K.s., McKercher, B., & Packer, T.L. (2004). Traveling with a disability: more than an access issue. *Annals of Tourism Research*, 31(4), 946–960.

Yeoman, I., Munro, C., & McMahon-Beattie, U. (2006). Tomorrow's world, consumer and tourist. *Journal of Vacation Marketing*, 12(2), 174–190.

II

Key Themes and Issues

5

Urban Tourism Precincts: An Overview of Key Themes and Issues

Deborah Edwards, Tony Griffin and
Bruce Hayllar

Introduction

The previous section illustrated that precincts are multifaceted environments that under analysis draw on a number of dimensions – geographic, political, economic, behavioural and sociocultural. Understanding how these issues manifest themselves in the urban environment, and influence consumption, experience, behaviour and design is critical. As the previous chapters highlighted, the issues are complex and cannot be seen as operating in isolation from one another. They are inextricably linked together by elements such as context, visitation, representations, social relationships, spatial development, flows of information, property markets, financial transactions, different levels of governance and specific local issues. Making sense of the urban environment and the way in which tourism takes place in it requires a framework which can help to organize thinking and facilitate a greater understanding of urban precincts. A framework that meets these aims can be useful for researchers, educators, policymakers and potential sponsors of any future research.

The purpose of this chapter is to outline a framework that provides the focus for the following chapters in this section. It is possible to study individual elements of urban tourism precincts and their specific consequences but as the chapters in Section I have identified, each element is in effect part of a dynamic urban tourism system.

Figure 5.1 is adapted from Edwards et al. (2007: 22). This conceptual framework presents key issues that could, or should, be addressed in an analysis of urban precincts. The framework comprises seven broad areas: the urban destination context; structure and form of the precinct; relationships within the city; the tourists' precinct experience and behaviour; environmental, sociocultural and economic impacts; conflicts and politics; and best practice. Each box encapsulates a key set of precinct related issues and the arrows indicate the multidirectional

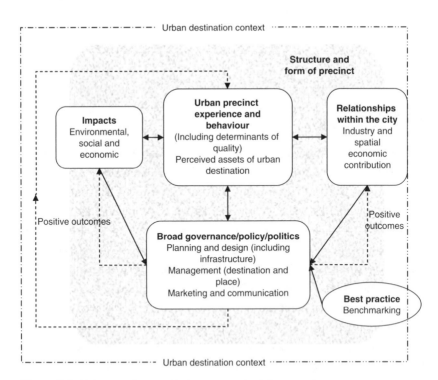

Figure 5.1 Urban tourism precincts: a conceptual framework

relationships that exist between them. An explanation of each element is developed further below.

Conceptual Framework

Urban Destination Context

The key set of issues within the framework is embedded in the context of the city destination itself. In any tourism destination, the physical, social and environmental 'setting' establishes the context for experience and the experience itself is part of that context. That is, our experience both shapes and is shaped by the setting/context. Stevenson (2003) captures the fluid nature of the setting when she notes that signs, images, surfaces, movement and temporary moments are the milieu that underpins a visitor's experience in which the possibilities of change and renewal are endless and open.

A city observed at different times can be busy, quiet, festive, sombre, serious or fun. The intrinsic activity of the city will influence the consumption of the urban precinct. The issues surrounding the urban destination context are explored by Kelly in Chapter 6 who states that 'no matter what happens, it must happen *somewhere*'. Kelly discusses the characteristics of urban tourism precincts that make precincts distinctive within cities.

Structure and Form of Precincts

Overlayed onto the context of the city is the structure and form of the precinct. While some precincts are clearly demarcated by development or specific cultural signs, many 'cities divide into geographically discrete precincts which rarely conform to imposed administrative or political boundaries' (Stevenson, 2003: 73). Since urban spaces are places in which people like to walk around with or without intent, it is the physical form, as defined by such things as individual buildings, facades and architecture, which defines the precinct with recognizable markers that help visitors to locate their experience. Layered over the physical structure, a precinct performs clear functions that service the physical and personal needs of visitors.

Increasingly precincts are being structured as centres of recreation and tourism, as places of consumption and economic competition to stimulate visitation and improve economic conditions. Most precincts aspire to be recognized as a place 'to go'. Regeneration strategies are formulated in order for leisure, enjoyment, spectacle and pleasure to be produced, packaged, marketed and consumed (Stevenson, 2003). The motivations for embarking on urban regeneration are varied. They may form part of a government's agenda for economic or cultural redevelopment; as a means of attracting investment and tourism; or regeneration projects may be a way of initiating wider environmental improvements and infrastructure developments (Smith, 2006). A key aspect of these motivations is the belief that regeneration will have a cumulative effect, acting as a catalyst for further business activity and development of other initiatives that will reinvigorate otherwise vacant urban spaces.

Ideally the features described above should come together in a way that marks each precinct as unique. However, more frequently it is noted that precincts are being replicated with a resultant 'evolutionary sameness' where it is increasingly difficult in the eyes of the visitor to differentiate one urban space from another. It is argued that cities like Hong Kong, Singapore, Kuala Lumpur and others compete to construct monumental edifices in the form of international hotels, shopping malls and entertainment complexes that are provoking debates about the problems of homogenization and the serial reproduction of culture in different destinations (Relph, 1976; Augé, 1995; United Nations Human Settlements Programme Staff (CB), 2004; Richards & Wilson, 2006; Smith, 2006; Piggin, 2007). Ironically, as Richards and Wilson (2006: 1210) have observed, 'even the strategies adopted by cities to avoid such serial reproduction and create a "distinctive" image are also converging'. Krolikowski and Brown tackle these issues in Chapter 7 with a discussion of the functional and spatial characteristics of precincts in reference to contrasts between precincts that exhibit mixed-use developments and those that reflect specialist themes and the clustering of attractions. Here, they argue that there is a relationship between form and structure of tourism precincts where different environments encourage different forms of behaviour and where 'spatial properties of tourism precincts constitute a stage which affords particular touristic performances'.

Urban Precinct Experience and Behaviour

Experience and behaviour incorporate a key set of issues required for developing a better understanding of the urban visitor. This set of issues is central to understanding the ensuing impacts that occur in an urban precinct and how the key elements of the industry can serve the visitors' needs and meet their expectations. Experience and behaviour are inextricably linked to structure and form.

Urban precincts are multifaceted spaces. The concept of urban is both virtual and real in that it encompasses places and spaces where people, as they move around, find themselves outside and inside structures. Yet, this movement creates a complex relationship between experiences, activities and interpretation. According to Raban (1974) there is no reality outside of the personal experience and the personal experiences people seek to gain are their own. Raban's analysis reminds us that urban space is always personalized and imbued with emotional meanings which according to Holmes (2001: 15) 'are produced in time on a moment by moment basis'. Balshaw and Kennedy (2000: 3) acknowledge this personalization arguing that interpretation of urban space always comes, 'almost as an afterthought to the production of social space; "reading" follows production in all cases except those in which space is produced especially in order to be read'. Selby, Hayllar and Griffin expand the personalization of space. In Chapter 9 they discuss the textual community, suggesting that visitors have varying experiences dependent on the way in which their encounters and reflections reconfigure the landscape and whether those experiences occur as an individual or as a social group.

In developing the urban tourism precinct, how do we engage local communities who are often packaged as passive assets to be consumed by the tourist? According to Maitland (Chapter 11) this can be achieved by providing the amenities that matter to local residents as they argue that tourists have a desire to share a similar set of consumption opportunities. This 'developmental dualism' ensures that the local community is socially included and their needs are not lost within the emerging tourism economy. At the same time the lived experience of the tourist is enhanced (perhaps just as they expected it to be) through the sharing of urban space with the local residents.

Relationships Within the City

Experience and behavioural issues are linked to the economic and spatial considerations of industry through product delivery and the economic benefits realized from visitors. In Chapter 6, Kelly argues that precincts can be examined as industrial complexes with the components of the complex being the tourists, the hotels, market places, shops and museums. In this chapter he highlights the spatial relationships that occur between the components and the external environment.

More contemporary considerations of precincts as places for visitors, rather than static spaces, have lead to the reconfiguration of spatial structures more centred around information, leisure, recreation and tourism (Thorns, 2002). It is the rise of the experience economy that is changing the shape of the urban landscape to one that emphasizes playfulness, accessibility, interaction and entertainment. These changes are evidenced by the staging of festivals and activities in open spaces, café culture that has spread onto the street, artwork that fills the gaps in the built environment and museums that have become *hands on* rather than *hands off*.

Tourism then has an influencing role in shaping the spatial characteristics of cities: it has driven precinct development towards the needs of tourists. Consequently, in examining the economic contribution of precincts Ritchie states that 'it becomes difficult to separate the tourism component (or even specific entertainment or cultural tourism components) from the local component, because of this multi-use aspect of the Tourism Business District or precinct' (Chapter 8).

However, the problem of replication is ever present. The increasing use of distinctive architectural features and public art across the urban landscape has been so successful that it has led to replication of the strategy itself. As Richards and Wilson (2006: 1210) observe, 'there is now a waiting list of 60 cities for a Guggenheim "kit" so perhaps "McGuggenheim" is now a more appropriate label for this museum chain'. The buildings may vary but the strategy is still the same: global producers that influence taste and control access. Or is this just a fear that development is out of control beyond any intervention from state or society? For Ritchie it is clear that while there are a number of potential economic benefits associated with developing tourism precincts, cities must be mindful that in their search for uniqueness and long-term brand equity they are not simply replicating the strategies of other cities.

What these perspectives suggest is that in developing precincts we should emphasize the particular – the local, and the cultural over the ubiquitous and global. Urban precincts clearly need to differentiate themselves in order to attract tourists, but they also need certain levels of familiarity, comfort and security.

Impacts

Tourists could be seen as a 'transient population' using cities either as gateways to other destinations or as a home for a fleeting period of time. The result is urban populations expanding and contracting as each new wave of visitors replaces the last. During their stay tourists interact with the host destination and from this interaction impacts arise. The consideration of impacts on the urban precinct is a relatively contemporary phenomenon. There have been models that sought to explain and determine what these impacts might be. The earliest of these include Doxey (1975) who explained host–guest interactions and relationships and Smith (1978) who analysed waves of tourist types and presented a seven-stage model to expand the understanding of community impacts. However, it can be argued that these models are now overly simplistic as Edwards et al. (2007: vii) state, 'a more dialectic engagement takes place between host and visitors and the question is whether or not urban centres, originally designed to accommodate permanent residents and concentrations of economic and physical activity, in actuality face their own set of consequences'. That is the same impact can be perceived in different ways by different people and host communities are often prepared to put up with temporary inconveniences and disruption given other positive consequences they are likely to receive (Edwards et al., 2007).

These are complex issues as visitation effects changes in both the visitor and the host community by influencing visitor perceptions, behaviour and patterns; a community's collective and individual value systems; and the community's structure, lifestyle and quality of life (Edwards et al., 2007). In effect, social learning through experience takes place. Maitland and Newman deal with these questions in Chapter 11. They conclude that there is strong overlap between the host and tourist experience of place and that the opportunity for convivial interactions between them should be celebrated and recognized.

Globalization has lead to rising numbers of high-income professional households, and the changing economic organization of visitors to different urban spaces (Thorns, 2002; Blum, 2003). Simultaneously, economic activity in urban areas has shifted from labour-intensive manufacturing to the production of consumer services many of which are centred on entertainment, recreation and tourism. Urban-based economic activities now account for 55 per cent of GNP in all countries, and up to 85 per cent in high-income countries of the developed world (United Nations Human Settlements Programme Staff (CB), 2007). As Thorns (2002: 144) notes, 'focused on the selling of pleasure, tourism is seen as one of the exemplars of contemporary consumerism'. Tourism and consumption activities are important elements in the promotion and advertising of all major cities. It is appropriate then that Ritchie in Chapter 8 should explore tourism's influence on the form of economic development of precincts. He demonstrates how the spiral of urban development within precincts is often stimulated by flagship projects and regeneration strategies.

Governance, Policy and Politics

The conceptual framework highlights the need to recognize that one of the purposes of conducting research is to provide appropriate guidance on the governance of precincts and the specific assets within them. This governance – policy, planning, design, management, marketing and communication activities – should be aimed at achieving positive outcomes with respect to: improved experiences for the visitors; reduction of negative impacts and greater net benefits for the host community; and improved functioning of the total, interdependent industry within the urban environment. Hence, while recommendations with regard to improved governance of urban tourism precincts must be informed by a fundamental understanding of visitor experiences and behaviour, impacts and industry linkages, they must also feed back to and influence these elements in a positive way.

In essence, these practices should be conceived as revolving around the long-term maintenance and effective functioning of the assets on which urban precincts are based. A practical problem with achieving these broad goals, however, is that there is a diverse array of stakeholders involved, many of whom may have different perceptions on the most desirable outcomes of governance processes. As a result of the reliance upon market signals, promotional activity and new forms of partnerships, debates about the nature of urban development have intensified. Decisions will often involve trade-offs and the favouring of particular sets of stakeholders' interests over others.

Conflicts between stakeholders and the political resolution of these are hence inevitable aspects of precinct governance. In Chapter 10, Searle explores these issues, highlighting that the development and management of urban precincts lead to differing sets of consequences for the various stakeholders, where some stakeholders are more equal than others. By considering a range of international examples, Searle identifies and discusses a number of conflicts associated with managing competing stakeholder interests and how these have been resolved. He argues that 'development outcomes can be understood as the product of stakeholder interaction in which differential ownership of, or access to, power is critical'. Searle forces us to re-think the constant debate around the precinct planning process, namely: should precinct development be a top-down process in which some groups in society decide what is appropriate for others or should it be a bottom-up design where planning occurs with the community?

Best Practice

Benchmarking and best practice are seen to inform urban planning and governance practices such that urban tourism can function efficiently whilst providing a quality experience for the visitor. Examples of best practice planning management and marketing form the final section of this book and will be discussed in Chapter 12.

Summary

The issues explored in the conceptual framework have not been exhaustive but rather used as a vehicle to explore the discussions that will unfold in the following chapters. The framework attempts to bridge the divide alluded to in previous chapters. It is hoped that the framework presented in this introduction will help to organize thinking and stimulate new ideas on what are inherently complex issues.

References

Augé, M. (1995). *Non-Places: An Introduction to an Anthropology of Supermodernity*. London: Verso.

Balshaw, M., & Kennedy, L. (2000). Introduction: urban space and representation. In L. Kennedy (Ed.), *Urban Space and Representation*. London: Pluto Press.

Blum, A. (2003). *Imaginative Structure of the City*. Montreal, PQ, Canada: McGill-Queen's University Press.

Doxey, G.V. (1975). A causation theory of visitor-resident irritants, methodology and research inferences. The impact of tourism. *Sixth Annual Conference Proceedings of the Travel Research Association*, San Diego, CA.

Edwards, D., Griffin, T., & Hayllar, B. (2007). *Development of an Australian Urban Tourism Research Agenda*. Technical Report, CRC for Sustainable Tourism Pty Ltd, Gold Coast.

Holmes, D. (2001). *Virtual Globalization: Virtual Spaces/Tourist Spaces*. London: Routledge.

Piggin, J.-B. (2007). Mourning Beiging's lost spirit. *The Nation*, Sunday edn, Bangkok.

Raban, J. (1974). *Soft City*. London: Hamish Hamilton.

Relph, E. (1976). *Place and Placelessness*. London: Pion.

Richards, R., & Wilson, J. (2006). Developing creativity in tourist experiences: a solution to the serial reproduction of culture? *Tourism Management*, 27, 1209–1223.

Smith, M.K. (2006). *Tourism, Culture, and Regeneration*. Cambridge, USA: CABI Publishing.

Smith, V. (1978). Eskimo tourism: micro models and marginal men. In V. Smith (Ed.), *Host and Guests*. Oxford: Blackwell.

Stevenson, D. (2003). *Cities and Urban Cultures*. Berkshire, England: McGraw Hill Education.

Thorns, D.C. (2002). *Transformation of Cities: Urban Theory and Urban Cities*. Gordonsville, VA, USA: Palgrave Macmillan.

United Nations Human Settlements Programme Staff (CB). (2004). *State of the World's Cities: Globalization and Urban Culture*. Toronto, Ont., Canada: Earthscan Canada.

6

Precincts Within the Urban Form: Relationships with the City

Ian Kelly

Introduction

Geographers justify the universality of their areas of investigation by maintaining that no matter what happens, it must happen *somewhere*. That is, every event (or occurrence) has locational attributes which may be analysed in the search for understanding and predictability. However, geographers also recognize the existence of non-spatial factors and are generally careful to avoid falling into the trap of spatial determinism whereby each event is explained as purely the outcome of its location. It is therefore emphasized that, despite its focus, this chapter does not reflect an exclusive reliance on spatial analysis and is intended as a contribution to a collection which demonstrates the multidisciplinarity of approaches through which urban tourism precincts may be examined.

The objective of this chapter is to contribute to our understanding of urban tourism by examining spatial elements pertaining to tourism precincts:

- The characteristics by which such precincts are distinguished
- The processes by which they evolve

- Precinct location and distribution
- Internal flows and interactions
- External linkages
- Impacts
- Variations
- Prospects

Characteristics of Urban Tourism Precincts

The identification of an area as a tourist precinct may be regarded as an application of the regionalization process, a device used by geographers to group and classify unique locations according to their similarity in terms of selected attributes and their proximity to each other (Kelly & Nankervis, 2001).

The editors of this book have described an urban tourism precinct as 'a distinctive geographic area within a larger urban area which is characterized by a concentration of tourist-related land uses, activities and visitation, within fairly definable boundaries'. This is a definition which, with allowances for scale differences, might be applied to a region, and in which there are clear references to elements of a spatial nature – area, concentration, land uses, visitation and boundaries.

The range of urban tourism precincts incorporates evolved and purpose-built developments, including inner city locations, revitalized waterfront and industrial (brownfield) areas, ethnic communities, entertainment complexes, marinas, beach resorts, and spaces centred on cultural and pilgrimage sites – a diversity which challenges our ability to generalize. Of course, although such areas may also be frequented by city residents, a defining element is the high-level presence of visitors from elsewhere; i.e., tourists and day-trippers.

A second common element is clustering. In addition to clustering of visitors, a tourism precinct may be identified as 'a concentration in space of at least one element of the tourist product and one or more supporting product elements' (Jansen-Verbeke & van de Wiel, 1995: 140). The authors note that 'spatial proximity facilitates combined use and therefore increases the opportunity spectrum in a particular site'.

Ashworth and Dietvorst (1995: 14) refer to the tourism place product as a 'place-bound package' of functionally associated and spatially clustered attractions and facilities, often involving a high degree of fragmentation in business ownership and used by residents as well as tourists.

Urban tourism clusters, like the tourism shopping villages (TSVs) described by Getz et al. (1994), may be identified visually and often comprise retail and service outlets with a visitor orientation such as bars and restaurants, and shops selling souvenirs, gifts, books, holiday clothing, craftware and confectionery. Some precincts may be described as specialized, for example, those based on heritage or cultural attractions. Adelaide, in South Australia, contains an educational tourism precinct which borders the central business district (CBD) and comprises three university campuses, botanic gardens, art gallery, a major library, the State museum, a migration museum and an Aboriginal centre. In addition to supply features, there may also be support services such as visitor information centres, restrooms and places in which to relax. A clearly defined example is Pacific Fair, located close to a large number of accommodation houses on Australia's Gold Coast, and comprising a precinct of mostly small shops and dining establishments, bounded by walls and with a limited number of access points.

Precincts differ in the extent to which they incorporate open public space in the form of walkways, parks, plazas and viewing areas. Griffin et al. (2006) examined the tourist experience in Melbourne's Federation Square, a purpose-built tourism site comprising cafes, restaurants, bars, a gallery and an information centre grouped around a large plaza in which events are regularly staged. Open spaces in which visitors congregate are also characteristic of precincts which have grown around cultural or religious attractions. For example, St Peters Square (Piazza San Pietro) in Rome was laid out in the 17th century as a meeting place for the thousands of pilgrims wishing to view the Vatican. Commercial development is, of course, severely restricted in the Square, but there is a tourist office where guided tours of the Vatican City can be arranged and a large number of tourist shops in the surrounding district. Visitors also congregate in Prague's Old Town

Figure 6.1 The John Huss Memorial in Prague's Old Town Square – public open space popular with tourists

Square, flanked by the Old Town Hall and the Astronomical Clock, and described by Simpson (1999) as 'imbued with significant social, political and cultural meanings'. Tourist retail services are supplied by stalls which contribute to a market atmosphere (Fig. 6.1).

Evolutionary Processes

Although it has spatial implications, evolution is a process perhaps more associated with time than with space, and it is clear from the examples used above that urban tourism precincts are spatial entities which have emerged as the result of different processes occurring over time. Ashworth and Dietvorst (1995: 2) refer to the significance of both space and time in the process of transformation, 'defined as the changing of the shape, appearance, quality or nature of something'.

Some tourist spaces may be regarded as tourism incidental in that they were designed originally as places of worship, commemoration or celebration of culture and located in places chosen by religious or political leaders seeking to optimize visual or spiritual impact. More recent developments are tourism specific, having been planned as places able to offer enjoyable visitor experiences. However, it is likely that in all cases political decisions were involved and these may be analysed through the perspectives of political geography which examines the spatial considerations entering into, and the spatial outcomes emerging from political decision-making.

The core attraction approach apparent in the older precincts has been adopted for more recent developments which often incorporate a convention or exhibition centre, casino, museum, sports arena or major art gallery. This may be seen as an adaptation of the growth pole strategy (Boudeville, 1966) whereby commercial developments are integrated around a 'leader' which generates spillover and multiplier effects throughout the area.

Among the most visible of spatial transformations are the numerous revitalization and rehabilitation projects which reflect political decisions following the deindustrialization of many inner city and port areas. Hall (1995) submits that the primary justification for such developments is the economic benefits associated with tourism and the perception that cities have become products to be sold. Part of the process is the 'reimaging' of city areas in order to attract tourism expenditure, generate employment and encourage investment in 'white-collar' industries.

An illustrative example of this redevelopment and reimaging process is Melbourne's Southbank, a former riverside industrial area which has been undergoing transformation since 1992. It now features a mix of tourism, leisure, dining, specialty shopping, entertainment, residential and commercial land uses, closely linked to the Crown Casino, a major gallery and three performing arts theatres. A similar approach is apparent in the neighbouring Docklands redevelopment (MCVB, 2006).

Savage et al. (2004) review the policy of Thematic Zone development pursued as a means of diversifying Singapore's economy and enhancing its competitiveness as a tourist destination. There are plans to develop 11 thematic zones comprising 'a marriage of old world landscapes with new commercial innovations, sustaining a local and tourist clientele seeking a slice of authentic Singapore' (p. 213). During the 1960s and 1970s, the Singapore River Zone experienced transformations involving a shift from shophouses, tenements, squatter colonies and entrepot activities to CBD skyscrapers. With redevelopment it is now presented

Figure 6.2 Charles Bridge, Prague – tourist activity in the transition zone

as 'The Night Zone', featuring ambient lighting, alfresco dining, night-life activities, festivals and family entertainment amenities.

The evolution of ethnic districts as tourist precincts follows a more organic process involving in-migration, difficulties with assimilation, preservation of certain culture elements and recognition of commer-cial opportunities, often associated with food. The Chinese diaspora is reflected in the large number of Chinatowns which commenced as havens for new arrivals but which are now appreciated, preserved and promoted for their restaurants, festivals and opportunities for visitors to experience 'the other'. Hall (2005) refers to this as a commodification process, dependent on 'place differentiation' involving planning to maintain shop-front visibility, prominent markers (e.g. gateways) and community acquiescence. Other examples of touristified ethnic districts include Malay Village and Little India which constitute islands of ethnic distinction in Chinese-dominated Singapore (Ismail & Baum, 2006).

There are instances of tourism precinct growth which appear to support the claims of geography's derivative gravity model which predicts expansion along the channels linking similar functional zones. For example, the tourist zones of central Prague (the Old Town Square, the Lesser Quarter and Prague Castle) appear to be coalescing as the streets and bridges linking them are progressively occupied by craftware stalls, buskers, painters and touts (Fig. 6.2). Similar trends are identifiable around the links between Melbourne CBD and the Yarra River developments.

Location and Distribution

It is interesting to speculate on the possible role of core-periphery forces in the origin and distribution of urban tourism precincts. The core-periphery model suggests that throughout history innovativeness and the intensity of human activity have tended to be greatest in locations where channels of spatial interaction (and hence communication of ideas) converge (Friedmann, 1973), and offers thereby an explanation for the differential growth of cities and the distribution of land uses within them. Tourism is clearly a human activity in which spatial interaction is important and there is abundant evidence of uneven distribution. Can urban tourism precincts therefore be regarded as cores arising from forces contributing to an intensification of tourist activity?

Some of the factors contributing to the location and distribution of urban tourism precincts have already been identified. These include the presence of an 'anchor' (Page & Hall, 2003) or growth pole around

113

which tourism operations may congregate, the availability of land for development or redevelopment, and a focus on tourism at the decision-making and planning levels.

Urban settlements have traditionally been regarded as central places, located where they can best meet the need for goods and services of the surrounding population (Christaller, 1933/1966). Differences in the size of settlements relate to the population of the area served, with some aided by natural situational advantages, advancements in communications and transport technology, and economies of scale acquired through development of a global reach. Gunn (1994) recognizes the role of parks, museums, theatres, etc. as longstanding urban venues for entertainment, but Page and Hall (2003) and Hall (2005) suggest that the modern demands of tourism have reinforced the central place function of cities and contributed to the establishment of new spaces designed for this new form of experience consumption. Page and Hall (2003: 49) note that '... tourism is subsumed and integrated into the postmodern city and while it may be a dominant element in those localities actively promoting its virtues, it is one aspect of the form of the city'.

Getz (1994) refers to the difficulties incurred by dispersed tourist shopping establishments and emphasizes the value of clustering in creating a critical mass of businesses and customers. With respect to the location of these clusters, decisions are based on the predicted demand for tourism products and services, the availability of land, the costs of clearance or rehabilitation, provision of utilities, the need for ongoing management and regulations pertaining to land uses. However, the major spatial consideration is accessibility to the precinct for those living in or visiting the city of which it is a part.

In general, inner city precincts whose site and situation factors incorporate proximity or transport links to the CBD are advantaged in attracting visitors. Many precincts appear also to benefit from proximity to water (rivers, lakes and seafronts) which, in addition to scenic attractiveness and recreational opportunities, provides for additional linkages using ferries and water taxis.

Suburban and rural fringe tourism precincts are relatively rare (Law, 2002; Page & Hall, 2003) although some (which may be regarded as sub-cores) have grown around attractions such as theme parks or near key gateways such as airports. The expansion of coastal metropolitan areas has led in some cases to the suburbanization of former beach recreation and holiday resorts, for example, Bondi and Manly in Sydney, Australia. Glenelg, a former beachside village now in the western fringe of Adelaide (South Australia) metropolitan area, continues to evolve as a tourist complex featuring a jetty, fun park, a range of other attractions, small tourist-oriented retail outlets, entertainment and dining establishments, hotels and residential apartments. Expansion of tourism land uses (and residential gentrification) is occurring parallel with the shoreline and inland towards the city. It is well served by public transport, including a recently modernized tram service which is itself seen as a tourist attraction.

Internal Flows and Interactions

If tourism is regarded as an industrial activity, tourism precincts may be examined as industrial complexes. According to Law (2002: 193):

> *... an industrial complex or cluster ... can be defined as a group of firms, geographically concentrated in space, which are linked through a focus on a particular activity and which gain strength and the potential for growth through those links.*

This is a view supported by Dietvorst (1995), Page (1995) and Hall (2005) who suggest further that a tourism complex may be seen as a system, an entity whose complexity can be reduced by identifying the interdependent components, their interrelationships and the factors affecting them. The components of a tourism complex as a system include the tangible entities such as the tourists and the hotels, market places, shops and museums visited by them. Spatial relationships among these can be identified by examining the interactions among visitors and the flows of visitors and information within the complex. There are also relationships between these elements and the external environment as discussed below.

The elements of visitor movement, as one form of spatial inter-action within a tourist precinct, may be categorized according to Gould's (1973) concept of mental maps (the images used by people in their organization of spatial routines and expression of preferences). These include gateways (entrances and exits), nodes (the places visited), paths or circulation corridors (the channels along which movement occurs), districts (subdivisions), edges (barriers or markers separating subdivisions) and landmarks (points of reference for navigation). Law (2002) emphasizes the importance of scale, suggesting that tourist complexes should be compact, with only essential vehicle traffic, allowing visitors to walk around them.

Analysis of internal visitor movements can be used to answer a range of questions relating to:

- duration and extent of visits;
- visitor preferences with respect to the activities, products and experiences offered in the precinct's urban tourism opportunity spectrum (UTOS) (Page & Hall, 2003);
- economic advantage attached to location within the precinct (e.g. proximity to a gateway, routeway intersection or central site);
- advantages pertaining to specialist groupings (e.g. of antiques, craft or clothing outlets);
- visitor convenience and safety (e.g. number and distribution of rest areas, hindrances to freedom of movement, areas of visitor vulnerability);
- carrying capacity (e.g. overcrowding, visitor dispersion);
- identification of weak links in the system.

Many tourist precincts are closed to vehicular traffic. With respect to the management of visitor movement in these tourist spaces, McManus (1998) developed the concept of Preferred Pedestrian Flow, a combination of the walking rate at which people are most comfortable and the distance they wish to place between themselves and strangers. Perceptions of crowding occur when these preferences are transgressed, something which may occur when pedestrians are channelled into paths which restrict the freedom to choose. The importance of pedestrian choice is also recognized by Boerwinkel (1995), who distinguishes between 'successive' and 'simultaneous arrangement'. The former refers to a system in which choices are progressively presented to the pedestrians as they move along, while the latter presents a range of choices from any particular location. The author's research indicates that simultaneous arrangement is preferred by visitors as providing greater freedom to explore, suggesting a need for precinct planners to be generous in the use of open space.

However, the competitiveness of a precinct as a place attractive to visitors also depends on less visible internal interactions contributing to the coherence (Dietvorst, 1995) and integration (Ashworth & Dietvorst, 1995) necessary for the achievement of synergies. Hall (2005) notes the need for cooperative networking in ensuring the optimal mix of product offerings, efficiency in the delivery of these and promotional activities.

External Linkages

It is recognized that understanding of a system cannot be acquired by identification of only its internal linkages. By their nature, the majority of systems are open, with inputs from and outputs into larger systems existing in the wider environment. An urban tourism precinct operates, therefore, as a component of the larger urban settlement, which is itself an element in a nested hierarchy of systems extending in some cases from local to global. Stilwell (1992: 141) uses a biological analogy whereby the city is viewed as an ecological environment involving interdependent elements reflecting 'territorial specialization, competition and adaptation, invasion, dominance and symbiosis'. Equilibrium in an element such as a tourism precinct is unavoidably affected by these external forces.

As noted above, some tourism precincts have been defined by local (or higher level) government legislation and boundaries which can be shown on maps are imposed. However, others have evolved and continue to evolve with edges marked by transition zones in which there is competition among different forms of land use. Land uses in the transition zone on which a tourist precinct may depend include provisions for visitor accommodation, car parking and access to public transport.

Precinct operators can develop collaborative networks to promote their interests with regional, state and national tourism organizations and with various levels of government.

Business links must be established between precinct retail and service outlets and their suppliers, and some of these may involve transnational franchises (e.g. fast food outlets and coffee bars).

However, the most obvious spatial link between a precinct and its external environment is with the origins of its visitors, and the most obvious spatial principle that of distance decay. It is well documented that, in general, the greater the distance between locations, the less frequent the interaction generated, a negative correlation explained by the costs, time, effort and intervening opportunities involved. Thus, it would be expected that, on a given day for any precinct, the majority of visitors would have travelled from somewhere nearby. However, it becomes necessary to distinguish between travel from a nearby hotel and that from the home of the visitor. The principle of distance decay will still apply but the success of the precinct is now seen to be dependent on the success of the city or destination region in attracting visitors.

This dependence on the city as the source of visitors may partially explain the apparent popularity of inner city precinct locations and the importance of transport or pedestrian links to the CBD and to other tourism precincts. It may also help explain the relative scarcity of such precincts in suburban locations lacking a core attraction or major transport hub.

Impacts

As noted, the increase in recognition of tourism in urban planning and of government involvement with urban tourism precincts reflect the positive impacts of resource development, enhanced business activity, increased employment opportunities, and improvements to the cityscape through the rehabilitation of derelict industrial and residential sites.

However, Stilwell (1992: 14) claims that '... concerns with space and place coexist uncomfortably with the dominant contemporary processes of international economic and social integration'. This view would appear to be supported by Simpson (1999) who points to the introduction of international characteristics through tourism as a threat to the expression of national identity in the built environment of Prague's inner city area. She asserts, furthermore, that:

> Land use is being rapidly transformed (often from residential to commercial use), the traditional residential population is being displaced and the overall atmosphere and congestion of the streets is being negatively influenced by the city's visitors. The research, therefore, illustrates a clear need to manage tourism-related activity within the historic core of Prague, if its quality of life for residents and the very character which attracted tourists in the first place are not to be eroded substantially (p. 182).

The gentrification of older residential areas (and the displacement of existing residential populations) is a clear example of spatial impact, as is the concurrent increase in the distance residents may have to travel to conduct their shopping for daily household needs (Law, 2002).

Other impacts with spatial implications include problems of increased criminal activity, traffic and pedestrian congestion in districts bordering tourism precincts, and changes in land value and associated taxation burdens. It is clear that concerns about carrying capacity should not be confined to areas within the boundaries of a tourism complex.

Variations

The range of urban tourism precincts is wide, and a comprehensive review of variations should be based on research and fieldwork more extensive than is possible in the present circumstances. However, some preliminary observations based on the literature and personal observation may be made.

The discussion above indicates that there are broad variations among tourism precincts relating to age, evolution, purpose, location and type of tourism.

Older precincts which have evolved around ethnic communities and religious, cultural or historic attractions differ greatly in appearance and impact from those planned and developed as urban rehabilitation projects. The architecture and layout of the former continue to reflect differences among cities in their history, culture and society, and thereby provide the visitor with an experience of authenticity. These older precincts are rich in meaning and may be described as 'survivals from the past' which constitute 'counterstructures in the *ephemerality* of fashions, products, values, etc.' (Gospodini, 2001: 928) (original emphasis). In these older precincts, differences in the forms taken by entrepreneurial activity can be seen. There are the open markets of Eastern European cities, the walled *souks* of Southwest Asia and the colourful bazaars of East Asia, popular with tourists and residents alike. Measures to preserve the atmosphere of *kampung* 'localism' in some tourism precincts of Kuala Lumpur, Singapore and Melaka are noted by Ismail and Baum (2006).

However, Simpson (1999) warns about the substantial erosion in Prague's inner city area of the attributes which attracted tourists in the first place, drawing attention to concerns about the homogenization of tourist spaces as the forces of globalization and internationalization operate in the direction of standardization and against a distinctive 'sense of place' (Gospodini, 2001).

Prospects

The future of urban tourist precincts is tied to that of urban settlements as tourist destinations, and the choices which are made with respect to urban land uses. Advances in communications technology permit (or even encourage) decentralization of some commercial activities, while tourism precincts reflect the perceived advantages of centralizing tourism business activity. Indeed, growth in the number of tourist precincts may continue to compensate for the deindustrialization of certain functional zones in cities.

It is apparent that tourist precincts benefit from and may even depend on, proximity to the CBD. However, as cities become larger (in population and areal extent), they develop satellite business districts in outer metropolitan areas, a trend which may lead to the establishment of additional tourism precincts alongside these.

On the other hand, there is a blurring of the distinction between tourism precincts and the large suburban shopping centres which increasingly cater for visitors as well as residents with a combination of retail, entertainment, dining, souvenir and gallery establishments and nearby accommodation for holiday and business travellers. An example of such developments is the West Edmonton Mall in Alberta, Canada; the world's largest shopping complex, incorporating all of the above plus theme-park-type recreation opportunities and event venues.

Summary

Table 6.1 lists the elements of urban tourism precincts and the tools (geographical concepts) used in identifying the operation of spatial factors involved in their evolution, functions, impacts and prospects.

It is re-emphasized that the emergence of tourism precincts as functional zones in urban settlements is a reflection of various factors, including a number categorized as spatial. These do not operate in isolation from non-spatial factors and, indeed, from each other. They are not of equal significance, and they may not be consciously involved in the planning for and management of tourism precincts.

Precincts have emerged as places in which tourists congregate and thereby constitute a resource which can be exploited by commercial interests, businesses supplying goods and services required or wanted by tourists. Some are planned developments, rehabilitating former industrial and port areas which have become economically non-viable. Others have evolved around sites with historical, cultural, religious or recreational qualities to which visitors have been drawn, in some cases for hundreds of years. The location and distribution of precincts may be partially explained by reference to such concepts as central place

Table 6.1 Spatial analysis in the examination of urban tourism precincts

Precinct attributes	Spatial analysis
Precinct identification	Regionalization process
Precinct boundaries	Land-use analysis
Transition zone	Scale
Precinct evolution and growth	
■ Evolution	Core-periphery model
■ Site redevelopment	Gravity model
■ Clustering	Central place theory
	Spatial transformation
	Spatial interaction
	Site and situation factors
Internal linkages	
■ Business coherence and integration	Systems analysis
■ Visitor movements – gateways, nodes, paths, districts, edges, landmarks	Spatial interaction
■ Use of space	Mental maps
■ Internal accessibility	
External linkages	
■ Hierarchical	Systems analysis
■ Business	Gravity model
■ Political/organizational	Network analysis
■ Visitor origins	Distance decay
■ Accessibility	Central place theory
■ Transport	Spatial interaction
	Intervening opportunity
Impacts	
■ Economic benefits	Land-use analysis
■ Gentrification	Carrying capacity
■ Displacement	
■ Standardization	
Variations	
■ Age	Land-use analysis
■ Evolution	Place differentiation
■ Location	Site and situation factors
■ Type	'Sense of place'
Prospects	
■ Continuing deindustrialization	Core-periphery model
■ Satellite developments	
■ Integration	

theory, growth pole strategy, the gravity model, core-periphery forces and spatial interaction.

There is a range of internal and external linkages related to the presence, maintenance, regulation and impacts of precincts as complexes devoted to tourism. In many precincts the comfort and convenience of pedestrian visitors is of paramount importance and attention is given to facilitate these, making use of the elements of mental mapping. There are also more extensive interactions (e.g. networks and collaborative arrangements) involving visitors, suppliers and regulators, some extending from local to global. Linkages can be examined as examples of spatial interaction and as reflections of component interdependence in a hierarchy of systems in which distance decay and gravity forces play a part.

The positive impacts associated with tourism precincts are primarily economic, but there are concerns about the displacement of resident populations driven out by crowding, gentrification processes and rising land values. In some areas efforts are directed to maintaining place differentiation as a counter to a trend towards homogenization in the design and architecture of tourism precincts.

The future of urban tourism precincts will be influenced by continuing deindustrialization, a relative decline in the gravitational force of CBDs, growth of satellite business districts in suburban areas, and the emergence of complexes combining central place functions, recreation and tourism services.

Discussion Questions and Exercises

(1) Using examples, discuss whether or in what respects, an urban tourism precinct is similar to a tourist destination region?

(2) Develop a list of spatial considerations which would influence a local council decision to allow or prohibit tourism developments alongside a cathedral.

(3) Explain, with the use of examples, how clustering such as that associated with urban tourism precincts contributes to expansion of the opportunity spectrum.

(4) In your opinion, would the adoption of the Singaporean Thematic Zone strategy be appropriate in Western cities. Explain your answer.

(5) Suggest, with an explanation, which internal element of an urban tourism precinct is, in your opinion, the most essential.

(6) Provide a statement of the principle of distance decay as a positive correlation.

(7) What problems might be incurred by residents living close to an urban tourism precinct?

(8) How might the decentralization of business activity in cities affect the form and distribution of urban tourism precincts?

References

Ashworth, D.J., & Dietvorst, A.G.J. (1995). Tourism transformations: an introduction, Chapter1. In D.J. Ashworth, & A.G.J. Dietvorst (Eds.), *Tourism and Spatial Transformations: Implications for Policy and Planning.* Wallingford, Oxon: CAB International.

Boerwinkel, H.W.J. (1995). Management of recreation and tourist behaviour at different spatial levels. In D.J. Ashworth, & A.G.J. Dietvorst (Eds.), *Tourism and Spatial Transformations: Implications for Policy and Planning* (pp. 241–263). Wallingford, Oxon: CAB International.

Boudeville, J.R. (1966). *Problems of Regional Economic Planning.* Edinburgh: University Press.

Christaller, W. (1966). *Central Places in Southern Germany*, trans. C.W. Baskin. Englewood Cliffs and London: Prentice Hall (German Edition, 1933).

Dietvorst, A.G.J. (1995). Tourist behaviour and the importance of time–space analysis. In D.J. Ashworth, & A.G.J. Dietvorst (Eds.), *Tourism and Spatial Transformations: Implications for Policy and Planning (Chapter10).* Wallingford, Oxon: CAB International.

Friedmann, J. (1973). *Urbanization, Planning and National Development.* London: Sage.

Getz, D., Joncas, D., & Kelly, M. (1994). Tourist shopping villages in the Calgary region. *Journal of Tourism Studies*, 5(1), 2–15.

Gospodini, A. (2001). Urban design, urban space morphology, urban tourism: an emerging new paradigm concerning their relationship. *European Planning Studies*, 9(7), 925–934.

Gould, P. (1973). On mental maps. In R.M. Downs, & D. Stea (Eds.), *Image and Environment: Cognitive Mapping and Spatial Behaviour.* Chicago, IL: Adine.

Griffin, T., Hayllar, B., & King, B. (2006). City spaces, tourist places: an examination of tourist experiences in Melbourne's riverside precincts. *To the City and Beyond, Proceedings of the CAUTHE Conference*, Melbourne 6–9 February, CD ROM, pp. 1036–1050.

Gunn, C.A. (1994). *Tourism Planning: Basics, Concepts, Cases.* Washington, DC: Taylor & Francis.

Hall, C.M. (1995). *Introduction to Tourism in Australia: Impacts, Planning and Development.* Melbourne: Longman.

Hall, C.M. (2005). *Tourism: Rethinking the Social Science of Mobility.* Harlow, Essex: Pearson.

Ismail, H., & Baum, T. (2006). Urban tourism in developing countries: the case of Melaka (Malacca) City, Malaysia. *Anatolia*, 17(2), 211–234.

Jansen-Verbeke, M., & van de Wiel, E. (1995). Tourism planning in urban revitalization projects: lessons from the Amsterdam waterfront development. In D.J. Ashworth, & A.G.J. Dietvorst (Eds.), *Tourism and Spatial Transformations: Implications for Policy and Planning (Chapter 8).* Wallingford, Oxon: CAB International.

Kelly, I., & Nankervis, T. (2001). *Visitor Destinations.* Milton, Qld.: Wiley.

Law, C.M. (2002). *Urban Tourism: The Visitor Economy and the Growth of Large Cities* (2nd edn). London: Continuum.

McManus, P.M. (1998). Preferred pedestrian flow: a tool for designing optimum interpretive conditions and visitor pressure management. *Journal of Tourism Studies*, 9(1), 40–50.

Melbourne Convention and Visitors Bureau (MCVB) (2006). *New Developments.* Available at www.mcvb.com.au (accessed 17 November 2006).

Page, S. (1995). *Urban Tourism.* New York: Routledge.

Page, S.J., & Hall, C.M. (2003). *Managing Urban Tourism.* Harlow, Essex: Pearson.

Savage, V.R., Huang, S., & Chang, T.C. (2004). The Singapore River thematic zone: sustainable tourism in an urban context. *The Geographical Journal*, 179(3), 212–225.

Simpson, F. (1999). Tourist impact in the historic centre of Prague: resident and visitor perceptions of the historic built environment. *The Geographical Journal*, 165(2), 173–183.

Stilwell, F. (1992). *Understanding Cities and Regions.* Leichhardt, NSW: Plato.

7

The Structure and Form of Urban Tourism Precincts: Setting the Stage for Tourist Performances

Christopher Krolikowski and Graham Brown

Introduction

Our level of knowledge about urban tourism is said to have suffered from 'double neglect' (Ashworth, 1989), with tourism research having failed to acknowledge the way tourists respond to environmental variables in cities and urban researchers largely ignoring tourism issues. Consequently, little is known about the tourist experience of urban destinations and how it is shaped by the specific spatial characteristics of urban environments (Dietvorst, 1995; Jansen-Verbeke & Van de Wiel, 1995; Jansen-Verbeke, 1998; Jansen-Verbeke & Lievois, 1999). This is surprising as tourism precincts, which often form the focal points of tourism activities in a city, represent a potentially insightful unit of analysis. The complexity of tourism experiences in urban precincts can be viewed as a product of the wide range of tourist interpretations and responses to the combination of physical features offered at each precinct.

This chapter will confront this complexity and will seek to provide a conceptual foundation for the analysis of tourism precincts. A discussion of the functional and spatial characteristics of precincts will be considered with reference to contrasts between precincts that exhibit mixed space-use developments and those that reflect specialist themes and the clustering of attractions. The notion of a tourism precinct as a stage for tourism performances is explored with a focus on the synergistic relationship between the spatial form of tourism precincts and the performances of tourists.

Defining Tourism Precincts: Spatial Characteristics

The term 'tourism precinct' is not widely understood and suffers from definitional confusion with use of the term subject to a multiplicity of interpretations. A recent enquiry at the tourist information centre in Melbourne about that city's tourism precincts caused consternation among the staff and a request for the term to be explained. This was despite the availability of the brochure entitled 'Discover Melbourne's Precincts'. For tourists, 'tourism precincts' are likely to be seen as artificial constructs which are not readily identifiable from the broader urban fabric. In a study of Sydney's Rocks a tourist stated: 'There's not a sort of sign that said 'this is The Rocks', we just sort of stumbled across it' (Hayllar & Griffin, 2005: 521). A statement such as this illustrates some of the problems associated with the demarcation of clear boundaries. It may also indicate the way tourists operate in unfamiliar environments and the significance of 'signs' as they seek to gain orientation within particular precincts.

In the academic literature, a 'tourism precinct' has been defined and described in a number of ways (see Stansfield & Rickert, 1970; Burtenshaw et al., 1991; Getz, 1993; Jansen-Verbeke & Lievois, 1999; Judd, 1999; Ashworth & Tunbridge, 2000; Hayllar & Griffin, 2005). Even though the various terms used by the authors broadly refer to a similar concept, each of them encapsulates a somewhat different meaning and thus implies distinct spatial qualities. For instance, many tourist-historic cities are characterized by less definite external boundaries than the newly developed tourism precincts.

In some historic cities, heritage resources serve as 'markers', endowed by agents such as local heritage resource managers, members of the tourist industry, or tourists themselves (Ashworth & Tunbridge, 2000: 63). Thus, the final shape of the tourist areas within the historic city is the result of political processes. This can be illustrated using the example of Prague. In contrast to many other cities of Central Europe, Prague emerged from World War II with a heritage base that was largely untouched. However, the city's current tourism precincts are a product of 'marking' that has occurred during the last 60 years. In the communist era, only certain parts of the city were made accessible to tourists. The controlling role of government in determining tourist flows into the country and its role in the conservation of particular historic buildings and sites determined the nature of tourism activity in Prague. After the fall of communism in 1989, the extensive growth of tourism has altered the map of the tourist areas in the city (Hoffman & Musil, 1999; Simpson, 1999). New areas have been discovered, revitalized and 'marked' for the purpose of tourism, extending existing borders of the tourist city and forming new tourism districts (Hoffman & Musil, 1999: 184).

The confusion in demarcating clear borders of tourism precincts in historic cities is also a result of the overlapping that occurs at different levels of the broader city, and particularly between its historic and commercial areas (Burtenshaw et al., 1991; Ashworth & Tunbridge, 2000). Such overlapping (represented in Fig. 7.1) tends to be more prominent in smaller towns where space limitations foster stronger links between various districts and their functions. The historically determined layout of many European towns has created a merging across multiple uses and users of space. Hence, the transition between tourism precinct and the broader urban area may be difficult to identify due to overlapping functions of the city and the fluidity of borders between the different urban districts.

Figure 7.1 may be particularly applicable to small- and medium-sized historic towns where tourism precincts have emerged naturally from the existing urban form (Ashworth & Tunbridge, 2000: 78). In larger cities there is often less extensive overlapping and greater physical separation. The polycentric nature of large cities which

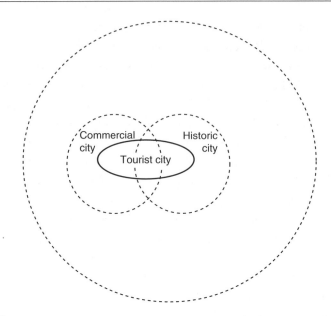

Figure 7.1 The location of the tourist city (Ashworth & Tunbridge, 2000: 74)

is characterized by wide spatial dispersion of historic and cultural attractions results in distinct and spatially separate tourism precincts (Ashworth & Tunbridge, 2000: 212). In cities such as London and New York, famous theatre districts have emerged over a long period of time to become prominent and distinctive components of tourist maps. In Paris, tourism precincts are spatially dispersed with functional links connecting them into a web of multi-precinct experiences (Pearce, 1998):

> *Within the polycentric tourist-historic city each individual tourist-historic district is not only distinctive but does not necessarily contribute towards a single consistent aggregate tourist-historic identity for the city as a whole, although it may be one part of the package of experiences assembled by the tourist (Ashworth & Tunbridge, 2000: 213).*

In purpose-built precincts, where new developments have been added to areas as part of a regeneration strategy, the identification of precinct boundaries may be more clearly defined. The physical distinctiveness of newly developed precincts often supplies an attraction in its own right: giving tourists a chance to gaze upon and admire cityscapes that are commonly accompanied by the presence of water and other natural attractions such as parklands. Law (1993: 131) recognizes the potential of combining land and water into aesthetically pleasing environments, whilst the success of developments such as the South Bank precincts in Melbourne and Brisbane testifies to the appeal of such juxtapositions.

In both heritage-based and purposefully developed tourism precincts the main 'pull' factors can be attributed to particular morphological features of a place including its built environment, architecture, urban form, artefact and public spaces (Jansen-Verbeke & Lievois, 1999: 93–94). Alexander (1979) in his groundbreaking book 'The Timeless Way of Building' provides an interesting perspective on the ability of the physical and architectural aspects of cities to generate what he has, enigmatically, described as a 'quality without name'. The author develops the concept of 'patterns', or repeating spatial elements of a city, which foster the emergence of 'quality without name' and, in so doing, create a distinctive urban identity:

> *Venice gets its life and structure from its patterns. A large number of islands, typically 1000 feet across, packed together houses, 3–5 stories, built right up to the canals; each island with a small square in the middle of it, the square usually with a church; narrow, irregular paths cutting across the islands; hump-backed bridges where these paths cross canals; houses opening onto the canals and onto the streets; steps at the canal entrance (to take care of variations in water level) ... Venice is the special place it is, only because it has these patterns of events in it, which happen to be congruent with all these patterns in the space (Alexander, 1979: 96–97).*

Urban tourism precincts are defined by their particular patterns of architectural design, layout, attractions and the overall configuration of the physical elements that then help to forge a particular sense of place. Maitland's (2007) research in the areas of Islington and North Southwark in London confirmed the importance of architecture, building streetscape and physical form, endowed with the particular atmosphere and sociocultural attributes of the locality in generating a sense of place that then forms a focal point of tourists' attention. Also Griffin and Hayllar in their investigations of two Australian waterfront heritage areas of Fremantle and Williamstown showed that most tourists visited the precincts not for specific attractions but rather for the atmosphere and ambience of those places (Griffin & Hayllar, 2006: 8).

Consistently with the above views, Costa and Martinotti (2003), in making reference to Venice, point out that most people visit the city not so much for its attractions but rather for its 'atmosphere' and the 'urban spectacle' that the city presents. Thus, the 'quaint' atmosphere of many historic towns rich in heritage presents a tourist attraction in itself. Evoking past eras and somewhat idealized versions of the past, they provide a focal point for a tourist gaze and an opportunity to reminisce and daydream. In purposefully developed urban precincts the focus appears to be of a different kind; revealing the lure of visual and material consumptions embedded in and designed to constitute an integral and often central part of those spaces.

Urry's (1990) distinction between what he termed the 'romantic gaze' and 'collective gaze' may be useful in categorizing the organic and new precincts according to the type of gaze they are likely to attract. Consequently, whilst the romantic gaze implies 'solitude, privacy and a personal, semi-spiritual relationship with the object of the gaze' and may involve 'nostalgia for heritage rescued from contemporary urbanism' (Costa & Martinotti, 2003: 65), the collective gaze refers to entertainment and amusement which is experienced in the presence of other people (Urry, 1990: 45). Even though this may be an overly simplistic view, the focus on entertainment and leisure of many newly developed precincts does help to distinguish them from the historic city, which in most cases offers a more 'layered' experience.

Characteristics of Tourism Precincts

The functional integration of tourism precincts, at both intra- and inter-precinct levels, is a crucial aspect determining the dynamics of tourism activity occurring within a precinct (Jansen-Verbeke & Van de Wiel, 1995). Whilst internal dimensions of a tourism precinct are the main focus here, it must be acknowledged that they cannot be considered in isolation from the broader environment of cities and the interlinkages with other tourism districts. For instance, in Singapore, a government programme sought to redesign districts that reinforced their distinctive ethnic identities (Chang, 2000: 38). This was achieved, in part, by fostering greater functional interaction between the precincts. The changed dynamics of the spatial urban product served to reinforce the specialization of the individual precincts, making their distinctive ethnic theme virtually a precondition of, and essential to, the wholeness of the urban experience in Singapore. In a similar manner, Melbourne's 15 urban precincts promoted by the city council (City of Melbourne, no date) are defined by strong spatial and functional links which ultimately affect the internal functioning of the precincts, their spaces and uses on a micro level. Thus, the 'Flinders Quarter' is 'Melbourne's designer paradise, where you will discover clothes, furniture, craft, art, organic food, film poetry bookshops, cigar bars, fishing rods, basement jazz and warehouse conversation' whilst the 'Yarra River' Precinct is the 'pulsating heart of entertainment and leisure … exciting, energizing and with spectacular views of the city' (City of Melbourne, no date). Consequently, it may be argued that the functional interaction of precincts on a broader level reinforces the development of a specific identity for each of the individual precincts.

Despite the ongoing debate on the increasing homogeneity of tourism spaces and the diminishing distinctness of urban areas (Judd, 1999; Middleton, 2000; Maitland, 2007; Richards & Wilson, 2007), the particular internal configuration of tourism precincts remains unique for each precinct. The morphology of existing urban fabric or specific design of newly established tourism precincts defines their particular characteristics and uses. Getz (1993) has discussed the importance of physical and functional integration of tourism precincts and his model of the tourism business district (TBD) highlights the role of spatial and functional integration of the core attraction, central business district (CBD) functions and essential services (Getz, 1993: 597). The role of access into and within the TBD is also emphasized as being crucial in facilitating the movement of tourists (Fig. 7.2).

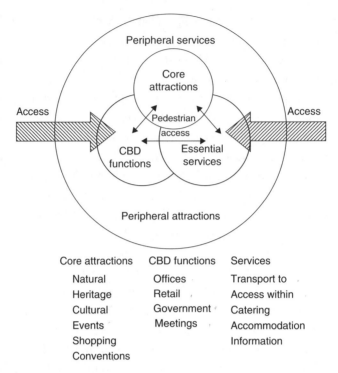

Core attractions	CBD functions	Services
Natural	Offices	Transport to
Heritage	Retail	Access within
Cultural	Government	Catering
Events	Meetings	Accommodation
Shopping		Information
Conventions		

Figure 7.2 Tourism business district (Getz, 1993: 597)

Getz argued that creating a critical mass by the spatial integration of attractions, tourist amenities and other functions of a city, including its commercial role helps to increase the attractiveness of precincts to tourists. His case study of Niagara Falls, New York and Niagara Falls, Ontario discussed the implications of different types of spatial organization of the TBD. The more concentrated form of the TBD on the US side offered a benefit of easier exploration of the area by the mostly pedestrian tourists, whilst the more dispersed Canadian Niagara Falls was thought to experience fewer problems with traffic congestion and land shortages.

Clustering of attractions and tourist facilities in both organic and purposefully constructed precincts has been seen as instrumental in achieving greater spatial and functional integration of urban tourism precincts (Getz, 1993; Jansen-Verbeke & Van de Wiel, 1995; Page, 1995a; Pearce, 1998). Concentrating tourist-oriented attractions and activities in one site helps to create a wide range of potential uses of an urban tourism precinct (Jansen-Verbeke & Van de Wiel, 1995). In a case study of London's Docklands, Page (1995a) warned against ignoring the importance of clustering, citing the Department of the Environment's view that:

> *Tourism projects appear to have greater impact when they are grouped with other tourism projects in a relatively small geographical area. This clustered approach gives a higher profile, enables links to be developed between projects and facilitates joint marketing (Page, 1995a: 70).*

The importance of clustering within tourism precincts is underlined by the fact that tourists' mental maps of an area are usually fragmented and restricted to a relatively small area (Burtenshaw et al., 1991: 212). In addition, the fact that most tourists do not possess their own transport and are often unfamiliar with local public transportation limits them to particular spatial confines. Clustering, as a form of concentrating attractions, tourist facilities and other elements of interest, allows for convenient access to and experience of tourism precincts. The role of pedestrian access to a wide range of attractions within a precinct presents a possibility to engage in diverse activities (Jansen-Verbeke & Lievois, 1999). Precincts that provide convenient linkages between their internal elements encourage exploration of the area and increase their attractiveness to mainly pedestrian tourists (Getz, 1993). The benefits of creating pedestrian linkages in cities have been advocated (Gehl & Gemzoe, 2001; Gehl, 2002) and finds support from the evidence of successful waterfront developments in Baltimore and Liverpool (Craig-Smith, 1995), (Fuller, 1995) and Brisbane (Fagence, 1995).

The results of studies conducted in Amsterdam (Jansen-Verbeke & Van de Wiel, 1995) and Paris's two neighbouring attractions – Notre Dame and Sainte Chapelle (Pearce, 1998) demonstrate in practice the importance of clustering and creating convenient pedestrian access within precincts. An example of failure to integrate adjacent sites is apparent in the latter study, wherein the two attractions (despite spatial proximity) exhibited significantly different visitation levels and almost no functional integration (Pearce, 1998: 56). This could be explained not only by the status of Notre Dame as one of the main tourist icons of Paris but also the district's confusing spatial structure and the poor pedestrian linkages between the two sites.

In heritage-based tourism, as a city adapts to new economic and regulatory conditions, so the functions and uses of its spaces change (Burtenshaw et al., 1991; Ashworth & Tunbridge, 2000; Page & Hall, 2003). Tourism is a relatively recent 'layer' added to an already established environment, sharing city spaces with other functions of a historic city.

The interweaving of urban space, heritage and leisure takes a unique course in each case. In the example of Amsterdam, the gentrification of the historic city centre, government regulations as well as the particular layout of the area characterized by small-sized land blocks, narrow streets and alleys (often inaccessible by car) ultimately determined the mix of land uses in the area. There was little opportunity to develop large offices and instead, a diverse range of leisure functions emerged; from antique shops to restaurants (Terhorst et al., 2003: 80). A similar process took place in York where the re-orientation of the city from a place of production to one of consumption resulted in a gradual incorporation of leisure and tourism functions in the city's structure (Meethan, 1996). In both cases, the existing spatial and social fabric of the city has played a significant role in determining the formation of a tourism precinct. A gradual amalgamation of tourism into heritage areas where tourism is 'injected' into an existing structure of a city facilitates a more diverse mix of uses with smaller, human-scale developments. Such organically developed areas create an assemblage of 'unlike' elements (Moltch et al., cited in Maitland, 2007: 31), combining unique and diverse uses of space that add to the touristic potential of a precinct. As a result, the organically developed precincts have been found to be more sustainable and resilient to changes in customer expectations as compared to areas which relied on specific attractions (Maitland, 2007; Murayama & Parker, 2007).

At the other end of the continuum, purposefully developed tourism precincts with no or little pre-existing spatial form are subjected to a deliberate planning process that determines a 'desirable' mix of developments and particular patterns of space use. Baltimore, where the integration of offices and residential units with tourism and leisure amenities was pioneered, has become a benchmark for similar type of developments around the globe (Craig-Smith, 1995: 19). The success of Baltimore can be explained by spatial as well as functional integration of diverse uses in a visually attractive setting. Utilizing a waterfront location and providing an array of activities, ranging from flea markets and boat races to international festivals, allowed Baltimore to generate a critical mass to attract a diversity of users (Craig-Smith, 1995). Creating accessible environments with convenient pedestrian access and attractive public spaces has also contributed to the development's popularity (Rubenstein, 1992).

The model of waterfront precinct development established in Baltimore has been exported to and replicated in places as varied as Darling Harbour in Sydney, Yokohama Bay in Japan and Barcelona's Ramblar del Mar (Jones, 2007). This raises the issue of homogenization and replication of urban spaces (Jansen-Verbeke, 1998; Judd, 1999; Jones, 2007; Maitland, 2007; Murayama & Parker, 2007; Richards & Wilson, 2007), as well as a possible disregard for the specific local (physical and sociocultural) context in which such precincts emerge (Judd, 1999; Jones, 2007; Richards & Wilson, 2007). Maitland (2007) questioned the authenticity of the purposefully developed precincts which, according to him, increasingly constitute a standardized tourism product reproduced on a global scale regardless of their geographic and cultural positioning. He argues that 'enjoyment of distinctive places may in part be the opportunity to determine the mix of the novel and local with the international and familiar – providing choices unavailable in pre-planned tourism bubbles or urban entertainment destinations' (Maitland, 2007: 28).

It appears that alternatives to existing models of creating new tourism precincts are needed. Creating tourism spaces that are complex, multidimensional, and unique is required in order to reverse increasingly homogenous and commodified tourist cities. The current literature emphasizes the need to move beyond the mixed-use planning purely in terms of supplying spatial diversity for potential uses, to interweaving cultural and place-specific elements into the physical form of such developments (Smith, 2007). The notion of developing creative spaces, creative spectacle and creative tourism, in which culture plays a central role has been raised (Richards & Wilson, 2007) and deserves further consideration. In the quest to become attractive to tourists, many urban areas have lost what initially made them a focus of interest – the richness of the urban spectacle, with the life of the city, its residents, and their culture at the core of the urban experience.

Integrating the Form and Uses of Tourism Precincts: City as Stage

The last part of this chapter considers an important, yet largely overlooked, aspect of the interrelationship between the spatial characteristics of urban tourism precincts and the tourist experience of precincts. The dominance of marketing and management perspectives in dealing with the urban tourism phenomenon appears to have diverted attention from the core issues of how the urban form and content shapes the experience of tourists. A request has been made to shift the debate from focusing on why tourists visit places to what they actually do and experience whilst at the destination (Middleton, 2000; Griffin & Hayllar, 2006). There is also a need to better understand the behaviour of tourists in urban precincts and to examine the way the physical setting may influence their behaviour.

Tourism precincts as an integral part of a broader urban context provide an interesting insight into the complex interaction of tourists, local residents and the city as the setting for the interaction. The spatial configuration of precincts as represented in their physical structure forms an arena for the behaviour and experience of visitors. It has been argued that themed places are particular kinds of stages upon which both tourists and workers in the tourism industry perform (Edensor & Kothari, 2003). Bærenholdt (2003: 150) suggests that 'there is a complex relationality of places and people that are connected through diverse performances' and that 'the 'place' itself is not as much fixed but is itself implicated within the complex networks by which 'hosts, guests, buildings, objects and machines' are contingently brought together so as to produce certain tourist performances in certain places at certain times'. The tourists perform at places and 'act out' their touristic scripts in relation to the stage as well as other performers, residents and visitors alike, thus shaping the spectacle of the urban experience (Bagnall, 2003).

Tourism precincts, as spaces of tourist performances, consist of an intricate web of relationships that link the stage with the performers and their performances. The space of tourism precincts can be envisaged as a stage supplying a context for the performances of tourists; a stage which is simultaneously re-contextualized and transformed by their performances. Goffman (1959) refers to the front stage, which provides the context of the performance, defining the situations that take place within its confines. Hence, it is the stage that provides a background for the enactment of tourists' roles through the presence and nature of the stage's physical setting; the décor, the props, as well as the performances of others. The role of sociocultural, temporal and space-specific norms regulating this performance is also crucial to the nature of the overall spectacle. Junemo (2004) in a description of 'playscapes', emphasized the significance of 'thematized' environments as 'interactive milieux' for social exchanges. Subsequently, it is not exclusively the touristic scripts of 'tourists as actors' that define their experience of a place, but to a significant extent the spatial and social contexts in which those scripts are written and enacted. The spatial and social settings act as regulators of the tourist performance – encouraging some while making others look out of context, and thus are crucial to the investigation of the nature of urban tourism.

The relationship between people and their environment has been explored in many fields, notably in environmental psychology. Some of the earliest and most fundamental works in the field confirmed a close interdependence between spatial structure and spatial behaviour (Berry, 1968). The ecological equation devised by Lewin (1951) illustrates this by construing behaviour as an outcome of environmental and person-related factors. Barker's theory of behaviour setting (1968) presumes a unity between physical setting and behaviour, conceiving the latter as an amalgamation of the physical environment (milieu), standing pattern of behaviour (re-occurring human activity) and spatio-temporal limitations of the previous two (Barker, 1968). According to Barker, each setting possesses a programming which enforces particular forms of activities, whilst discouraging others. The theory resonates with the previously mentioned notion of tourist spaces as a stage for tourist performances; both allowing conceptualizing tourist spaces and events that occur within it as a holistic and mutually dependent process.

Barker (1968) observed that a person in a church exhibits different behaviour from a person in a marketplace. This may seem simplistic, yet it does clearly demonstrate the point that different environments encourage different forms of behaviour. From the tourism point of view, the relationship between form and structure of tourism precincts and the corresponding activities that occur within them, remains of particular interest for two main reasons. First, as mentioned previously, the tourists' experience, or performance, is to a large extent shaped by the nature of spatial context, or the stage, in which it takes place. Consequently, a particular tourism space and its internal arrangement also promotes different activities and experiences. On the other hand, the same space along with its corresponding activities also forms an object of the tourist gaze. The gaze is directed as much towards the urban scene as to the performance of others. As a result, the tourists can be seen simultaneously as performers and an audience for the performance of others (Goffman, 1959). The space of urban tourism precincts along with re-occurring performances demonstrates the relationality of space and activity, and the way it contributes to developing a distinctive identity of a given place, simultaneously providing content for the tourist gaze. Alexander's notion of patterns which was mentioned earlier in this chapter captures this phenomenon with grand insightfulness:

> *[T]here is a fundamental inner connection between each pattern of events, and the pattern of space in which it happens. For the pattern in the space is, precisely, the precondition, the requirement, which allows the pattern of events to happen. In this sense, it plays a fundamental role in making sure that just this pattern of events keeps on repeating over and over again, throughout the space, and that is, therefore, one of the things which gives a certain building, or a certain town, its character (1979: 92).*

The concepts of patterns as well as the theory of behaviour setting introduced by Barker carry implications for the way urban tourism, including tourism precincts, can be viewed. In particular, by linking urban spaces with corresponding activities it is possible not only to establish supply-demand representation of an urban locality, but more importantly to conceptualize the whole phenomenon of urban tourism as a holistic process of interweaving place-related qualities with multi-dimensional experiences of individual tourists. Tourism precincts are performed, as their space is inhabited, given meaning and thus transformed into place by fleeting groups of visitors.

Selectivity of vision which determines 'marking' of particular sites by tourists (Ashworth & Tunbridge, 2000: 76) and the pattern in which they are experienced (Jansen-Verbeke & Van de Wiel, 1995) is another important consideration in the analysis of the interplay between tourism spaces and tourist performances. Gibson's research on visual perception and the resulting theory of environmental affordances links particular properties of the environment with behavioural opportunities, as mediated by individual (visual) perception (Gibson, 1977; Gibson, 1979). Environmental affordances can be envisaged as specific opportunities for behaviours, which result from a congruence between certain environmental properties and the abilities of a person, as well as their needs, wants and motivations (Greeno, 1994: 340). In this light, the environment can be seen as 'full of opportunities and constraints because of its characteristics' (Lang, 1987: 81); like a theatre's stage, it enables certain performances and interactions to occur, whilst making others more difficult to stage due to inappropriate settings and a lack of relevant props. Haldrup and Larsen (2006) discuss affordances in terms of experiencing physical landscapes as a stage:

> *[Tourists] step into the 'landscape picture', and engage in bodily, sensuous and expressive ways with their materiality and 'affordances'. Landscape as a 'way of seeing' must be complemented by an idea of 'landscape as stage'. This landscape has a dense materiality of scenery, sets and so on that crucially not only signifies and stirs the imagination, but enables things and enactments (p. 281).*

The tourist-opportunity spectrum (Jansen-Verbeke & Van de Wiel, 1995; Jansen-Verbeke, 1998; Jansen-Verbeke & Lievois, 1999) reflects the concept of affordances within an urban tourism context. It accounts for the complexity of interactions between the stage and the performers, linking the structure and content of urban tourism spaces with the actual pattern of their use. The model combines core elements of urban tourism which may include a range of historical, cultural or recreational attractions with secondary elements which encompass a broadly understood hospitality sector, entertainment and others. The clusters of spatial elements represented in the tourist-opportunity spectrum entail different uses of the same place by different groups of people (Jansen-Verbeke & Van de Wiel, 1995; Jansen-Verbeke & Lievois, 1999). It is also interesting to note that the factors which constitute the urban tourist-opportunity spectrum parallel to a large extent the issues discussed in the first part of the chapter from functional integration of tourism precincts to their accessibility. More specifically, Jansen-Verbeke and Lievois (1999) envisage the tourist-opportunity spectrum as comprising:

- accessibility to and within the destination area;
- the possibility of choosing from a wide range of activities and meeting a diversity of preferences;
- the combination of activities within a specific time–space budget;
- the spatial arrangement of interesting places (networks, trails);
- the functional synergy between urban facilities; and
- interaction between activities.

What seems to be of particular value in the tourist-opportunity spectrum is the linking of the structure and form of urban precincts with the functions they play for different groups of visitors. Along with the theory of affordances the tourist-opportunity spectrum exposes the significance of individualized space, where factors such as gender, race, age, sexuality, disability and others influence the lens through which the same touristic space can be read and experienced. The concept of choraster (Wearing & Wearing,1996) points to an interactivity and transformation of space where qualities of a city and a tourist are in a state of constant flux and exchange. The notion of 'chora' conceptualizes space as being open to transformation, permitting a wide range of human performances and embracing diversity. This concept, however, is yet to be fully recognized in urban planning, where the emphasis in designing spaces is often on the aesthetic rather than human element.

The case of the revitalization of North Terrace in Adelaide, one of South Australia's most prominent urban tourism precincts, illustrates in practice the failure of urban design to create spaces that foster interactions between people and a city. A subsequent call made by the mayor of the city to 'identify what is the human activity that will make North Terrace an icon in our hearts' appeared to be overdue. Presently, North Terrace remains a place of underutilized space and unrealized potential because its rejuvenation did little more than update its façade. Seeing beyond 'aesthetic coatings' (Sheller & Urry, 2004: 8) of urban spaces and conceptualizing them as stages of human performance, where residents and tourists alike seek to express their complex roles, is a potentially fruitful alternative. For a tourism precinct to be engaging and lively its spatial design should enable a diverse range of human performances. Gehl divides them insightfully into necessary, optional (urban recreation) and social activities:

> *In good quality city areas one will find not only necessary activities (carried out under decent conditions) but also a multitude of recreational and social activities people love to do while in cities. However these activities will only happen if the circumstances are right; i.e. if the city offers tempting, good quality spaces. This is why a good city can be compared to a good party – people stay for much longer than really necessary, because they are enjoying themselves (2002: 9).*

Clearly, while some tourism precincts encourage diverse touristic activities, others do so to a lesser extent. The interconnectedness between tourism spaces and tourist performances means that stimulating places are the ones that allow tourists to become involved in a wide array of activities, addressing diverse human needs to play, to relax, to socialize and so forth. The previously discussed mixed-style developments, and their prevalence in current planning, proves the appeal of tourism precincts which assemble diverse uses of space and allow for a mixture of activities to take place. The example of festival marketplaces in cities such as Baltimore and Sydney (Craig-Smith, 1995) provides a suitable illustration of tourism precincts as places of activity. The interdependency of both, the space and activity, is fascinating but, at the same time, it adds complexity to the analysis of the phenomena.

Conclusion

The aim of this chapter was to discuss the main themes related to the structure and form of urban tourism precincts. It appears that the term 'tourism precinct' suffers from definitional 'fuzziness'; a characteristic that is reflected on a spatial level of precincts, notably those of which have emerged organically from an existing urban fabric. Previous studies point to the importance of strong spatial and functional integration as well as mixed-use developments and clustering as some of the defining features of precincts. These are likely to vary from precinct to precinct creating particular arrangements of sites and sights thus giving rise to divergent tourist gazes.

The variety and complexity of individual tourism precincts complicates the task of analysing the phenomenon. This represents the fundamental dilemma faced by urban tourism research which is characterized by a lack of strong theoretical foundations. As suggested in the second part of the chapter, this can be overcome by conceptualizing urban tourism as an interaction between the environment of cities and the tourists. The notion of a tourist performance is explored through its application to urban tourism precincts and a number of theoretical approaches are drawn to provide a framework for the examination of precincts. It has been argued that spatial properties of tourism precincts constitute a stage which affords opportunities for particular touristic performances. The relationship between the stage and enacted performances of tourists is seen as synergistic with the stage contextualizing the performances of tourists, and conversely, the performances shaping the nature of a touristic space. The proposed approach offers an opportunity to shift the currently dominant focus on spatial distribution of different supply elements to a more comprehensive examination of the phenomenon. Such a perspective is needed at a time when the continuing growth and revitalization of urban areas presents both potential and challenges for creating tourist spaces. This is also accentuated by the fact that 'a global stage is emerging, bringing the curtain up on new places and experiences for play. Upon that stage, towns, cities, islands and countries appear compete, mobilize themselves as spectacle, develop their brand and attract visitors, related businesses, and 'status' (Sheller & Urry, 2004: 8). Consequently, it is critical to go beyond 'aesthetic coatings' (Sheller & Urry, 2004: 8) of tourist spaces, and conceive them as complex places of human activity, imagery and performance.

Discussion Questions and Exercises

(1) What are the differences between organic and purposefully developed urban tourism precincts? How does this impact on the spatial distinctiveness of both types of precincts from the surrounding urban fabric?

(2) List and discuss factors that have been found to contribute to the successfulness of tourism precincts.

(3) How is spatial form and structure of tourism precincts relevant for the experience of precincts? Support your answers with examples.

(4) How can different theoretical approaches augment existing research in urban tourism and urban tourism precincts? Elaborate on some perspectives discussed in the second part of the chapter.

References

Alexander, C. (1979). *The Timeless Way of Building*. New York: Oxford University Press.

Ashworth, G.J. (1989). Urban tourism: an imbalance in attention. In C.P. Cooper (Ed.), *Progress in Tourism, Recreation and Hospitality Management* (Vol. 1, pp. 33–54). London: Belhaven.

Ashworth, G.J., & Tunbridge, J.E. (2000). *The Tourist-Historic City: Retrospect and Prospect of Managing the Heritage City.* Amsterdam: Pergamon.

Bærenholdt, J.O. (2003). *Performing Tourist Places.* Aldershot, Hants: Ashgate.

Bagnall, G. (2003). Performance and performativity at heritage sites. *Museum and Society*, 1, 87–103.

Barker, R. (1968). *Ecological Psychology: Concept and Methods for Studying the Environment of Human Behavior.* Stanford, CA.

Berry, B. (1968). A synthesis of formal and functional regions using a general field theory of spatial behaviour. In B. Berry, & D. Marble (Eds.), *Spatial Analysis: A Reader in Statistical Geography.* Englewood Cliffs, NJ: Prentice-Hall.

Burtenshaw, D., Bateman, M., & Ashworth, G.J. (1991). *The European City: A Western Perspective.* London: David Fulton Publishers.

Chang, T.C. (2000). Theming cities, taming places: insights from Singapore. *Geografiska Annaler*, 82, 35–54.

City of Melbourne (no date). *Discover Melbourne's Precincts*, pp. 1–18.

Costa, N., & Martinotti, G. (2003). Sociological theories of tourism and regulation theory. In L.M. Hoffman, S.S. Fainstein, & D.R. Judd (Eds.), *Cities and Visitors. Regulating People, Markets, and City Space* (pp. 53–71). Oxford: Blackwell.

Craig-Smith, S.J. (1995). The role of tourism in inner-harbour redevelopment: a multinational perspective. In S.J. Craig-Smith, & M. Fagence (Eds.), *Recreation and Tourism as a Catalyst for Urban Waterfront Redevelopment: An International Survey* (pp. 15–35). Westport, CT: Praeger.

Dietvorst, A.G.J. (1995). Tourist behaviour and the importance of time–space analysis. In G.J. Ashworth, & A.G.J. Dietvorst (Eds.), *Tourism and Spatial Transformations* (pp. 163–181). Wallingford, CT: CAB International.

Edensor, T., & Kothari, U. (2003). Sweetening colonialism: a Mauritian themed resort. In D.M. Lasansky, & B. McClaren (Eds.), *Architecture and Tourism* (pp. 189–205). Oxford: Berg.

Fagence, M. (1995). Episodic progress towards a grand design: waterside redevelopment of Brisbane's South Bank. In S.J. Craig-Smith, &

M. Fagence (Eds.), *Recreation and Tourism as a Catalyst for Urban Waterfront Redevelopment: An International Survey* (pp. 71–87). Westport, CT: Praeger.

Fuller, S.S. (1995). Planning for waterfront revitalization – the Alexandria experience, Virginia, the United States. In S.J. Craig-Smith, & M. Fagence (Eds.), *Recreation and Tourism as a Catalyst for Urban Waterfront Redevelopment: An International Survey* (pp. 37–52). Westport, CT: Praeger.

Gehl, J. (2002). *Public Spaces and Public Life: City of Adelaide 2002.* Adelaide: South Australian Government, City of Adelaide Capital City Committee.

Gehl, J., & Gemzoe, L. (2001). *New City Spaces.* Copenhagen: The Danish Architectural Press.

Getz, D. (1993). Planning for tourism business districts. *Annals of Tourism Research*, 20, 583–600.

Gibson, J.J. (1977). The theory of affordances. In R. Shaw, & J. Bransford (Eds.), *Perceiving, Acting, and Knowing: Toward an Ecological Psychology.* Hillsdale, NJ: Erlbaum.

Gibson, J.J. (1979). *The Ecological Approach to Visual Perception.* Hillsdale, NJ: Erlbaum.

Goffman, E. (1959). *The Presentation of Self in Everyday Life.* New York: Anchor.

Greeno, J.G. (1994). Gibson's affordances. *Psychological Review*, 101, 336–342.

Griffin, T., & Hayllar, B. (2006). Historic waterfronts as tourism precincts: an experiential perspective. *Tourism and Hospitality Research*, 7(1), 3–16.

Haldrup, M., & Larsen, J. (2006). Material cultures of tourism. *Leisure Studies*, 25, 275–289.

Hayllar, B., & Griffin, T. (2005). The precinct experience: a phenomenological approach. *Tourism Management*, 26(4), 517–528.

Hoffman, L., & Musil, J. (1999). Culture meets commerce: tourism in postcommunist Prague. In D. Judd, & S. Fainstein (Eds.), *The Tourist City* (pp. 179–197). New Haven: Yale University Press.

Jansen-Verbeke, M. (1998). Tourismification of historical cities. *Annals of Tourism Research*, 25, 739–742.

Jansen-Verbeke, M., & Lievois, E. (1999). Analysing heritage resources for urban tourism in European cities. In D.G. Pearce, & R.W. Butler (Eds.), *Contemporary Issues in Tourism Development: Analysis and Applications*. London and New York: Routledge.

Jansen-Verbeke, M., & Van de Wiel, E. (1995). Tourist behaviour and the importance of time–space analysis. In G.J. Ashworth, & A.G.J. Dietvorst (Eds.), *Tourism and Spatial Transformations:Implications for Policy and Planning*. Wallingford, CT: CAB International.

Jones, A. (2007). On the water's edge: developing cultural regeneration paradigms for urban waterfronts. In M.K. Smith (Ed.), *Tourism, Culture and Regeneration* (pp. 143–150). Wallingford, CT: CAB International.

Judd, D. (1999). Constructing the tourist bubble. In D. Judd, & S. Fainstein (Eds.), *The Tourist City* (pp. 35–53). New Haven: Yale University Press.

Junemo, M. (2004). 'Let's build a palm island!': playfulness in complex times. In M. Sheller, & J. Urry (Eds.), *Tourism Mobilities: Places to Play, Places in Play* (pp. 181–191). London and New York: Routledge.

Lang, J.T. (1987). *Creating Architectural Theory: the Role of the Behavioral Sciences in Environmental Design*. New York: Van Nostrand Reinhold.

Law, C.M. (1993). *Urban Tourism: Attracting Visitors to Large Cities*. London: Mansell.

Lewin, K. (1951). *Field Theory in Social Science*. New York: Harper & Row.

Maitland, R. (2007). Culture, city users and the creation of new tourism areas in cities. In M.K. Smith (Ed.), *Tourism, Culture and Regeneration* (pp. 25–34). Wallingford, CT: CAB International.

Meethan, K. (1996). Consuming (in) the civilized city. *Annals of Tourism Research*, 23, 322–340.

Middleton, M.C. (2000). The tourist maze: people and urban space. In M. Robinson (Ed.), *Reflections on International Tourism: Developments in Urban and Rural Tourism* (pp. 111–123). Sunderland: Centre for Travel and Tourism in association with Business Education Publishers.

Murayama, M., & Parker, G. (2007). Sustainable leisure and tourism space development in post-industrial cities: the case of Odaiba, Tokyo, Japan. In M.K. Smith (Ed.), *Tourism, Culture and Regeneration* (pp. 69–84). Wallingford, CT: CAB International.

Page, S.J. (1995a). Waterfront revitalization in London: market: led planning and tourism in London Docklands. In S.J. Craig-Smith, & M. Fagence (Eds.), *Recreation and Tourism as a Catalyst for Urban Waterfront Redevelopment: An International Survey* (pp. 53–70). Westport, CT: Praeger.

Page, S.J., & Hall, C.M. (2003). *Managing Urban Tourism*. Harlow: Prentice-Hall.

Pearce, D.G. (1998). Tourist districts in Paris: structure and functions. *Tourism Management*, 19, 49–65.

Richards, G., & Wilson, J. (2007). The creative turn in regeneration: creative spaces, spectacles and tourism in cities. In M.K. Smith (Ed.), *Tourism, Culture and Regeneration* (pp. 12–24). Wallingford, CT: CAB International.

Rubenstein, H. (1992). *Pedestrian Malls, Streetscapes, and Urban Spaces*. Canada: John Wiley & Sons.

Sheller, M., & Urry, J. (2004). Places to play, places in play. In J. Urry., & M. Sheller (Ed.), *Tourism Mobilities: Places to Play, Places in Play* (pp. 1–10). London: Routledge.

Simpson, F. (1999). Tourist impact in the historic center of Prague: resident and visitor perceptions of the historic built environment. *Geographical Journal*, 165, 173–183.

Stansfield, C.A., & Rickert, J.E. (1970). The recreational business district. *Journal of Leisure Research*, 2, 213–225.

Terhorst, P., van de Ven, J., & Deben, L. (2003). Amsterdam: It's all in the mix. In L.M. Hoffman, S.S. Fainstein, & D.R. Judd (Eds.), *Cities and Visitors. Regulating People, Markets, and City Space* (pp. 75–90). Oxford: Blackwell.

Urry, J. (1990). *The Tourist Gaze*. London: Sage.

Wearing, B., & Wearing, S. (1996). Refocussing the tourist experience: the flaneur and the choraster. *Leisure Studies*, 15, 229–243.

8

Contribution of Urban Precincts to the Urban Economy

Brent W. Ritchie

Introduction and Context

Urban areas offer a geographical concentration of facilities and attractions that are accessible to both visitors and residents alike. Urban precincts have existed for as long as urban settlements themselves. However, in the last few decades many of these precincts have received heightened attention from government as key components in urban revitalization and place marketing strategies. As Page and Hall (2003: 2) suggest 'it is only since the 1970s with the concern associated with cities affected by industrial restructuring induced by re-industrialisation, that the interest in the form and nature of the post-industrial city emerged'. Cities are increasingly looking for new economic activities to help them to overcome unemployment, deprivation and decline; all as a result of changing economic fortunes. As Law (2002) notes, the worst affected areas have been the older industrial cities in the 'northern' parts of their countries. Unemployment levels in some of these cities have remained high, and this coupled with intra-urban patterns of growth towards the outer suburbs, have left run down housing and a lack of retail activity in downtown areas further exacerbating urban decline.

However, in an effort to address these issues and respond to global pressures to modernize and develop service sector economies, governments (through public and/or private partnerships) have attempted to create new economic activities to assist in (re)developing the post-industrial or creating the post-fordist city (Hutton, 2004). In particular, government and the private sector have developed precincts as city spaces that cater for a range of different users including both locals and tourists. According to Page and Hall (2003) urban tourism has benefited from changing consumption patterns of post-industrial society with the public sector attempting to create places for investment as well as for the consumption of leisure, entertainment and tourism experiences. Entertainment or cultural industries linked to tourism have often been the core foundations of such strategies (Judd, 1995).

The Central Tourist District (CTD) outlined by Burtenshaw et al. (1991) or the Tourism Business District (TBD) identified by Getz (1993a), suggest that tourism activities in cities are located in certain areas where a relationship is evident between CBD (Central Business District) functions, tourist attractions and essential services (see Fig. 8.1). Getz (1993a) notes that a critical mass of attractions and services is required in order to encourage tourists to stay longer and increase their economic impact to the area and city. TBDs are often subjected to intense planning by municipal authorities (Getz, 1993a) integrating tourism into the broader economic context of the city.

However, while the concentration of tourism and non-tourism resources in precincts or the TBD can attract tourists, they can also create an interesting area for locals and workers through the provision of street entertainment, special events and ultimately provide a sense of place. As Judd (1995: 178) notes in referring to American downtown areas, 'Tourist and entertainment facilities coexist in a symbiotic relationship with the corporate towers, and there is some

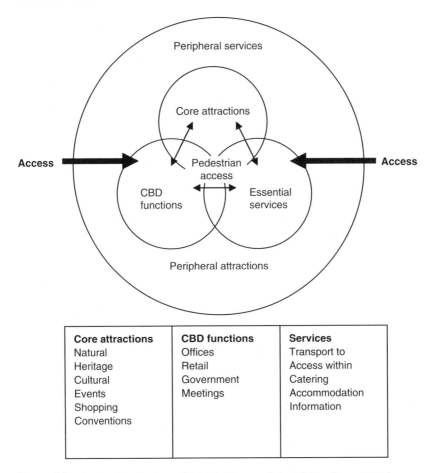

Figure 8.1 The Tourism Business District (Source: Getz, 1993a; Page, 1995)

overlap: shopping malls, restaurants and bars cater to daytime professionals who work downtown as well as to visitors'. As Savage et al. (2004: 215) explain in relation to Singapore, 'tourism thematic zones like the Singapore River are therefore multiple purpose landscapes: tourist attractions, heritage sites, residential areas and retail/entertainment precincts'.

Therefore, in examining the economic contribution of precincts it becomes difficult to separate the tourism component (or even specific entertainment or cultural tourism components) from the local component, because of this multiuse aspect of the TBD or precinct. Furthermore, not all tourist precincts are in the inner city or CBD, with enclaves often found in neighbourhood areas. However, as this chapter outlines, it is often inner city areas that are the focus for precinct (re)development. This focus raises questions about the wider distribution of economic benefits from precinct development for a city and its near environs.

In addition, Page and Hall (2003) and Law (2002) suggest some common economic benefits and costs of tourism in urban areas which can be applied to tourist precincts in urban areas. These costs and benefits are outlined in Table 8.1 and discussed in this chapter through the use of examples. The economic benefits and costs that arise from urban precincts can be considered in three major periods:

(1) Construction or (re)development of the precinct.
(2) The period several years after the precinct development – the short- or medium-term economic cycle.
(3) Decades after the precinct development – the long-term economic cycle.

This chapter discusses the interrelationship between precinct development and its impacts on the local economy using the three periods above and discussing the potential benefits and costs outlined by Page and Hall (2003). It will consider the costs and benefits associated with precincts, assess the value of precincts as part of the city's tourist attraction base and include consideration of agglomeration economies emerging from precinct development. The next section of the chapter begins with a discussion of the construction costs and benefits of tourism precinct development.

Construction or (Re)development of Precincts

A number of government initiatives and public–private sector partnerships have been developed to facilitate the construction of tourist precincts, often focusing on the redevelopment of derelict inner city or

Table 8.1 Potential economic benefits and costs of urban tourism precincts

Potential benefits	Potential costs
■ The generation of income for the local economy and local community	■ The potential for economic over dependence on one particular form of activity in the inner city or unequal distribution of benefits to inner city area
■ Creation of new employment opportunities for inner city area and expansion into new districts surrounding the precinct	■ Inflationary costs as new consumers drive demand for real estate and gentrification occurs displacing small business and residents
■ Improvements to the structure and balance of economic activities in the locality through new urban economic development	■ Growing dependency on imported products or services if the local economy is not self-sufficient and has high economic leakages
■ Encouraging entrepreneurial activity and the informal economy especially for ethnic groups	■ Seasonality in consumption and production leading to limited returns on investment
■ Regeneration led repopulation to the inner city area and growth of economic activity	■ Additional indirect costs or opportunity costs for city authorities including security and surveillance costs

Source: After Page and Hall (2003).

fringe industrial areas. In doing so, the public sector are able to attract capital from private investors and help stimulate longer-term economic development and employment services (Harvey, 1989). However, there have been criticisms of how partnerships between the public and private sector work with respect to urban and social regeneration (Goodwin, 1993), with some cities having weak private sector investment and lacking entrepreneurial activity (Law, 2002).

Economic data on the construction phase of such precincts are often difficult to find, particularly as incentives, grants or tax relief are commonly provided to the private sector and are typically not disclosed. In some cases public–private sector agencies are created specifically to develop precincts, such as the London Docklands and the Quincy Market in Boston. The Quincy Market in Boston illustrates the ability of the public sector to make profits in such developments, with the city of Boston providing $12 million (or 30 per cent of the cost of the project) for a 99-year lease, in exchange for a minimum cash payment and a portion of income from store rents above this figure (Judd, 1995). The role of the government in the London Dockland development has been substantial, with the total public cost of regenerating Docklands estimated to be approximately £3900 million, nearly half of which is related to transport, while private sector investment was estimated at £8700 million by March 1998 (DETR, 1998). Research estimates from DETR (1996) suggest that for every £1 million of public sector cost generated, there is a threefold increase in employment and a fivefold increase in the number of firms.

Consultants estimated that as part of the regeneration of the South Bank of the Thames River in London, the Tate Modern Gallery development was estimated to have provided an economic benefit of £100 million and 3000 jobs for the local community in the construction phase alone (Kennedy, 2001). As part of the legacy from the 2002 Manchester Commonwealth Games, the *SportCity* site in North East Manchester is expected to attract £400 million worth of investment, including £90 million of public money over the next 10–15 years to build a 160 hectare technology business park, provide 12,500 new homes and a new town centre with restaurants and retail facilities. In developing Birmingham's Jewellery Quarter, a total of 300 city grants totalling £1.6 million were leveraged with £3 million in private sector investment through the Jewellery Quarter Action Project (Pearce, 1994), although as discussed later, this project has been deemed a failure due to the lack of local business support.

In Detroit in the mid-1990s, an entertainment led regeneration project to develop a cultural and sports precinct involved a public contribution package of 48 per cent of the $505 million project, while in 1996 proposals for between $500–700 million worth of gambling casinos were made and were expected to create 3000–4000 jobs (McCarthy, 2002). The world's largest shopping centre, West Edmonton Mall in Alberta, Canada, combines leisure, tourism and retail in one facility. Estimates suggest the total cost of building the West Edmonton Mall was $1.2 billion.

European Union funding has been used in some cases to help regeneration efforts in countries such as Ireland, Portugal and Liverpool (UK) as part of the strategy for economic restructuring. For instance, Porto in Portugal received European Funding under the European Union Support Framework to refurbish public spaces, create new cultural facilities and public works prior to it being the European Capital of Culture (Balsas, 2004). Dublin received an initial grant of £4 million from the European Union as part of a £100 million package over 10 years to turn Temple Bar into a cultural quarter (Montgomery, 2003). As Judd (1995: 184) notes, the melding of public subsidies and private dollars through new public–private entities makes it difficult to evaluate the economic costs and benefits. Further issues, such as the fact that many developments are undertaken incrementally, also may lead to a lack of data.

Shorter/Medium-Term Economic Cycles

Tourist Visitation, Spending and Employment

More data is available on the short- to medium-term economic cycles created by tourist precincts by examining the income, employment and economic activity generated by urban tourist precincts after they are completed. These data provides more of an insight into the economic costs and benefits of precinct development. The generation of income and new employment opportunities are a direct result of attracting tourists and their money to the city or specific districts and are dependant on the links and relationships between sectors within the economy and the 'flow' of money through the economy as a result of these links. The co-location of links between tourism-related businesses in tourist precincts can stimulate the economy and provide employment opportunities and entrepreneurial activities amongst residents, often due to the concept of agglomeration economies.

Economists note that agglomeration economies occur when the location of any one economic unit depends on the location of all the others (Heilburn, 1981), while Jansen-Verbeke and Ashworth (1990) suggest that when spatial association and functional links are made in a tourist location, agglomeration economies occur. For instance, as Ashworth and Tunbridge (1990: 65) note 'restaurants and establishments combining food and drink with other entertainment ... have a distinct tendency to cluster together into particular streets of districts, what might be termed the "Latin-quarter effect"'. As Pearce (1998: 56) notes, with respect to the Ile de la Cité district in Paris, 'the linear concentration of tourist orientated shops and services – souvenir shops, restaurants, cafes and foreign money exchanges ... along the Rue du Cloître Notre Dame and the Rue d'Arcole suggest agglomerative forces are at work'. According to local data, Pearce (1998) suggests that this precinct alone generated 12 million visitors a year in the mid-1990s; however, the historic attractions themselves only received between 187,393 and 567,545 visitors (Pearce, 1998: 54). Plate 8.1 provides a visual presentation of the Louvre museum precinct in Paris. In Amsterdam the coffee shops selling cannabis have attracted other retail premises, including tattoo and body-piercing studios that deliver services to the same clientele creating 'a few hundred of these shops and studios in the historic city center' (Terhorst et al., 2003: 86).

This agglomerative effect has been noted by Judd (1995) who suggested that agglomeration economies apply to tourist districts because a full mixture of services and businesses are required to make the space maximally attractive to consumers of the space as well as providing lower costs or improving business efficiency. As Hutton (2004) notes, economic agglomeration in inner city districts creates strong backward and forward linkages between industry firms and supporting industries located in situ or in adjacent districts, as illustrated in the case of the TBD in Fig. 8.1. The creation of tourism districts or clusters has several advantages as they allow the use of shared infrastructure, public transport and access roads and lead to greater visibility

Plate 8.1 Louvre museum precinct, Paris

of tourism resources or products (Rogerson & Kaplan, 2005: 219). Furthermore, the physical proximity of a number of tourism products provides visitors with an opportunity to engage in multiple activities in a short period of time (Law, 2000). Montgomery (2003) in his discussion of success factors of cultural quarters notes that complementary daytime and evening uses, an evening economy and a diversity of land uses are important in developing an active cultural quarter to attract visitors. Therefore, a group or cluster of tourist resources may increase their attractiveness more than individual operators, helping to potentially boost visitation, tourist spending and employment.

In some cities an individual or group of attractions are able to increase visitation, not only to the attraction or precinct, but also the region. The building of the landmark Guggenheim Museum in Bilbao, northern Spain, is part of a strategy to attract tourists, business and employment to the city. Initial data indicated a monthly increase of 28,989 arrivals of which 34 per cent were foreigners (Plaza, 2000). However, more sophisticated analysis, taking into consideration external factors, estimated that visitor increases to the Guggenheim Museum accounted for 58 per cent of tourism growth and 54 per cent of overnight stays in the Basque Country from October 1997 to July 1999 (Plaza, 2000: 1057).

Flagship attractions, such as Moulin Rouge in the Montmartre precinct of Paris, help attract visitors to the district while the Tate Modern Art Gallery on London's South Bank attracted 5.25 million visitors in its first year of operation alone (Kennedy, 2001). This also led to international hotel chains, art galleries and venues moving into the area (Teedon, 2001; Hutton, 2004) to benefit from this interest. Such economic benefits are also discussed in relation to the Temple Bar District in Dublin where it was estimated to employ 2000 people in 1996 an increase of 300 per cent from 1991 when regeneration activities and construction of hotels, shops and cultural centres were completed (Montgomery, 2003).

In Canberra, Australia, attractions in the Parliamentary Zone Precinct accounted for the majority of visitation from holiday and leisure visitors (Ritchie and Dickson, 2006). Subsequently, the research indicated that 62.6 per cent of leisure and holiday visitors to the destination were motivated to visit the destination by the attractions and 38.5 per cent indicated that they would have travelled elsewhere if the attractions did not exist. The authors suggested that the location of the attractions in close proximity to each other was instrumental in their tourist attractiveness. Applying visitor spend data to secondary data the authors estimated that $256 million of direct expenditure was attributable to the attractions and $99 million per annum would have been foregone if they had not existed (Ritchie and Dickson, 2006). A total of 33 per cent of total spending was on accommodation, 30 per cent on food and beverages, and 17 per cent on shopping outside of the attractions.

As Kent et al. (1983) claim, tourists spend more on shopping than on accommodation and food! In 2000, the Travel Industry Association of America found that 63 per cent of all travellers went shopping as part of their tourist activity (Gentry, 2001). Malls and waterfront developments also provide '... a choice of shopping and entertainment facilities within a post-modern habourscape, visitors (be they local or tourists) are almost certain to find something on which to spend their money and time' (Dodson & Killian, 1998: 158). Moscardo (2004) noted that 29 per cent of visitors to Far North Queensland stated that shopping was an important or very important factor in their destination choice. Visitation took place at shopping centres as well as local markets and craft shops. Serious shoppers, who rated shopping as important and undertook both general shopping and arts/crafts shopping, represented 41 per cent of the sample. Serious shoppers were more likely to indicate the importance of nightlife/entertainment, high quality restaurants, a resort area, and were more likely to participate in commercial tours and visit attractions, indicating the potential link and value between shopping precincts and visitors.

Approximately 20 per cent of hotel leisure guest expenditure is estimated to be spent on shopping in Paris while the space between major tourist attractions such as the Opera and the Louvre have been identified as primarily tourist shopping sites for passing foot traffic with some streets specializing in luxury items such as perfume, clothing and fashion accessories (Pearce, 1998). According to Getz (1993b) the concentration of specialty shops together with entertainment and dining services defines tourist shopping villages, which are small communities that attract visitors because of their tourist retailing opportunities and their natural or cultural amenity. Examples include St Jacobs, Ontario (Canada), where it is estimated that more than 1 million people visit each year bringing between $15 million and $20 million into the village economy (Mitchell et al., 1998). However, in Amsterdam in the 'cannabis district' in the central city precinct, Terhorst et al. (2003) estimate that 50 per cent of all soft drugs are sold to foreign visitors.

Mega malls also provide distinct precincts which provide entertainment, leisure and retail opportunities for visitors. West Edmonton Mall consists of 7 major tourist attractions, theme streets, over 800 stores, 26 movie theatres, hotels and activity centres including an indoor lake and outdoor parking for over 20,000 vehicles (Timothy, 2005). The retail and entertainment opportunities provided by the Mall attract tourists as well as locals, with an estimated 35 million people visiting annually (Timothy, 2005). Data indicate that the Mall employs 23,500 people directly, while authors note that it is one of Canada's top tourist attractions averaging more than 100,000 people a day with an impact of $12 billion per annum (Finn & Erdem, 1995; Timothy, 2005). Unlike other examples of villages such as St Jacobs, between 40 and 50 per cent of all visitors to the Mall are from outside of Alberta, a greater number than visits the iconic Banff National Park or Niagara Falls. Similarly at the Mall of America, 43 million people visit the mall every year with 10–15 million from outside of a 200 km radius, providing $1.6 billion per year with 8 per cent contributed by foreign visitors (Mall of America, 2002 in Timothy, 2005; Goss, 1999). The mall has its own tourism department and tour organizers to promote mall tourism, demonstrating the importance of tourism to the Mall precinct (Goss, 1999).

Retail tourism is also occurring in developing countries. Cohen (1995) describes localized ribbon development in Thailand as short stretches of a road in a city offering similar products made by locally owned stalls, shops and workshops. The government is recognizing the importance of tourism retailing by crating a 'cultural centre' to display local products, which Cohen (1995) believes will create more regular and organized tourist visits. In one ribbon development alone, 200 workers are employed in local factories with 40 per cent of their product sold locally to tourists, while the remaining 60 per cent is exported (Cohen, 1995: 233). Furthermore, he notes that 'the ease with which tourists can directly observe production and the considerable choice of products offered by many closely adjoining establishments has made some ribbons into a tourist attraction in their own right ...' (Cohen, 1995: 234), creating links to manufacturing and exporting to provide economic development for Thailand.

Night markets are also often located in tourism precincts and their combination of diversity, on-site business activities and friendly atmosphere are drawcards for visitors to eat, play games, shop or experience authentic customs and culture (Hsieh & Chang, 2006). From a survey undertaken with Hong Kong visitors to the night markets in Taipei (Hsieh & Chang, 2006), 88 per cent of respondents stated that their preferred leisure activities at the night markets were eating followed by everyday shopping (56 per cent) and entertainment (23 per cent).

Although data were collected on visitor expenditure patterns they were not reported in the paper. According to Lau and McKercher (2004) repeat visitors to Hong Kong were more motivated by, and participated in greater numbers in shopping and visiting shopping districts or markets than first time visitors. However, research conducted on the clientele of businesses along the Singapore river precinct demonstrated that only a quarter of businesses had tourists comprising at least half of their customers and for most (63.6 per cent), Singaporeans constituted the majority of their customers (Savage et al., 2004: 220).

As Pearce (1998) suggests, the visitor services and attractions in precincts tend to spread to other adjoining streets and inner city districts with the development of cabarets and sex tourism evident in the Pigalle district. Judd (1995) terms these areas as 'carousal zones' or districts which comprise strip clubs, topless bars and stores that sell sex paraphernalia and pornography. Well-known examples include the French Quarter in New Orleans, Rush Street in Chicago, North Beach in San Francisco, the Amsterdam red light district and Kings Cross in Sydney.

An area which is often ignored in examining the economic benefits of tourist precincts is the informal economy. Hawkers, street vendors or itinerant sellers may receive economic benefit from selling goods or services to tourists at precincts or in districts. In many instances these hawkers or street vendors operate illegally as they are unlicensed. Timothy and Wall (1997) discovered that the largest items sold by street vendors in Yogyakarta, Indonesia, were clothing and leather jewellery and belts. Pearce (1998) notes that in Paris itinerant sellers and hawkers were often located close to key attractions such as Notre Dame or in districts such as Montmartre. In developing countries the informal sector is believed to account for a significant share of the local economy (Henderson, 2000), with some evidence suggesting that street vendors receive above average incomes (Lynch, 1999) and run successful businesses (Ibrahim & Leng, 2003).

Economic Costs and Issues

Although tourist precincts provide agglomeration economies that may increase business efficiency and attract tourists and their spending, they can also have negative economic effects in the short to medium economic cycle. However, data on the negative impacts or costs of tourism precincts are difficult to locate. Nevertheless, tourists attracted to precincts may influence the price of goods and services located in tourist precincts affecting both tourists and locals. For instance, in Montmartre, Paris, the growth of tourism to the district has created higher prices, lower standards and greater competition amongst local businesses (Pearce, 1998), which could lead to negative word of mouth and reduced visitor numbers.

One of the drawbacks or criticisms of the concept of agglomeration economies and the clustering of tourist facilities and services in tourist precincts is that often they are located in inner city or downtown areas, and therefore because of their location, they may create economic enclaves with limited trickle down impacts to other districts. Temple Bar in Dublin has been criticized for being too trendy and popular, with some criticism on the ruthless redevelopment and marketing of this area at the expense of other parts of the city (Montgomery, 2004). Mega malls may reduce spending that may have occurred in other parts of the city and reduce the economic benefits to local smaller-scale retail outlets in suburban areas. As McCarthy (2002: 108) states, '[s]uch displacement effects have been recognised even in Baltimore, often cited as the paradigm of tourism-related regeneration'.

Subsequently, residents may perceive that the proposed economic benefits and impacts are unevenly distributed. For instance, Ritchie and Inkari (2006) identified that residents of the Lewes District in England who lived further away from the Lewes town centre (the major tourist precinct) perceived that the economic benefits of tourism were unevenly distributed and were more cautious about the benefits of tourism. However, those located closer to the town centre were more supportive of tourism but also perceived congestion and traffic parking issues due to increased visitation to the TBD.

Not surprisingly, little data is provided on tourist precinct failures. However, studies on the economic impact of stadiums conclude that they often have limited economic impact and may even have a negative effect by replacing spending with expenditures that exit the economy more quickly due to leakages (Euchner, 1993: 71). As Richards and Wilson (2006) note, many of the tourist numbers and revenue predicted for cultural and regeneration projects often fail to materialize leading to changes to the projects. According to 1991 data, an estimated 12 million people visited the South Street Seaport in New York, with one-third comprising tourists, although projected government revenue and jobs were both lower than anticipated (Metzger, 2001). Increased investment and more public subsidies were committed to redevelop the festival marketplace with most of its shops closing within the first year and the 'flagship' Seaport museum withdrew from its joint venture with the developer because of a lack of financial return (Judd, 1995; Metzger, 2001). The Birmingham Jewellery Quarter has been labelled unsuccessful due to a lack of support from the jewellery trade itself due to security concerns, time and a lack of interest (Fields & Humphreys, 2002), despite public and private sector investment.

Even those businesses that do attract tourists to precincts may be unable to capture the full benefits of tourist spending. For instance, the attractions sector in Canberra only captured 7 per cent of holiday/leisure visitors direct spending despite nearly 63 per cent suggesting that the attractions were important or very important in their decision to visit Canberra (Ritchie and Dickson, 2006). In this sense, although they benefit from increased visitor numbers through agglomeration economies, they find it challenging to capture the economic benefits associated with this attractiveness. Furthermore, local entrepreneurs may be displaced from tourist precincts due to increasing rents and prices related to business operations as tourist demand and competition increase.

Long-Term Economic Cycles

Tourist Precincts as Economic Regeneration Tools

The concept of regeneration includes both physical, i.e. concerned with architecture and image, and social dimensions, i.e. concerned with improving the quality of life of those who already live in target areas (Page & Hall, 2003). The longer-term goal of cities is often to 'pump prime' tourist precincts in inner city areas to create broader urban development which may spread beyond the initial precinct area. As discussed earlier in the chapter, these are often created by the public sector or through public–private sector partnerships. The approach is often to promote physical growth or regeneration, in the form of high profile visible schemes or 'flagship projects' to maximize the impact on the city's image (McCarthy, 2002). As Zukin (1999) suggests, image is an important component of the broader strategy to market cities to potential investors. Cultural, entertainment, sport or leisure precincts are often linked to production, consumption and place making. As Montgomery (2003) argues, cultural quarters have been deliberately used as a model for urban regeneration in declining inner urban areas as they help establish cultural production (making objects, goods, products and providing services) as well as cultural consumption (people going to shows, visiting venues and galleries). Table 8.2 provides an overview of some of the tourism led approaches to urban regeneration, while Fig. 8.2 outlines the proposed spiral of urban development associated with precincts or what Law (2002) terms the 'strategy of urban tourism'.

Regeneration strategies have been used in many urban destinations throughout the Western world. In Australia, Sydney has also redeveloped its former waterfront area (Darling Harbour) with the use of cultural attractions including a National Maritime Museum, Aquarium and the Powerhouse Museum, while its fierce rival Melbourne has developed a similar strategy along its riverside. Flagship projects such as these are often used to stimulate further development through agglomeration economies, as in the case of convention centre development which may encourage hotels and other tourist services to locate nearby. As Montgomery (2003) suggests with respect to cultural quarters, many venues and galleries have developed organically through local entrepreneurs or have been planted as strategic elements in the development of the area by public/private partnerships.

Law (2002) suggests that these may be named 'public sector anchors' and notes that Baltimore has four including an aquarium, a science museum, a convention centre and the Harborplace festival

Table 8.2 Tourism led approaches to urban regeneration

Visitor attractions
New physical attractions, such as waterfront developments, new museums or casinos are used to attract tourists.

Cultural attractions
Expanding and using cultural attractions, such as the arts, theatre or music in order to attract visitors.

Events
Creating new festivals or attracting 'mega-events' such as major festivals and sports events.

Leisure shopping
Developing new shopping–retailing complexes.

Promoting the city as a host venue
Attracting local and international fairs, conferences and exhibitions.

Nightlife
Improving nightlife in order to attract particularly younger tourists for clubbing as part of creating a 24-hour city.

Industrial attractions
Redeveloping industrial attractions and related retail outlets.

Local food and drink
Promoting distinctive local cuisine.

Source: Based on Swarbrooke (1999, 2000) in Rogerson and Kaplan (2005).

market (which received a large public sector subsidy). Baltimore has transformed its harbour by replacing abandoned buildings with tourist facilities. HarborPlace, a two block-long translucent pavilion which opened in 1980, earned $42 million in its first year (Judd, 1995). Between 1980 and 1986 the number of tourists visiting the site and the number of hotel rooms tripled, while over a decade an estimated 15 million visitors were attracted to the precinct (Judd, 1995). Private investment began to flow and in the 1980s and 1990s the project continued to extend the regeneration by attracting the Orioles baseball

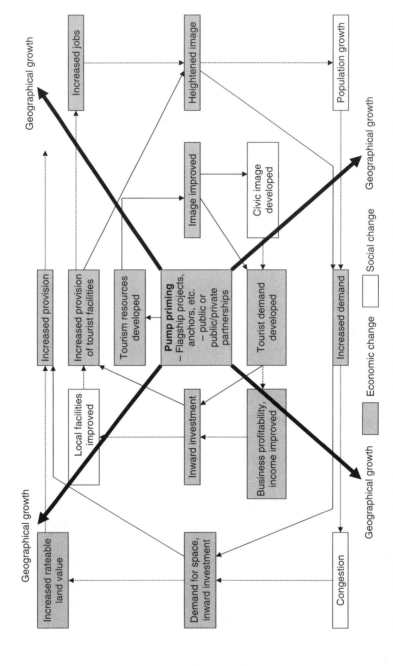

Figure 8.2 The proposed strategy of urban precinct development (Source: Modified from Fields and Humphreys, 2002: 48)

team and the Ravens football team. In the late 1990s more attractions were opened and the convention centre was extended. According to Law (2002) the precinct attracted 2.9 million overnight tourists who stayed for an average of 3.3 days in 1999.

Parts of the former ethnic enclaves of Chinatown and Little India in Singapore have been conserved, in projects that combine redevelopment and adaptive reuse and are important tourist precincts (Henderson, 2003) as they provide important tourist experiences. In San Francisco, tourist interest in the Chinatown precinct has been instrumental in providing long-term economic development for Chinese Americans (Page & Hall, 2003). Hutton (2004) suggests that social, cultural and environmental amenities are important in providing local area regeneration. He notes that important secondary regeneration benefits exist in terms of derived demand for restaurants, coffee houses, shops, galleries, recreation facilities and the like because of regeneration of inner city industrial districts (Hutton, 2004: 99).

According to Hall (2004), despite some misgivings a number of cities have embarked on large-scale sporting developments associated with regeneration strategies usually related to the hosting of major sports events such as the Olympics (e.g. Sydney, Barcelona), the Commonwealth Games (e.g. Manchester, Melbourne) or they have created sports infrastructure for sport competitions. According to Jones (2001) some cities have concentrated on the beneficial effects of media coverage, international visitation and investment rather than on servicing local orientated teams and sporting interests. As Logan and Molotch (1987) suggest, sports teams are a distinct asset to cities in view of the strong image they present the tourist traffic they attract. As Gratton et al. (2000) note, hosting major sporting events generate economic activity through the construction of facilities and infrastructure as well as through the events themselves. The facilities can also be used for hosting other events on an ongoing basis and provide additional economic activity and employment for local residents.

Ritchie and Hall (1999) suggest that Manchester's bid for the 2000 Summer Olympics was seen as a possible contribution to solving some

Table 8.3 Long-term regeneration and urban restructuring plans resulting from hosting Manchester Commonwealth Games 2002

Regeneration
- Forty hectares of land reclaimed for *Sportcity* (in North East Manchester), which has become Institute of Sport for sport training and development after the Games.

Facilities for sporting and local use
- Swimming complex used for training, research and local community use.
- City of Manchester Stadium (funded by Sport England at £77 million, Council £26 million) is now the home ground for the Manchester City Football Club.
- Athletics, squash and tennis facilities can be used for regional and local club competitions.

Tourist facilities
- Salford Quays regeneration including the Lowry Museum, Imperial War Museum North and an arts centre.
- A new convention centre (which hosted the weightlifting event initially).

of the city's 'inner city problems'. Table 8.3 indicates some of the major long-term impacts expected from the successful bid and hosting of the 2002 Manchester Games. The 1992 Barcelona Olympics was used to regenerate a derelict coastal area through the development of a new marina, leisure facilities and sandy beaches (Essex & Chalkley, 1998). The new marina, which includes restaurants and a cinema complex, is pictured in Plate 8.2. Unemployment in the city decreased during and after the Olympics from 128,000 to 78,000 mainly through the development of new business as a result of the rejuvenation (Standeven & De Knop, 1999). Additional hotels attracted more tourists to the area, which added to the city's economy, while the Barcelona Olympic Village also provided two thousand flats, three parks, offices and a conference centre, which all added to the economy of Barcelona (Standeven & De Knop, 1999: 193). As Balsas (2004) notes, many cities are using cultural, retail and entertainment developments to help repopulate declining inner city areas.

Smaller destinations have also used events as a catalyst to regenerate their inner city or waterfront areas to repopulate derelict areas.

Plate 8.2 Barcelona Olympic led waterfront development

For instance, Southampton in England is drawing on its past history as a port to help it host sporting events to regenerate and use derelict marina facilities. In terms of physical regeneration, many activities have been undertaken to beautify the inner city area. Central parks have been improved, a pedestrian precinct refurbished and transport improvements made. The creation of St Mary's Stadium, and its link to the waterfront area, has created £12 million in regeneration of St Mary's Street, attracted a new £7 million Travel Inn hotel next door and is now one of the most popular conferencing and hospitality venues on the south coast (Southampton City Council, 2003). Between 1999 and 2001, £2.8 million of spending by visitors took place. In 2000, and for the first time, the accommodation sector generated £700 million worth of earnings for the local community (Southampton City Council, 2003).

In some destinations waterfront areas (the former location of ports or industry) have been identified as being culturally significant and conserved for both visitor and local use (Hoyle, 2001). In England, destinations such as Liverpool have developed cultural tourism attractions along their waterfront and port areas to help regeneration including the Beatles Museum and Liverpool Maritime Museum, while other abandoned warehouses were replaced with shopping, recreational and apartment facilities. This work started in the 1980s with considerable national assistance (Judd, 1995). In London the South Bank of the Thames has been recently redeveloped with the recreation of Shakespeare's Globe Theatre and the development of the Tate Modern Gallery and retail, restaurants and apartments. In an effort to modernize their economies, Hoyle (2001) indicates that waterfront development is also occurring in the developing world for urban redevelopment and conservation purposes, although he concedes that it is not yet been accorded a high priority. Often beautification and clean up operations are required to create pollution free areas which are costly investments often borne by government to encourage private investment. This is exemplified in the Singapore River development (Savage et al., 2004).

Economic Costs and Issues

The longer-term costs associated with precinct development are hotly debated. This is particularly problematic because of the opportunity costs associated with using tourist precincts for achieving broader objectives such as regeneration or urban restructuring, and the lack of clear data on the long-term costs or benefits of such projects. This lack of data coupled with the long-term nature of (re)imaging or (re)developing the inner city makes economic evaluation difficult. As Hoyle (2001) suggests, costs are high, progress is slow and return on investment is not immediate.

Hall (2004) notes that the use of sport as a regeneration tool or in creating sport precincts often revolves around the external benefits (e.g. civic pride, tourism and leisure time options) brought to a city. However, in the context of sport tourism led regeneration, he notes that there is a lack of empirical evidence of the longer-term benefits. Coalter et al. (2000: 6–7) concluded, that 'there is little evidence about the medium to long-term economic effects of such sports event-led economic regeneration strategies ... In particular, there is a lack of available data on the *regenerative impact* of sports investments on local communities'. As Judd and Swanstrom (1998: 370) suggest while discussing the Greektown area of Detroit, the new restaurants and tourism-related developments represent an 'island in a sea of decay' which may occur when *induced* clusters or precincts are created by government or private investors. Some argue that cultural quarters or sporting precincts are just another means of creating high property values in newly gentrified urban areas with often little benefit to most local residents (Evans, 2003; Montgomery, 2003; Hall, 2004). In Lamu, East Africa, Hoyle (2001) suggests that the growth of urban waterfront tourism can present the juxtaposition of very rich visitors and apparently poor local people leading to social/cultural problems.

Rosentraub et al. (1994: 225) noted that 'it is very difficult, if not impossible to completely disentangle the sports strategy from the non-sports elements of the downtown development program'. Although the strategy 'generated a substantial number of service sector and hotel jobs' and benefits (Rosentraub et al., 1994: 237) they calculated that sports-related jobs accounted for only 0.32 per cent of all jobs in the Indianapolis economy (an increase of 0.03 per cent) and the sports-related payrolls accounted for less than 0.5 per cent of the total payrolls of all Indianapolis businesses. Local demand for labour may require highly skilled professionals, many recruited from outside of the local labour market, as in the case of Manchester's *Sportcity* and proposed IT precinct. Criticizing such strategies can result in the labelling of residents as 'disloyal' according to McCarthy (2002), and therefore the benefits are often taken as a 'given'. This is often because civic elites or politicians are involved in entertainment or cultural led regeneration often leading to a lack of equality, social justice and inclusivity, as Newman (2002) indicates in relation to Atlanta and the city's black residents.

The serial reproduction of urban precincts, often consisting of similar museums and waterfront developments is often considered a major issue in tourist precinct development. According to Zukin (2004: 8 in Richards & Wilson, 2006: 1210) 'the so-called cultural cities each claim distinctiveness but reproduce the same facilities in any number of places'. Judd (1995) and Newman (2002) suggest that with few exceptions the tourism strategy for downtown areas has become an extraordinarily standardized phenomenon in the United States and are simply dull and boring. In some cases the same consultants have provided input into such developments. For instance, the Australian-based Cox Group (who were responsible for the King Street Wharf at Darling Harbour, Sydney) provided input into the Singapore River development in 2001 (Savage et al., 2004). Many cities have simply copied Baltimore's tourism-related waterfront schemes, while the process of gentrification and development has pushed out sex clubs in major American cities, ensuring that cities 'look and feel as squeaky clean as any suburban mall' (Judd, 1995: 185).

This may be in part due to the concept of regulation theory (Hoffman et al., 2003) where local governments regulate and create a tourist precinct which creates predictability and safety for the visitor but also sanitizes and makes the space dull. The feeling of safety and predictability may require investment in surveillance, security and policing to reduce crime and make the tourist feel at ease in the city. As Judd (2003: 29) suggests, enclave tourist spaces are designed to regulate their inhabitants through the control of four principal aspects of agency – desire, consumption, movement and time:

> *Desire and consumption are regulated by promotion and marketing. Time and movement are strictly confined (by corridors, turnstiles, escalator, tunnels and tubes) and monitored (by security cameras and security guards). The use of time is also constrained by the scheduling of staged spectacles and performances and by physical features such as the availability or absence of seating and gathering places. The experiences and products on offer combine homogeneity and heterogeneity – enough of the former to give a sense of comfort and familiarity, enough of the latter to induce a sense of novelty and surprise.*

Therefore, it is no wonder then that such developments may lose their unique appeal, history and culture and therefore their longer-term economic viability due to over 'regulation'. Moreover, tourist precincts that rely on 'flagship' attractions and 'public sector anchors' as their main image and brand, could lose their appeal as their brand disperses and the image dilutes. For example, the Guggenheim museum has spread throughout the world to places such as Berlin, Bilbao and Las Vegas (Evans, 2003). Visitor numbers in Bilbao have started to fall from 1.3 million in the first year to 875,000 in 2003, with the original Guggenheim in New York also facing falling visitor numbers and staff cuts (Richards & Wilson, 2006).

Culturally led regeneration projects that focus on the inner city area can reinforce development inequalities. For instance, in discussing the extent and nature of culturally led regeneration in Paris, Evans (2003) noted that flagship projects in Paris were estimated to consume 58 per cent of the national culture budget in total while leaving the suburbs neglected. Balsas (2004) suggests that Porto, Portugal placed too much emphasis on attracting public investment to regenerate public space, replacing infrastructure and modernizing cultural facilities at the expense of institutional capacity building and boosting local civic creativity. In many cases the real economic benefits and costs will not be known for decades.

Cost–benefit analysis should be used to weigh up the direct and possible indirect costs and benefits of tourist precinct development at the three major economic cycles: precinct construction/(re)development, the short to medium economic cycle and the long economic cycle. This should also include private and wider social costs and benefits (Tribe, 2005), especially as government appears to be taking a major lead in the development and maintenance of tourist precincts in inner city areas. However, according to Newman et al. (2003), measuring or translating social benefits into economic dollar figures is often a difficult and complex process.

Conclusion

The chapter has outlined and discussed the potential economic costs and benefits of urban tourism precincts. The agglomeration of facilities and services which attract urban tourists also provide an interesting environment for residents, which makes it difficult to separate and assess in isolation the tourism value or costs associated with such developments. Nevertheless, this chapter has acknowledged that some insights can be gained by examining the construction costs and benefits associated with precincts and the short, medium and longer-term economic impacts after construction is completed. Tourism precincts can create and attract tourists and their associated expenditure which leads to a growth in employment and income for the city. However, the agglomeration economies associated with tourism precincts may also increase prices, create inflation and contribute towards unequal economic development.

Furthermore, this chapter has discussed the potential economic benefits associated with using tourism precincts to regenerate inner city areas and their contribution to long-term economic cycles. However precinct development has tended to focus on the core inner city area close to the Central Business (Tourist) District neglecting, and in some instances, marginalizing other parts of the city. As cities search for uniqueness and long-term brand equity the paradox is that many are simply replicating the strategies of other cities.

Urban planners and government should cautiously evaluate the potential benefits and costs of tourism precincts through cost–benefit analysis to ensure that their contribution is worthy of such investments and that projections on the economic benefits are not overestimated. Precincts should attempt to encourage mixed use so that locals and tourists can use the space during the day and night in order to create a more interesting and economically viable setting. This requires foresight in planning the built environment associated with tourism precincts. Furthermore, economic leakages need to be limited by encouraging local entrepreneurs and ensuring a local labour force is used in tourism precinct developments.

Finally, more research is required into the economic contribution of tourism precincts and the costs and benefits associated with urban precinct development. Such information will be able to provide more insights into whether such precincts really do help the city to meet their medium or long-term economic goals or whether they simply exacerbate existing economic problems.

Discussion Questions and Exercises

(1) What are the costs of tourism precincts as an urban regeneration mechanism?

(2) In what ways can urban destinations develop unique selling points to promote themselves through the use of tourism precincts?

(3) What methods or tools can be used to evaluate the economic contribution of tourism precincts, and how reliable are they?

(4) How could government go about valuing the social costs and benefits of precinct development?

References

Ashworth, G.J., & Tunbridge, J.E. (1990). *The Tourist-Historic City.* London: Bellhaven.

Balsas, C. (2004). City regeneration in the context of the 2001 European capital of culture in Porto, Portugal. *Local Economy*, 19(4), 396–410.

Burtenshaw, D., Bateman, M., & Ashworth, G. (1991). *The European City.* London: David Fulton Publishers.

Coalter, F., Allison, M., & Taylor, J. (2000). *The Role of Sport in Regenerating Deprived Urban Areas.* Edinburgh: Centre for Leisure Research, University of Edinburgh, The Scottish Executive Central Research Unit.

Cohen, E. (1995). Touristic craft ribbon development in Thailand. *Tourism Management*, 16(3), 225–235.

Department of the Environment, Transport and the Regions (DETR) (1996). *Four World Cities: A Comparative Study of London, Paris, New York and Tokyo (Urban Research Summary No. 7).* London: DETR.

Department of the Environment, Transport and the Regions (DETR) (1998). *Regeneration Research Summary: Regenerating London Docklands (No. 16)*. London: DETR.

Dodson, B., & Killian, D. (1998). From port to playground: The redevelopment of the Victoria and Alfred Waterfront, Cape Town. In D. Tyler, Y. Guerrirer, & M. Robertson (Eds.) *Managing Tourism in Cities: Policy, Process and Practice* (pp. 1139–1162). Chichester: John Wiley & Sons.

Essex, S., & Chalkley, B. (1998). Olympic Games: catalyst of urban change. *Leisure Studies*, 17(3), 187–206.

Euchner, C. (1993). *Playing the Field: Why Sports Teams Move and Cities Fight to Keep Them*. Baltimore, MD: John Hopkins University Press.

Evans, G. (2003). Hard branding the cultural city: from Prado to Prada. *International Journal of Urban and Regional Research*, 27(2), 417–440.

Fields, K., & Humphreys, C. (2002). Birmingham's Jewellery Quarter: Is spatial integration a key requirement for success?. In N. Andrews, S. Flanagan, & J. Ruddy (Eds.), *Innovation in Tourism Planning* (pp. 39–53). Dublin: Tourism Research Centre, DIT.

Finn, A., & Erdem, T. (1995). The economic impact of a mega-multi mall: estimation issues in the case of West Edmonton Mall. *Tourism Management*, 16(5), 367–373.

Gentry, C. (2001). The sport of shopping. *Chain Store Age*, 77(9), 137–138.

Getz, D. (1993a). Planning for tourism in business districts. *Annals of Tourism Research*, 20(4), 583–600.

Getz, D. (1993b). Tourist shopping villages: development and planning strategies. *Tourism Management*, 14(1), 15–26.

Goodwin, M. (1993). The city as a commodity: the contested spaces of urban development. In G. Kearns, & C. Philo (Eds.), *Selling Places: The City as Cultural Capital, Past and Present* (pp. 145–162). Oxford: Pergamon Press.

Goss, J. (1999). Once-upon-a-lifetime in the commodity world: an unofficial guide to the Mall of America. *Annals of the Association of American Geographers*, 89(1), 45–75.

Gratton, C., Dobson, N., & Shibl, S. (2000). The economic importance of major sports events: a case study of six events. *Managing Leisure*, 5(1), 17–28.

Hall, C.M. (2004). Sports tourism and urban regeneration. In B.W. Ritchie, & D. Adair (Eds.) *Sport Tourism: Interrelationships, Impacts and Issues* (pp. 192–206). Clevedon: Channel View Publications.

Harvey, D. (1989). *The Urban Experience*. Oxford: Blackwell.

Heilburn, J. (1981). *Urban Economics and Public Policy* (2nd edn). New York: St Martin's Press.

Henderson, J. (2000). Food hawkers and tourism in Singapore. *International Journal of Hospitality Management*, 19, 109–117.

Henderson, J. (2003). Ethnic heritage as a tourist attraction: the Peranakans of Singapore. *International Journal of Heritage Studies*, 9(1), 27–44.

Hoffman, L., Fainstein, S., & Judd, D. (2003). *Cities and Visitors: Regulating People, Markets and City Space*. Oxford: Blackwell Publishing Ltd.

Hoyle, B. (2001). Lamu: waterfront revitalization in an East African port-city. *Cities*, 18(5), 297–313.

Hsieh, A., & Chang, J. (2006). Shopping and tourist night markets in Taiwan. *Tourism Management*, 27, 138–145.

Hutton, T. (2004). The new economy of the inner city. *Cities*, 21(2), 89–108.

Ibrahim, M., & Leng, S. (2003). Shoppers perceptions of retail developments: suburban shopping centres and night markets in Singapore. *Journal of Retail and Leiure Property*, 3(2), 176–189.

Jansen-Verbeke, M., & Ashworth, G. (1990). Environmental integration of recreation and tourism. *Annals of Tourism Research*, 17(4), 618–622.

Jones, C. (2001). A level playing field? Sports stadium infrastructure and urban development in the United Kingdom. *Environment and Planning A*, 33, 845–861.

Judd, D. (1995). Promoting tourism in US cities. *Tourism Management*, 16(3), 175–187.

Judd, D. (2003). Visitor and the Spatial Ecology of the City. In L. Hoffman, S. Fainstein, & D. Judd (Eds.), *Cities and Visitors: Regulating People, Markets and City Space* (pp. 23–38). Oxford: Blackwell Publishing Ltd.

Judd, D., & Swanstrom, J. (1998). *City Politics: Private Power and Public Policy*. New York: Longman.

Kennedy, M. (2001). This is the favourite exhibit in the world's favourite museum of modern art. *The Guardian*, 12 May.

Kent, W., Shock, P., & Snow, E. (1983). Shopping: tourism's unsung hero(ine). *Journal of Travel Research*, 21(4), 2–4.

Lau, A., & McKercher, B. (2004). Exploration versus acquisition: a comparison of first-time and repeat visitors. *Journal of Travel Research*, 42, 279–285.

Law, C. (2000). Regenerating the city center through leisure and tourism. *Built Environment*, 26, 117–129.

Law, C. (2002). *Urban Tourism: the Visitor Economy and the Growth of Large Cities* (2nd edn). New York: Continuum.

Logan, J., & Molotch, H. (1987). *Urban Fortunes: The Political Economy of Place*. Berkeley, CA: University of California Press.

Lynch, B. (1999). Street foods: urban food and employment in developing countries. *Gender and Society*, 13(4), 563–565.

McCarthy, J. (2002). Entertainment-led regeneration: the case of Detroit. *Cities*, 19(2), 105–111.

Metzger, J. (2001). The failed promise of a festival marketplace: South Street Seaport in lower Manhattan. *Planning Perspectives*, 16, 25–46.

Mitchell, C., Parkin, T., & Hanley, S. (1998). Are tourists a blessing or bane? Resident attitudes towards tourism in the village of St Jacobs, Ontario. *Small Town*, 28(6), 18–23.

Montgomery, J. (2003). Cultural quarters as mechanisms for urban regeneration. Part 1: Conceptualising cultural quarters. *Planning, Practice and Research*, 18(4), 293–306.

Montgomery, J. (2004). Cultural quarters as mechanisms for urban regeneration. Part 2: A review of four cultural quarters in the UK, Ireland and Australia. *Planning, Practice and Research*, 19(1), 3–31.

Moscardo, G. (2004). Shopping as a destination attraction: an empirical examination of the role of shopping in tourists' destination choice and experience. *Journal of Vacation Marketing*, 10(4), 294–307.

Newman, H. (2002). Race and the tourist bubble in downtown Atlanta. *Urban Public Affairs*, 37(3), 301–321.

Newman, T., Curtis, K., & Stephens, J. (2003). Do community-based arts projects result in social gains? A review of the literature. *Community Development Journal*, 38(4), 310–322.

Page, S. (1995). *Urban Tourism*. London: Routledge.

Page, S., & Hall, C. (2003). *Managing Urban Tourism*. Harlow: Prentice-Hall.

Pearce, D. (1998). Tourist districts in Paris: structure and functions. *Tourism Management*, 19(1), 49–65.

Pearce, G. (1994). Conservation as a component of urban regulation. *Regional Studies*, 28(1), 88–94.

Plaza, B. (2000). Guggenheim museum's effectiveness to attract tourism. *Annals of Tourism Research*, 27(4), 1055–1058.

Richards, G., & Wilson, J. (2006). Developing creativity in tourist experiences: a solution to the serial reproduction of culture? *Tourism Management*, 27, 1209–1223.

Ritchie, B., & Hall, C.M. (1999). Mega events and human rights. *Proceedings of Sport and Human Rights Conference*, Sydney, Australia, 1–3 September, pp. 102–115.

Ritchie, B.W., & Dickson, T.J. (2006). Assessing the economic impact of built attractions: the case of the Australian Capital Territory, Australia. Paper for *Cutting Edge Research in Tourism*, June, University of Surrey, Surrey.

Ritchie, B.W., & Inkari, M. (2006). Host community attitudes toward tourism and cultural tourism development: the case of the Lewes District, Southern England. *International Journal of Tourism Research*, 8, 27–44.

Rogerson, C., & Kaplan, L. (2005). Tourism promotion in 'difficult areas': the experience of Johannesburg inner-city. *Urban Forum*, 16(2/3), 214–243.

Rosentraub, M.S., Swindell, D., Przybliski, M., & Mullins, D. (1994). Sport and downtown development strategy: If you build it, will jobs come? *Journal of Urban Affairs*, 16(3), 221–239.

Savage, V., Huang, S., & Chang, T. (2004). The Singapore River thematic zone: sustainable tourism in an urban context. *The Geographical Journal*, 170(3), 212–225.

Southampton City Council (2003). *Community Regeneration Projects.* http://www.southampton.gov.uk/CommunityRegeneration/Our Approach/ (accessed 12 December 2003).

Standeven, J., & De Knop, P. (1999). *Sport Tourism.* Champaign, IL: Human Kinetics.

Teedon, P. (2001). Designing a place called Bankside: on defining an unknown space in London. *European Planning Studies*, 9(4), 459–481.

Terhorst, P., van der Ven, J., & Deben, L. (2003). Amsterdam: it's all in the mix. In L. Hoffman, S. Fainstein, & D. Judd (Eds.) *Cities and Visitors: Regulating People, Markets and City Space* (pp. 75–90). Oxford: Blackwell Publishing Ltd.

Timothy, D. (2005). *Shopping Tourism, Retailing and Leisure.* Clevedon: Channel View Publications.

Timothy, D., & Wall, G. (1997). Selling to tourists: Indonesian street vendors. *Annals of Tourism Research*, 24(2), 322–340.

Tribe, J. (2005). *The Economics of Recreation, Leisure and Tourism* (3rd edn). Oxford: Elsevier.

Zukin, S. (1999). Cultural strategies and urban identities. Remaking public space in New York. In A. Reed Jr. (Ed.), *Without Justice for All. The New Liberalism and Our Retreat from Racial Equality* (pp. 205–217). Boulder, CO: Westview Press.

9

The Tourist Experience of Precincts

Martin Selby, Bruce Hayllar and Tony Griffin

Introduction

In this chapter, we turn to the experience of precincts amongst visitors and other consumers of 'place'. Whilst the precinct itself has received the attention of urban tourism researchers, particularly from planning, economic, and geographic perspectives, the experience of tourists within these spaces has been somewhat neglected.

In this chapter we briefly review research into the experience of urban tourism precincts from a number of disciplinary perspectives. From there we draw upon both cultural geography and then phenomenology to examine and theorize the precinct experience in more depth.

Research into Urban Tourism Precincts

Since Ashworth and Tunbridge (1990) conducted their seminal analysis of tourist-historic cities, the urban tourism precinct has received increased attention in the literature. However, rather like Ashworth and

Tunbridge's study, the emphasis has often been on examining demand and visitor management, rather than the experience of visitors per se (e.g. Laws & Le Pelley, 2000). As Pearce (2001) noted, spaces as diverse as redevelopment zones, sacred spaces, entertainment districts, and functional tourist districts have each attracted attention.

Research into redeveloped areas is exemplified by Mellor (1991), who provides a critical evaluation of the waterfront of Liverpool, UK. In a similar vein, Craig-Smith and Fagence (1995) in an internationally focused study, examined the development of precincts primarily based on the reclamation of former waterfront industrial sites where a 'wholesale exodus from the older port areas has left a major infrastructure to decline' (p. 6). Briggs (2000) enthusiastically describes ethnic tourism precincts, whilst Ram et al. (2000) demonstrate the problems and contradictions bubbling under the surface of the 'Balti Quarter' in Birmingham, UK. Research into tourists' experiences of sacred spaces is exemplified by the fascinating account of the Taj Mahal by Edensor (2000). Edensor's study was particularly notable for identifying the ways in which tourists of various cultures differ in their 'performances' at the site, a theme to which we will return later in the chapter. An important contribution to the experience of urban tourism precincts is the work of Judd, who developed the concept of the 'urban tourist bubble' (1999: 39), an area of a city exclusively developed and managed for tourists. This bubble consists of a contrived and carefully managed tourism landscape which may also be insulated from the city's environmental and social problems such as dereliction, crime, and poverty.

The service quality model, developed by Parasuraman et al. (1985) has been influential to several researchers interested in the experience of urban tourists (e.g. Gilbert & Joshi, 1992; Page, 1995; Page, 1999) As Bramwell (1998) explains, gaps may exist between the expectations of urban tourists and their perceptions when the destination is experienced at first-hand. This may result in either satisfaction or dissatisfaction with the destination. Whilst the crucial gap is between initial expectations and the perceived quality of experiences at the destination, underlying this are another four possible gaps. These are influenced by a manager's perception of visitor expectations, service quality specifications, service delivery, and external communications to visitors. The service quality approach to experience recognizes that destination image plays an important role in the experience of the urban environment. Although different types of image exist (see Selby, 2004b: 69–73), it would seem that expectations are formed not just through official marketing communications, but also through unofficial 'organic' images. The latter, which are often both powerful and persistent, are formed through representations of the destination in newspapers, magazines, television programmes, literature, art, and the like.

Whilst the service quality approach has the potential to inform destination management and marketing, there are also some serious limitations in the context of the experience of urban tourism precincts. There is considerable debate within the service quality literature over whether service quality is actually related to expectations, and there are further complications when gap analysis is applied to tourist destinations (see Williams, 1998). In the context of tourist destinations, it is difficult to ensure that constructs (or attributes) are salient to specific groups of visitors. Despite the fact that satisfaction and service quality do influence tourist experience, they are far from synonymous. Cultural researchers demonstrate the complexities inherent in experiencing the urban tourist landscape, and authors such as Crouch (2000) argue that the experience of tourist destinations is surprisingly active, creative, and purposive.

The Landscape of Urban Tourism Precincts

Cultural geography's traditional emphasis on representations and landscapes provides some useful insights into the experience of urban tourism precincts. More recent work on the 'performativity' of tourism is also useful. In many ways, the reading of landscapes and representations is fundamental to the tourist experience. Central to representational cultural studies is the 'landscape as text model', which draws upon both linguistics and semiotics. The metaphor of text is used to conceptualize the reading of both the landscape and representations of the landscape (e.g. through literature, guidebooks, and maps) as if they were documents. In the context of tourism, as Ringer (1998: 6) argues, the visible structure of a place expresses the emotional attachments held by both residents and visitors, and 'the means by which it is imagined, produced, contested, and enforced'. Furthermore, it is sometimes the deliberate manipulation of history and culture in precincts that creates a unique and attractive environment.

The basis of the textual model is semiotics, a means of understanding the use of signs to produce meaning. According to early pioneers such as de Saussure (1966), the sign consists of two components, the signifier and the signified. Whilst the signifier is the expression carrying the message, the signified is the concept that it represents. As Echtner (1999) explains in the context of tourism, a more socially orientated version introduces the 'interpretant' to form the semiotic triangle. Authors such as Urry (1990) and Culler (1981) have pointed out that all tourists are, in effect, amateur semioticians, seeking out landscapes 'in search of the signs of Frenchness, typical Italian behaviour, exemplary Oriental scenes ...' (Culler, 1981: 127). This suggests that precincts consist of concentrations of signs that represent particular histories and cultures. In Lockart Road in Hong Kong, for example, the tourist is offered a plethora of signs representing exotic, 'oriental', and hedonistic experiences, including restaurants, bars, and strip shows. This is accompanied, however, by an efficient and high quality tourism and transport infrastructure, including the MTR train station, overhead walkways, five star hotels, and convention centres. It is worth noting, however, that signs have different meanings to different interpretants. The term 'textual community' is useful in referring to social groups that interpret signs in similar ways. As Stock (1983: 294) argues, different textual communities 'organise aspects of their lives as the playing out of a script'.

Reading the Urban

Urry (1990) urges researchers to evaluate 'the typical contents of the tourist gaze' and he argues that tourists' ways of looking is both socially organized, and that it differs between different social groups. The tourist gaze is partly structured by the representations produced by the tourism industry, including promotional material, guidebooks, and tourist maps. Pritchard and Morgan (2001) demonstrate how through signs the tourism advertisement 'directs expectations, influences expectations, and thereby provides the preconceived landscape for the tourist to discover' (Weightman, 1987: 230, cited in Pritchard & Morgan, 2001: 168). As researchers such as Watson (1991), Goss (1993) and Bramwell (1998) demonstrate, urban tourism precincts are promoted through the use of signs that symbolize a high quality gentrified landscape (including restaurants, bars, boutique hotels), heritage, the arts, festivals, and sanitized ethnic and regional identities. Often these signs are used to counteract the negative images often associated with cities that have suffered de-industrialization. As Shields (1996: 231) argues, 'a shroud of representations stands between us and even the concrete objects which are elements of the city'. Urry (2001) draws upon Foucault's (1977) work on surveillance, but also acknowledges a greater variety of ways of experiencing the tourist landscape, including different ways in which bodies move in the space of tourist destinations.

Some precincts use signs and symbols in a way that produces the 'hyperreality' described by Eco (1986). The use of signs and symbols by the developers of tourism precincts has the potential to create landscapes that seem more 'real' than the actual places that the signs represent. While Disneyland may be considered an archetypal example, the totemic monoliths of Las Vegas substantially challenge experiential sensibilities. Reconstructions of 'Egyptian' temples, the 'Wild West', and 'Victorian England' create a hyperreal spectacle for urban tourists. Such experiences are consistent with Judd's (1999) assertion that cities are increasingly providing a tourist bubble to entertain visitors through the creation of spectacle. Interestingly, many heritage sites are also using hyperreality in order to engage and entertain visitors, even if authenticity and historical accuracy may be lost. As Rojek (1997) and Ritzer and Liska (1997) argue, the more that life in the urban tourist precinct resembles 'play', the greater the attraction to the tourist. Ironically, hyperreality may actually diminish the attraction (and aura) of the actual landscapes being simulated.

Foucault (1986) provides further insight into the signs and symbols of the urban tourism precinct. 'Of Other Spaces' discusses socially constructed 'external' sites, which have a function that is different to others. This practice of juxtaposing in a real place, several places and several sites that are in themselves incompatible is a common practice amongst the planners, developers, and marketers of urban tourism precincts (Foucault, 1986: 23–25). Precincts around the world incorporate different times and places that are 'simultaneously represented, contested, and inverted' (ibid.: 24). The area around Boat Key in Singapore, for example, consists of Chinese shop houses converted to bars and restaurants; the British Colonial District, dating from 1819; and the contemporary Central Business District. The area simultaneously functions as a tourism precinct and a playground for city bankers. The boundaries blur further as tourists flock to Harry's Bar, the 'one time hangout of Barings Bank breaker Nick Leeson' (Richmond, 2004: 498).

Representing the Urban

It could also be argued that the landscapes of urban tourism precincts are increasingly 'phantasmagoric'. As Benjamin (1979) explained, a phantasmagoria is an endless steam of images that appear to take on a magical and ghost-like nature. Whether it is the use of multimedia effects in heritage sites, or the creation of myths and ghost stories, cities appear to use phantasmagorias to attract and entertain visitors. As Pile (2005) demonstrates, dreams, magic, ghosts, and even vampires are as much a part of cities as bricks, mortar, concrete, and asphalt. In tourism districts such as New Orleans, stories of voodoo and ghosts entertain visitors whilst obscuring the brutality and suffering of the black population since the days of slavery. Pile also draws upon Freud's dream analysis, an inherently spatial approach in which the meaning of an individual's dream is not fixed, but dependent on the way an individual interprets and links together the various elements (or signs).

There are, of course, limitations in relying too heavily on the representational (and visual) in order to understand experience. Rojek and Urry (1997) argue that we need to evaluate the use of different senses in experiencing tourism, and avoid over-privileging the visual. As Veijola and Jokinen (1994) point out, it is easy to forget that tourists are 'lumpy, fragile, aged, gendered, and racialized bodies'. The urban tourism precinct, therefore, is experienced by visitors who draw upon their imaginations and memories to reconfigure the landscape, and the landscape is therefore grasped through a 'kaleidoscope' (Crouch, 2000: 96). Crouch argues that tourism involves encounters with other people and that a destination is more like a kaleidoscope and a patina, than a disembodied landscape. This process is also a social one, and this leads to shared encounters in urban tourism precincts.

The 'non-representational' approach to understanding urban tourism also emphasizes practices that cannot easily be put into words by tourists or residents. These practices may be better understood in terms of the complex styles, rhythms, steps, and gestures of different groups of people within tourism places. According to Thrift and Dewsbury (2000: 425), there are certain places where practices are acted out, celebrated, and reinforced. It would seem that such a place, termed a 'vortex', is very relevant to urban tourist precincts. An urban tourist precinct such as the square of Jemaa l-Fna in Marrakesh, Morocco, for example, brings together visitors, residents, vendors, magicians, buskers, snake charmers, fortune tellers, faux guides, and numerous other groups. Furthermore, each person simultaneously acts out their role, as if following a script. Whilst the performativity of places such as heritage sites has received attention in the literature (e.g. Bagnall, 2003), it is argued here that the urban tourism precinct better exemplifies the ideas embedded in the notion of the 'experience economy' developed by Pine and Gilmore (1999).

Whilst an analysis of the landscape and culture of urban tourism precincts does provide useful insights, it is clear that the ways in which people encounter and act within tourism environments is also important. Indeed, a critique of textual or representational studies relates to the tendency to read landscapes on behalf of people, rather than seeking to understand how they experience such places. Even non-representational cultural studies of tourism sites have been accused of developing new metaphors whilst neglecting 'the ordinary people out there who just act' (Nash, 2000: 662). Whilst cultural studies continue to add considerably to our understanding of the experience of urban tourism precincts, it is also necessary to focus on how tourists interact within the urban tourism precinct.

Experiencing the Urban Tourism Precinct

Despite the fact that both tourists and residents have '... views and feelings, develop values and make choices that affect the landscape' (Kaplan and Kaplan, cited in Ringer, 1998), there are relatively few humanistic studies of urban tourism. As authors such as Jamal and Hollinshead (2001) argue, the experience of tourism has been seriously neglected. One exception is the work by Veijola and Jokinen (1994), which conceptualized tourists as dynamic social actors, interpreting and embodying experience, whilst also creating new realities (including the urban environment) through their actions. Consequently, the tourist destination is arguably 'a negotiated reality, a social construction by a purposeful set of actors' (Ley, 1981: 219, cited in Ringer, 1998: 5).

Even though the landscape of urban tourism precincts has an important influence on experience, interpretations of representations and landscapes vary significantly between different individuals (and groups) of visitors. For example, if we were to analyse the Las Vegas landscape, focusing on the tomb of Tutankhamun at the Luxor Casino, we need to know how visitors interact and make sense of the landscape, and not just the characteristics of the landscape itself (see Ryan, 2000). Researchers such as Crang (1997) in his study of tourist photographs also argue that we should not dichotomize experiences and representations of tourism. Tourists have an active role in tourism precincts, binding sights (and sites) into a series, including 'the anxious demonstrations of doing' (Bourdieu, cited in Crang, 1997: 365).

Individualizing the Urban Experience

For some time, Kelly (1955) has been influential to researchers interested in environmental experience. A number of studies have drawn upon Kelly's 'personal construct theory' which, in short, states that individuals can construe events and the environment in a multitude of ways. One method for understanding the way in which tourists both construct and understand the environment is through the use of repertory grid analysis. Repertory grid analysis was used in a study conducted in tourism precincts in the cities of Cardiff, Edinburgh, and Bristol (Selby, 2004a).

The 60 conversational interviews generated nearly 700 constructs to describe the salient features of the urban tourism precincts under investigation. Although constructs are always bi-polar there was a consensus on the 11 most salient attributes. The positive attributes included 'old/historical', 'arts and culture', 'unique/interesting', 'impressive buildings', and 'good atmosphere'. Attributes of destinations that detracted from the experience included 'unsafe/high crime' and 'congested/crowded'.

Several studies conducted at heritage sites suggest that emotion and memory are important to the precinct experience. Bagnall (1998, 2003) draws upon the work of Campbell (1987) who showed how emotion provides a vital link between mental images and the physical environment. Bagnall's (1998) study of two heritage sites in North West England demonstrates how 'consumption is as much a matter of feeling and emotion as rational behaviour' (Bagnall, 1998: 68). Bagnall revealed how visitors used their memories and life histories to enhance the experience.

Rojek and Urry (1997: 14) also show how reminiscence is important when they argue that the concentrated viewing of objects and performances has the effect of reawakening dreams that connect the past to the present. Past experiences, in the context of work, family, and various social relationships were found by Bagnall (1998) to be used to either confirm or dispute the interpretations offered by the sites. The active role of the tourist is also emphasized by Crouch (2000: 96), who argues that the tourist 'imagines, plays with places and the content, subjectively, on their own terms, refiguring them'.

The performative nature of urban tourism is consistent with Bauman (1994: 29) who argues that 'the purpose is new experience; the tourist is a conscious and systematic seeker of experience, of a new and different experience'. Crouch's (2000) concept of the kaleidoscope is useful, with memory drawn upon as different events and experiences unfold. Making sense of the city involves a feeling of doing; and obviously memories are influenced by social factors such as gender and ethnicity.

Conceptualizing the Urban Experience

It is significant that writers such as Crang (1997), Ryan (2000), Fullager (2001), MacCannell (2001), and Hayllar and Griffin (2005) are turning to phenomenology in order to understand tourist experience. Phenomenology, concerned with how people experience and understand the world, suggests that our experience of a precinct is shaped dialectically (and dynamically) through our interactions with both the physical and essentially human dimensions of the space. This interpretive model of phenomenology owes much to the work of Martin Heidegger (1927/ 1977). Heidegger argued that the conceptualization of an experience is always grounded in prior experience, what he called the *fore-structure*. He argues that whenever something is interpreted, the 'interpretation will be founded essentially upon fore-having, fore-sight, and fore-conception. An interpretation is never a presuppositionless apprehending of something presented to us' (Heidegger, 1927/1977: 191–192).

In a similar way, Merleau-Ponty (cited in Crang, 1997: 371), argued that experience should be understood 'according to the way we settle ourselves in the world and the position our bodies assume in it'. According to Merleau-Ponty (1962: xviii), individuals are neither completely knowledgeable of their surroundings (objective), nor psychologically constituting their environment (subjective). Instead, in the context of tourism, it is necessary to look at the whole mode of existence of tourists, and the way that tourists cast an environment around themselves. It is what Merleau-Ponty describes as an 'intentional arc' that 'projects around us our past, our future, our human setting, our physical, ideological and moral situation' (ibid.). The phenomenological concept of 'operative intentionality' is useful in understanding tourist experiences as it is '… apparent in our desires, our evaluations, and in the landscape we see, more clearly than in objective knowledge' (ibid.).

Existentialists such as Merleau-Ponty and Sartre (1969) argue that perceptions are patterned into fields, and the content of these fields depends on how the individual focuses their gaze. This depends on the prevailing interests of the actor, as much as the objects themselves. Our perception of urban tourism precincts is therefore embodied, and 'images, sights, activities are all linked through the embodied motion of the observer' (Crang, 1997: 365). This suggests that what is salient in urban tourism precincts is closely linked to the operative intentionality of each tourist. It also suggests that we might be able to group tourists according to their different operative intentionalities.

It follows, for example, that tourists visiting the city of Amsterdam may cast an arts and cultural environment, a coffee shop, and cannabis-smoking environment, or a red-light environment around themselves, according to their prevailing interests. Yet Merleau-Ponty reveals a further implication for tourist experience. The perspectival nature of tourism, combined with an individual's lack of awareness of perspective, means that experience is based on profiles of objects, chance encounters, and glimpses of representations and landscapes. Although these chance encounters are difficult to regulate by tourism authorities and the industry, it would seem that the atmosphere, openness, and style of tourism precincts will have an influence on how individual components are perceived. An individual's positioning within, gaze upon, and openness to the city creates its form, and tourists rearrange what they are seeing to make it more interesting and consistent with their version of history (see MacCannell, 2001: 34). To this extent the tourist experience of precincts is a dialectical relationship where individual and collective 'ways of seeing' help to shape and reshape the physical world.

Representations of tourism precincts, whether guidebooks or advertisements, still have an influence. These may have the effect of directing what is produced at the destination as Urry (1990) argues. Yet visitors also contest what is on offer, using their own knowledge, experiences, and memories (see MacCannell, 2001). As Sartre (1969: 11) demonstrates, expectations of the city that are not met upon visiting can result in a feeling of 'non-being' when expectations are jolted by what they actually find.

Socializing the Precinct Experience

It is important to remember that visiting an urban tourist precinct is a shared not solitary act. Schutz's (1973) concept of 'stock of knowledge' is useful in understanding the shared experiences of urban tourist precincts. Tourists partly experience tourist destinations individually, and partly through shared knowledge common to specific cultures and social groups. Following Schutz and Luckmann (1974), it is only when a tourist is faced with new or contradictory information that they make an active attempt to accumulate further information. In familiar situations (and popular tourist destinations), tourists can relay upon proven recipes for acting, which have been socially transmitted. These recipes include, for example, the acting out of tourist rituals, include taking photographs at famous landmarks, and joining guided tours that "can't be missed". The tourism industry and authorities provide some of these recipes through guidebooks and promotional material. As Voase (2000) illustrates, the use of promotional clichés is part of this process, as tourists are invited to "step back in time", "rediscover", or "trace the steps". Yet the stock of knowledge also differs within different cultures and social groups. This, of course, was observed by Edensor (2000) at the Taj Mahal, as different nationalities tend to follow very different recipes.

These recipes are often influenced by a person's role within society. A tourist's social class, gender, ethnic group, age, occupation, lifestyle, personality, and the ways that people define themselves influence the 'degree of freedom in the choice of various courses' (Schutz & Luckmann, 1974: 95). Authority figures, such as parents, teachers or, increasingly, television presenters, are influential in forming social knowledge, yet they too are influenced by society's norms and values. From early child-hood, even first-hand experiences are embedded in 'socially determined and predelineated contexts' (ibid.: 247). As Ringer (1998: 6) argues, it is important to understand the multiple realities of social groups within a destination, and the way that they interpret and articulate experiences of the destination.

Schutz's (1973) concept of *multiple realities* is also apposite to discussions of the precinct experience. According to Schutz (1973), each 'reality' in which we live is a 'finite province of meaning' (Schutz, 1973). In using this terminology he remained consistent with some of his earlier theorizing which emphasized that it is the 'meaning of our experiences which constitutes reality' (Schutz, 1970: 252). According to Schutz (1973) the *paramount reality* refers to the finite province of meaning which we call everyday life. Schutz argued that we remain in the 'natural attitude' of the paramount reality until we receive a specific 'shock' which compels us to shift the accent of reality from one to another.

The 'shocks' discussed by Schutz are transition points between the paramount reality and other finite provinces of meaning. Theoretically, an urban tourism precinct represents a finite province of meaning. For example, as Hayllar and Griffin (2005) argued, as visitors move from the paramount reality of the adjacent city into *The Rocks* historic precinct, there are 'signs' which convey transition or 'shock' points; older buildings, a reorientation of scale; decreased traffic, and a slowing of pace. Once entered, visitors are 'suspended' in this new reality by the nature of the historical experience being undertaken.

The maintenance of the experience in this non-paramount world rests on the extent to which the precinct itself sustains its non-paramount character during the visit. A clash of architectural form, a cacophony of external noise, or an 'out of character' social intrusion may challenge (phenomenologically speaking) the experience being experienced. Through such an intrusion we theoretically revert back to the paramount reality.

Actioning the Urban Experience

Schutz's theorizing also highlights the active and ongoing nature of experience. The action of tourists helps to 'construct places, spaces, landscapes, regions, and environments' (Anderson and Gale, 1992: 4). As Werlen (1993: 16) argues, too many researchers focus on behaviour rather than action (see Selby, 2004b: 159). The action of urban tourists is actually embedded in the everyday home culture of tourism. As Franklin and Crang (2001: 16) argue, we commence planning, talking to friends and family, reading novels and guidebooks, watching television programmes, the combined effect of which is to produce a phantom landscape which guides our understanding of the one we eventually see.

'Places … are chosen because there is anticipation, especially through daydreaming and through fantasy' (Urry, 1990: 3). Schutz (1970: 153) explains this process in some detail when he argues that potential visitors, when they are not following the recipes of tourism, place themselves at a future time (and place), and each act 'takes its turn in projecting itself upon the screen of the imagination'. Whilst 'propulsive tendencies' may still allow a role for habit or 'recipes', the projected acts are compared and evaluated until a course of action is chosen. A tourist destination or an itinerary within an urban tourist precinct is very different from a tangible product where the qualities and possibilities are well known. Action therefore requires the use of the imagination, social knowledge, and in many cases, representations.

Summary

In order to understand the experience of urban tourism precincts, this chapter has primarily focused on the existential dialectic – the relationship between tourists and their experience of the tourism precinct. Whilst there has been some engagement with the experience of the tourism precinct in the urban tourism literature, it has been necessary to cast the net rather wider, and draw upon cultural studies and phenomenology. The chapter has therefore examined salient features of the landscape and environment of tourism precincts, drawing upon the work of cultural researchers. We have also engaged with phenomenology in order to understand how tourists perceive, experience, and act in the tourism precinct. It also became apparent that experiencing the tourism precinct is not a solitary experience, but a social one. In order to understand the important features of experiencing tourism precincts, it has been necessary to consider tourists' entire 'mode of existence' in relation to the precinct. The chapter has done this by exploring in detail the landscapes and representations of precincts, individual experience of precincts, and the influence of social relations and intersubjective knowledge.

Discussion Questions and Exercises

(1) Think about an urban tourism precinct that you have visited in the context of Schutz's ideas on multiple realities. What were the specific signs or 'shocks' in the physical and social environment that moved you from the 'natural attitude' of the paramount reality into the realm of the precinct?

(2) Foucault's idea of 'other spaces' is a commentary on the practice of juxtaposing in a real place, several places, and several sites that are in themselves incompatible. Does this practice, which is common amongst planners, developers, and marketers of urban tourism precincts, add to or diminish the experience of tourists?

(3) Consider the experience of visiting the Luxor Casino precinct in Las Vegas (visit Wikipedia for a description of the site). Contrast this type of experience with a visit to an historic precinct. Next, think of key words, phrases, and indeed your own prior experience, that might shape a visit to either of these places. Compare these with others. What are the differences and similarities?

(4) 'Phantasmagoria' may substantially impact on the experience of a visitor to an historic or redeveloped precinct. Do these allusions to 'history' enrich an experience? What would be the experiential impacts on the authenticity of a site?

(5) Discuss the distinction between reality and hyperreality. Where is the 'line drawn' between these two concepts?

(6) Phenomenologists argue that to understand our own experience requires us to engage in a process of active reflection. Either visit an urban tourist precinct (or think about one previously visited) and then write a detailed narrative of your visit. In this narrative take into consideration factors such as: the built environment; the natural environment; the relationships between the natural and the built; your interactions with others; your observations of others; texture; light; colour; aspect; and 'markers' and 'signs'. The narrative should tell the story of your visit, in detail, from beginning to end. Next, consider what are some common ideas or themes that are contained within your story. Now compare these with the stories of others. Are there any consistent sets of ideas, themes, or threads within the stories? What are these, and what might they say about the experience of an urban tourism precinct?

References

Anderson, K., & Gale, F. (Eds.) (1992). *Inventing Places: Studies in Cultural Geography*. Melbourne: Longman Cheshire.

Ashworth, G.J., & Tunbridge, J.E. (1990). *The Tourist-Historic City*. London: Belhaven.

Bagnall, G. (1998). Mapping the museum: the cultural consumption of two north west heritage sites. Unpublished PhD thesis, University of Salford: Salford.

Bagnall, G. (2003). Performance and performativity at heritage sites. *Museum and Society*, 1(3), 1–33.

Bauman, Z. (1994). Fran pilgrim till turist. *Moderna Tider*. September, 20–34.

Benjamin, W. (1979). *One Way Street* and *Other Writings*. London: Verso.

Bramwell, B. (1998). User satisfaction and product development in urban tourism. *Tourism Management*, 18(1), 35–47.

Briggs, S. (2000). Destinations with a difference – attracting visitors to areas with cultural diversity. *Insights*, July 2000, C1–C8 English Tourism Council.

Campbell, C. (1987). *The Romantic Ethic and the Spirit of Modern Consumerism*. Oxford: Blackwell.

Craig-Smith, S.J., & Fagence, M. (Eds.) (1995). *Recreation and Tourism as a Catalyst for Urban Waterfront Redevelopment: An International Survey*. Westport, CT: Praeger.

Crang, M. (1997). Picturing practices: research through the tourist gaze. *Progress in Human Geography*, 21(3), 359–373.

Crouch, D. (2000). Tourism representations and non-representative geographies: making relationships between tourism and heritage active. In M. Robinson, N. Evans, P. Long, R. Sharpley, & J. Swarbrooke (Eds.), *Tourism and Heritage Relationships: Global, National and Local Perspectives* (pp. 93–104). Sunderland: Business Education Publishers.

Culler, J. (1981). Semiotics of tourism. *American Journal of Semiotics*, 1, 127–140.

de Saussure, F. (1966). *Course in General Linguistics*, C. Bally, & A. Secheehaye (Eds.), trans. W. Basking. New York: McGraw-Hill.

Echtner, C.M. (1999). The semiotic paradigm: implications for tourism research. *Tourism Management*, 20(1), 47–57.

Eco, U. (1986). *Travels in Hyper-reality*. London: Picador.

Edensor, T. (2000). Staging tourism – tourists as performers. *Annals of Tourism Research*, 27(2), 322–344.

Foucault, M. (1977). *Discipline and Punish*. London: Tavistock.

Foucault, M. (1986). Of other spaces. *Diacritics.* Spring, 22–27.

Franklin, A., & Crang, M. (2001). The trouble with tourism and travel theory? *Tourist Studies*, 1(1), 5–22.

Fullager, S. (2001). Encountering otherness: embodied affect in Alphonso Lingis' travel writing. *Tourist Studies*, 1(1), 171–183.

Gilbert, D., & Joshi, I. (1992). Quality management in tourism and hospitality industry. In C. Cooper, & A. Lockwood (Eds.), *Progress in Tourism, Recreation and Hospitality Management* (pp. 149–168). London: Belhaven.

Goss, J.D. (1993). Place the market and marketing place. *Environment and Planning D: Society and Space*, 11, 663–688.

Hayllar, B., & Griffin, T. (2005). The precinct experience: a phenomenological approach. *Tourism Management*, 26(4), 517–528.

Heidegger, M. (1927/1977). *Being and Time.* Oxford: Blackwell.

Jamal, T., & Hollinshead, K. (2001). Tourism and the forbidden zone: the underserved power of qualitative inquiry. *Tourism Management*, 22, 63–82.

Judd, D.R. (1999). Constructing the tourist bubble. In: D.R. Judd, S.S. Fainstein (Eds.), *The Tourist City.* (pp. 35–53). New Haven: Yale University Press.

Kelly, G.A. (1955). *The Psychology of Personal Constructs.* New York: Norton.

Laws, E., & Le Pelley, B. (2000). Managing complexity and change in tourism. *International Journal of Tourism Research*, 2(4), 229–245.

MacCannell, D. (2001). Tourist agency. *Tourist Studies*, 1(1), 23–37.

Mellor, A. (1991). Enterprise and heritage in the dock. In J. Corner, & S. Harvey (Eds.), *Enterprise and Heritage: Crosscurrents of National Culture* (pp. 93–115). London: Routledge.

Merleau-Ponty, M. (1962). *Phenomenology of Perception.* London: Routledge and Kegan Paul.

Nash, C. (2000). Performativity in practice: some recent work in cultural geography. *Progress in Human Geography*, 24(4), 653–664.

Page, S.J. (1995). *Urban Tourism.* London: Routledge.

Page, S.J. (1999). Urban recreation and tourism. In C.M. Hall, & S.J. Page (Eds.), *The Geography of Tourism and Recreation* (pp. 160–177). London: Routledge.

Parasuraman, A., Zeithaml, V., & Berry, L. (1985). A conceptual model of service quality and its implications for future research. *Journal of Marketing*, 49, 41–50.

Pearce, D.G. (2001). An integrative framework for urban tourism research. *Annals of Tourism Research*, 28(4), 926–946.

Pile, S. (2005). *Real Cities: Modernity, Space and the Phantasmagorias of City Life.* London: Sage.

Pine, B.J., & Gilmore, J.H. (1999). *The Experience Economy.* Boston, MA: Harvard Business School Press.

Pritchard, A., Morgan, N.J. (2001). Culture, Identity, and Tourism Representation: marketing Cymru or Wales. *Tourism Management*, 22, 167–179.

Ram, M., Abbas, T., Sanghera, B., & Hillin, G. (2000). 'Currying favour with the locals': Balti owners and business enclaves. *International Journal of Entrepreneurial Behaviour and Research*, 6(1), 41–55.

Richmond, S. (2004). *Malaysia, Singapore and Brunei (Lonely Planet Country Guide).* Melbourne: Lonely Planet Publications.

Ringer, G. (Ed.) (1998). *Destinations: Cultural Landscapes of Tourism.* London: Routledge.

Ritzer, G., & Liska, A. (1997). 'McDisneyization' and 'post-tourism'. In C. Rojek, & J. Urry (Eds.), *Touring Cultures: Transformations of Travel and Theory* London: Routledge.

Rojek, C. (1997). Indexing, dragging and the social construction of tourist sights. In C. Rojek, & J. Urry (Eds.), *Touring Cultures: Transformations of Travel and Theory.* London: Routledge.

Rojek, C., & Urry, J. (1997). Transformations of travel and theory. In C. Rojek, & J. Urry (Eds.), *Touring Cultures: Transformations of Travel and Theory.* London: Routledge.

Ryan, C. (2000). Tourist experiences and phenomenographic analysis. *International Journal of Tourism Research*, 2, 119–131.

Sartre, J.-P. (1969). *Being and Nothingness*, trans. H. Barnes. London: Methuen.

Schutz, A. (1970). *On Phenomenology and Social Relations*, R. Wagner (Ed.). Chicago, IL: University of Chicago Press.

Schutz, A. (1973). *Collected Papers 1: The Problem of Social Reality* The Hague: Martinus Nijhoff.

Schutz, A., & Luckmann, T. (1974). *Structures of the Life-World*, trans. R.M. Zaner, & H.T. Engelhardt Jr. London: Heinemann.

Selby, M. (2004a). Consuming the city: conceptualizing and researching urban tourist knowledge. *Tourism Geographies*, 6(2), 186–207.

Selby, M. (2004b). *Understanding Urban Tourism*. London: I.B. Tauris.

Shields, R. (1996). A guide to urban representation and what to do about it: alternative traditions of urban theory. In A.D. King (Ed.), *Representing the City*. Basingstoke: Macmillan.

Stock, B. (1983). *The Implications of Literacy: Written Language and Models of Interpretation in the Eleventh and Twelfth Centuries*. Princeton, NJ: Princeton University.

Thrift, N.J., & Dewsbury, J.D. (2000). Dead geographies – and how to make them live. *Environment and Planning D: Society and Space*, 18, 411–432.

Urry, J. (1990). *The Tourist Gaze: Leisure and Travel in Contemporary Societies*. London: Sage.

Urry, J. (2001). *The Tourist Gaze: The New Edition*. London: Sage.

Veijola, S., & Jokinen, E. (1994). The body in tourism. *Theory, Culture and Society*, 6, 125–151.

Voase, R. (2000). Explaining the blandness of popular travel journalism: narrative, cliché and the structure of meaning. In M. Robinson, N. Evans, P. Long, R. Sharpley, & J. Swarbrooke (Eds.), *Tourism and Heritage Relationships: Global, National and Local Perspectives* Sunderland: Business Education Publishers.

Watson, S. (1991). Gilding the smokestacks: the new symbolic representations of the de-industrialised regions. *Environment and Planning D: Society and Space*, 9, 59–70.

Werlen, B. (1993). Society, Action, and Space: An Alternative Human Geography, trans. G. Walls. London: Routledge.

Williams, C. (1998). Is the SERVQUAL model an appropriate management tool for measuring delivery quality in the UK leisure industry? *Managing Leisure*, 3, 98–110.

10

Conflicts and Politics in Precinct Development

Glen Searle

Introduction

This chapter examines the urban tourism precinct development process in the context of the conflicts associated with managing the competing interests of the various stakeholder groups. Tourism development can take a variety of potential forms with differing sets of consequences for the diverse stakeholders. Conflicts arise because the costs and benefits of development differ between stakeholders. The resolution of these conflicts takes place in a socio-political context in which some stakeholders are more equal than others and have greater influence in determining the outcomes of development. The chapter will highlight how development outcomes can be understood as the product of stakeholder conflicts, alliances and agenda-setting in which those with more money and power, be it market based or political, have better chances of success.

The analysis is based on six central city tourist precinct developments that are waterfront redevelopment schemes and/or are centred on retail marketplace development. The six developments are:

- Faneuil Hall Marketplace, Boston
- Harborplace, Baltimore
- Covent Garden, London
- South Bank, Brisbane
- Southbank, Melbourne
- Darling Harbour, Sydney (see also Chapter 14 in this volume).

Development Politics

Urban tourism precinct development invariably involves contestation and conflict between stakeholders. In this general context, stakeholder alliances can strengthen the chances of success. At the same time, each stakeholder and their allies must operate within city contexts that vary according to local culture and politics, market opportunity, and inter-governmental support (Savitch & Kantor, 2002: 172).

The most significant alliances concerned with city development have been conceptualized, initially by Stone (1993), as urban regimes. Savitch and Kantor (2002: 53) define these as 'regularized pattern[s] of political cooperation for mobilizing city resources in support of a common, identifiable agenda'. The archetypal urban regime is the 'growth machine' version, as elaborated by Logan and Molotch (1987). In practice there can be several other types of regimes that form in response to the city context. Thus, while growth regimes respond to a disadvantaged market context by doing whatever is needed to facilitate business, other regimes may choose to use inter-governmental aid to offset or ease the pain of market disadvantage (Savitch & Kantor, 2002).

A central function of urban regimes is to set the agenda for a city's approach to development. This involves the generation of various public discourses – for example, rhetoric in favour of development. These discourses can take a number of forms, such as speeches reported in the media, articles in newspapers and magazines, press statements picked up by the media, and planning and other official reports and documents. They can hide or distort information to achieve dominance in arguments about city development (Flyvbjerg, 1998), such as the community effects of tourism development.

Governments at some level are invariably central in the city development process, arising from their power to enact rules and regulations that control development to a greater or lesser degree. Such government power is frequently used to the advantage of business and capital, as the source of wealth, prosperity and jobs. But governments must also retain their legitimacy with voters to stay in power, and so are also concerned with acting to keep the support of the electorate (Mollenkopf, 1994).

These concepts are used in the remainder of this chapter to understand how particular facets of conflict and politics in tourist precinct development influence the final outcomes. The ensuing analysis starts with the ways in which proponents justify the projects and set up development mechanisms, and the political influences involved. The influence of the business sector in promoting development is briefly reviewed. The chapter then looks at the role of community opinion and activism, and associated media influence. Next, the role of professionals is considered. The way in which conflicts between different levels of government are handled is then surveyed, followed by analysis of the role of key individuals in particular cases.

Development Justification and Implementation Mechanisms

The strength with which the case for developing a tourist precinct is made has a critical influence on the extent of any opposition to the scheme. The justification might be so obvious that it hardly needs stating, as in the case of economically depressed areas. In other cases it might involve several dimensions, including an implicit justification given by the project's symbolic role.

The economic situation of a city has a significant effect on the degree to which new tourism developments are opposed. In times of economic downturn, the justification and pressure for new developments is all but irresistible, and the political leverage of citizen groups virtually disappears (Hoyle, 2000). This was the case in Boston and Baltimore in the 1950s and 1960s, when both cities were experiencing losses of population and jobs, producing pressure for redevelopment that eventually led to central city tourist-based projects (Mollenkopf, 1983; Barnekov et al., 1989). The loss of federal grants for redevelopment of Baltimore's Inner Harbour was the specific trigger that turned the city to tourist-based habourside development. In Sydney, the recession of 1982–1983 caused the state government to respond with a programme of extra public works. The Darling Harbour scheme was conceived against this backdrop.

In Melbourne, the character of the Southbank redevelopment scheme changed significantly after 1992 when the new state government took action to pull Melbourne's economy out of a recession. It introduced new projects to Southbank that were intended to revitalize the city's economy. Instead of a relocated museum to anchor the western end of the scheme, an exhibition centre was constructed. In the central section, the government decided to invite tenders to build a major casino and associated retail and restaurant space and hotel accommodation (Sandercock & Dovey, 2002; Dovey, 2005). The casino had originally been rejected in 1982 because of its likely social damage and potential for corruption, but with the state economy in decline the decision was reversed in 1989. By 1992, the new state government saw the casino as the lynchpin of Melbourne's economic recovery (Dovey, 2005: 58). Nevertheless, there was soon a public outcry over the lack of financial and urban design details of the two preferred casino tenders, even if the principle of a casino as economic saviour was broadly accepted.

By contrast, central London in the 1970s, with its global financial, corporate and tourist role, was largely insulated from the sclerotic economy of the time in the rest of Britain. Redevelopment of the Covent Garden quarter proposed in government plans threatened the urban fabric of an area populated by an articulate and resourceful community linked into London's global role. The plans were eventually abandoned after protracted community opposition (Christensen, 1979), which ultimately led to the rehabilitation rather than redevelopment of the market area as a tourist precinct.

Whether the local economy really needs new jobs and investment or not, the mechanisms set up by authorities to bring development of tourism precincts to fruition have the potential to reduce or exacerbate conflict with other stakeholders. In general, development mechanisms that allow little scope for other stakeholders to have a say in processes and outcomes agreed between governing authorities and key investors reflect the power of the authorities in particular. Where the authority is a government agency or is local/state/national government itself, such power comes from the legal status of government decisions, from the professional, money and other resources of governments, and from some sense of popular legitimation for the government to act in an authoritarian way. Drawing on such authorization, the city-backed development corporations used for tourism precinct development in Baltimore and Boston were given wide powers to achieve their goals, such as zoning power in the case of the Boston Redevelopment Authority. In Baltimore, powers of eminent domain were available to the city, allowing it to compulsorily acquire private property.

An example of a powerful tourism precinct agency is the former Darling Harbour Authority. The authority was given power by the state government to redevelop Darling Harbour with its own act of parliament that overrode the state planning act with its various investigatory, participatory and environmental impact requirements (see Chapter 14 in this volume). In this case, the state government had a high capacity to exercise authoritarian power because of its popular Premier and large parliamentary majority, the potential job gains from the project following a recession, the prospect for the city of transforming a run-down port area into a modern multi-facility destination for local visitors and international tourists alike and, not least, the imposition of a deadline of 1988 to finish development when Darling Harbour was designated as the focal point of the state's national bicentennial celebrations. The success of the Darling Harbour redevelopment set a precedent for similar schemes in Melbourne and Brisbane, particularly the latter.

In Brisbane, the South Bank project was overseen by similarly powerful development authorities. The main trigger for the precinct's redevelopment was its choice as the site for Expo 88. To stage Expo, the state government passed the Expo 88 Act and established the Brisbane Exposition South Bank Redevelopment Authority (BESBRA) to acquire and develop the site for Expo 88, organize the event and dispose of the site afterwards. It was a requirement of the authority that redevelopment would achieve a satisfactory return on the government's substantial investment in Expo (Fagence, 1995: 80). Thus, a strong authority with specially legislated powers was needed to ensure that redevelopment achieved a high commercial return, involving no public consultation. At the time the Expo 88 Act was passed (1984), the long-standing state government of Premier Bjelke-Peterson was continuing to pitch itself as very pro-development, and such an Act would have been seen as a typical reflection of the government ethos. However, public outcry in 1989 over BESBRA's preferred post-Expo scheme (involving a world trade centre, casino and international hotel) (Craik, 1992; Fagence, 1995) and the replacement of Bjelke-Peterson by an interim Premier after the findings of an inquiry into government corruption shifted the balance of power. Another development authority, the South Bank Corporation (SBC), was set up to develop the site, but this time its remit was the less authoritative one of ensuring that development met the highest possible standards and was in the public interest (Craik, 1992). Wider consultation and planning processes were subsequently carried out for a new plan.

Where precinct development agencies lack powerful structures given by government – or even if there are such structures – there may be attempts to actively construct legitimacy for tourism development via rhetoric and other discourse and thus reduce opposition. The casino on Melbourne's Southbank fed into a transformed urban discourse, involving placement of the (private) casino's name on public street signs, for example (Dovey, 2005). More generally, the casino was central to the government's Agenda 21 manifesto for central Melbourne development, with its rhetoric of 'flagship projects' being essential in global inter-city competition justifying the stifling of public debate (Sandercock & Dovey, 2002: 157). Rhetoric can also be used simply to deflect criticism of tourism development. Criticism of the lack of housing in the Darling Harbour scheme was countered by the responsible minister's claim that the scheme's 'immensely attractive prestige development' would 'attract renovation and renewal' in adjoining residential areas (*Sydney Morning Herald*, 4 March 1985, cited in Daly & Malone, 1996: 100). In Melbourne, legitimation of projects was reinforced by simultaneous legitimation of the policy approach of the government itself. The development of the Southbank Exhibition Centre was seen as symbolizing the 'can-do' authoritarian development approach of the new state government (Dovey, 2005: 55).

The Role of Business

With its capacity to make investments and generate jobs, the business sector has a central role in the way conflicts about development are generated and played out. All tourism precincts require private sector investment to function, which places business in a powerful position to influence the nature of the precinct development. The way this potential influence is exercised becomes crucial to whether conflicts between business and the development authority or other stakeholders are generated. In this, the power of business relative to other stakeholders is critical. If business is very powerful because it is tightly organized and closely linked to the city government, and its investment is badly needed to rescue a central city economy, for example, other stakeholders will be much less willing to provoke disputes with business about the kind of development it will require. This was the situation in Baltimore leading up to the development of Harborplace, when the Mayor worked closely with elite company heads on the Greater Baltimore Committee to ensure that local politics did not conflict with business priorities and thus risk exacerbating economic decline (Barnekov et al., 1989). A similar situation prevailed in Boston, where the Mayor met a select group of leading businessmen, known as the 'Vault', every 2 weeks, and assigned to the Greater Boston Chamber of Commerce the task of rehabilitating the waterfront and developing the Faneuil Hall district (O'Connor, 1993). Development in both cities was thus effectively directed by growth regimes. Where the business sector's power is not so predominant, the potential for stakeholder conflict is likely to be greater.

Brisbane's South Bank development illustrates this perspective. There was strong business lobbying for Expo 88 based in particular on the redevelopment potential of the site post-Expo. Eventually, the government was persuaded to endorse the plan by arguments about the redevelopment potential (Craik, 1992). The government's redevelopment authority, BESBRA, operated in the manner of a private developer with the appointment of entrepreneurial staff, the contracting-out of many functions, secrecy and lack of community consultation, and statutory freedom to buy and develop the land. This was but one of many instances of authoritarian state government facilitation of business investment during the long tenure of Premier Bjelke-Peterson. This effectively constituted another urban growth regime in which government collaborated closely with business, intervening as necessary to ensure an on-going high rate of investment in the city. The cases of Baltimore, Boston and Melbourne after 1992 had a similar dimension. With the demise of Bjelke-Peterson as State Premier, the tight nexus between state government and business was loosened. Conflicts about the nature of redevelopment emerged. The $200 million scheme of a private consortium with close links with the government was selected by BESBRA, but drew sustained criticism from local government, architects and planners, the media and community (Craik, 1992). A new scheme involving wide public consultation and incorporating public uses and open space across half the site was eventually adopted.

Community Opinion

The extent to which community opinion generates conflict depends on a range of factors at different levels. At a general level, communities can be in conflict with major development projects because they want something different from urban development, such as adequate housing or more parks and other community facilities. In this sense, community conflict is conflict over urban meaning – what different groups want from a city (Castells, 1983). While this generates differences over development projects, the extent to which this sets up actual conflicts depends on further factors. At a basic level, there may be impediments to turning anti-development feeling in a community group into action that creates conflict (Kilmartin & Thorns, 1978; Burnett, 1984). A political economy approach would suggest that the time and money necessary for community involvement and action are in short supply for many, because of long or exhausting work hours, family responsibilities, lack of knowledge, expertise or social competence (Pickvance, 1976). Powerful neighbourhood associations are unlikely to be set up in poor areas with low resources, or in areas with a fragmented, heterogeneous or highly mobile population (Burnett, 1984). If there is a sufficient level of community activism, the conversion of that potential into active participation or protest then depends on further factors. These include consideration of the extent to which the issue is one that can be 'solved' by community action, and the likelihood of action being successful. Part of the calculus of likely success might be the degree to which the area is electorally marginal (Burnett, 1984).

The contrasting histories of community involvement in the Brisbane South Bank and Covent Garden cases illustrate such issues. In the former, the development of the site for Expo 88, was marked by the displacement of low income renters, perceived degeneration of the social fabric in the area, and the experience of political powerlessness (Day, 1988). As well as an increase in traffic and noise, there was also felt to be inadequate compensation for expropriated businesses and land. The area had housed low income and migrant groups, and their skills, knowledge and other resources were never going to be enough to cause a pro-development, authoritarian state government to modify its course to ameliorate the social costs of the Expo phase of South Bank's transformation.

By contrast, local residents were able to defeat a massive redevelopment plan for Covent Garden, which allowed the historic built fabric to be kept and refurbished as a tourism precinct. Plans published in 1968 called for 60 per cent of the area to be demolished. Community resistance was strong, using press conferences, public rallies and the national media to fight the plans (Christensen, 1979). This forced the government to hold a public inquiry in 1971 that led the Secretary of State to disallow the new roads necessary for redevelopment. The Greater London Council (GLC) elections of 1973 saw the Labour Party take control, resulting in new guidelines emphasizing conservation and housing provision. Even so, the new plan of 1976 still proposed demolition of 25 per cent of the building stock. The community association published its own plan that featured more rehabilitation, which was supported by local government. Later in 1976, the

GLC Covent Garden Committee approved a revised plan that adopted the community association's wishes, and which was approved by the full GLC in 1977 (Christensen, 1979). The plan emphasized sensitive renewal and rehabilitation and maintenance of the existing community.

A number of specific factors can be identified for the success of community resistance to the Covent Garden redevelopment. Among them were strong leadership of some 'catalytic personalities', including a renegade planner and an architectural student (Christensen, 1979: 345). The public inquiry of 1971 gave community organizers 'an event on which to focus and a means for educating the community, the Press and public opinion' (Christensen, 1979: 345). Christensen (1979: 345) sees the 'extraordinary organizational skills' of the community association as being especially critical. This involved: block by block organizing; using the media to exploit the growing interest in conservation and planning politics; taking the offensive by using their own expertise to propose solutions that were often superior to the planners'; building a rapport with the Labour GLC committee and the local council; and finding powerful allies such as the Town and Country Planning Association and the leading national conservation groups. In turn, the underlying socio-economic composition of the community gave the potential for such community organization and leadership to occur. Central London and its fringes had always had a significant population of intellectuals and professionals, and by the late 1960s this had been reinforced by more than a decade of gentrification (Savage & Warde, 1993). This was also reflected in membership of the Covent Garden Forum, comprising community-elected local representatives and set up in 1974 to provide formal advice to the GLC on the area's planning. According to Christensen (1979: 345), the Forum played an important role in defeating the plan because it 'legitimized many neighbourhood demands, demonstrating that concern for neighbourhood survival was not limited to radicals and working-class residents but included business people, property owners and middle-class residents'.

Whether such intense community opposition to redevelopment would happen today in London and other major western cities is a moot point. The late 1960s saw a reaction against demolition of older inner city buildings by local communities (Hall, 1988), as well as broader disillusion with comprehensive redevelopment and an emerging commitment to maintain heritage. Intensified competition between cities for major development projects since the 1980s has generated a countervailing tendency against such opposition, especially in cities lacking a strong market context. A related central point regarding Covent Garden is that its transformation into a tourist precinct was not sought by the community. Rather, the precinct languished after the produce market moved out in 1974, until it was discovered by property renovators who replaced local shops with boutiques and craft shops (Esher, 1981). This new tourism focus was capped off in 1980 with the re-opening of the central Market building as Europe's first speciality shopping centre.

A general consideration here is that the extent and nature of conflict with communities over tourism precinct development proposals very much depends on the size of the local community. Where the proposed precinct is occupied by commerce, industry or transport facilities rather than housing, community pressure will tend to be less because there is no local population threatened with the loss of residences. The Southbank project in Melbourne could be classed in this category, as could the Darling Harbour scheme. Nevertheless, Darling Harbour's redevelopment still faced wide opposition from Sydney's general public. This focused on the potential cost of the project and, in particular, the construction of a monorail from Darling Harbour to the Sydney CBD (central business district) (Daly & Malone, 1996). The Sydney City Council opposed the monorail because of its negative visual impacts on city streetscapes. However, the state government intervened and exempted the development from the state planning legislation in order to circumvent city council rejection of the plan. There were two public protest marches against the monorail proposal. The media, particularly the daily broadsheet the *Sydney Morning Herald*, prominently reported the anti-monorail discourse. The Darling Harbour example illustrates the kinds of reasons why the wider community may get involved in opposing tourism development proposals in an urban precinct. One is potential impacts on nearby, valued areas (in this case, central Sydney). Another is related to effects on government legitimation via perceived misuse of public funds.

The case of South Bank, Brisbane suggests a further perspective here: how consciousness about the public worth of a designated tourism precinct can evolve and thereby generate public expectations (and potential conflict) about final project outcomes. Expo 88 increased the public's appetite for the use of South Bank for leisure and tourism (Fagence, 1995). The advent of a weaker state government after Premier Bjelke-Peterson's downfall removed one constraint to a scheme giving priority to public waterfront access and leisure uses. However, the imperative to recoup the large public investment resulted in an initial post-Expo scheme, River City 2000, with an explicit tourist focus that included a 50-storey world trade centre, casino and five star hotel. There was sustained criticism from the general community, local government, architects and planners, and the media because of the lack of open space, the lack of activities for the ordinary public and the proposed casino (Craik, 1992). The state government was forced to re-tender the scheme, create the SBC with a public interest remit, and adopt a wider consultation and planning process (Craik, 1992). The SBC's new plan, which reserved half the site for open space and public uses, included specific features to distinguish it from major leisure projects overseas (Fagence, 1995). By 1992, riverfront parklands with a theme park orientation had been developed (Noble, 2001). Thus, in the Brisbane South Bank instance, rising community expectations and power and a weakened state government combined to produce a tourism precinct with the flavour of a regional park rather than an international up-market destination.

Professional Opinion

Professional opinion can often serve to support community opposition to tourism precinct proposals, although it rarely seems to be an independent source of conflict creation or reduction. In giving such support, however, its role can be crucial as a counter weight to development agency expertise. Thus, it can empower communities by adding expert knowledge or giving legitimation to community positions that challenge professional plans and discourses of agencies.

This role was most strongly shown in the Covent Garden case. Professional conservation and planning associations were among the objectors to the original redevelopment plan at the 1971 public inquiry. Conversely, planners on the government side adopted a traditional posture whereby planning was seen as something done by a professional elite, and fought a rearguard action to defend their plan all the way (Christensen, 1979). To counter this, the community association and the Forum confronted the planners with superior (professional) expertise and challenged them on their own ground.

Criticism by architects and other professionals helped to bring about the demise of the River City 2000 scheme for Brisbane's South Bank. Similar criticism was less successful in the development of Melbourne's Southbank precinct. In particular, the final design of Southbank's centrepiece, the casino, was negatively received by professionals (Dovey, 2005). The floor space of the complex had more than doubled from that of the winning tender, and the high rise section increased from 25 to 43 storeys. The government had attempted to head off professional critique and legitimate the casino design by appointing a Design Panel to approve the design of the winning tender, and to review subsequent design changes. But ultimate approval powers rested with the Minister, making it unclear if the panel had approved the final design (Dovey, 2005).

The views of professionals were also disregarded in a critical part of Darling Harbour's redevelopment. Studies had shown that a new public transport facility was needed to the city centre to handle projected Darling Harbour trips. Planners in the State Department of Environment and Planning recommended a light rail line to the city centre, linking with the existing rail system, but this would have required the government to pay an operating subsidy. To avoid this it accepted a bid from the TNT transport company, which had political links to the government, to build and run a monorail at no government cost. As noted, this proposal produced strong public opposition which was circumvented by the government.

Inter-government Conflicts

The development of urban tourism precincts commonly involves several levels of government. This creates the potential for inter-government conflicts arising from the different agendas and power bases of local, regional, state and national governments. Local government, for example, is likely to have greater empathy for local community views whereas higher levels of government might have a wider strategic perspective.

The Covent Garden case is an example of this, where the GLC was responsible for the redevelopment plan that was fiercely opposed by the community, with local government supporting an eventually triumphant community position. In Brisbane, there was similar local government support to community and other opposition to the state's preferred River City 2000 scheme, leading to its abandonment. In Melbourne, local council recalcitrance to state government plans was not able to subvert the state's intentions, given the state's imperative of attracting global investment (Dovey, 2005). The original mid-1980s state government strategy for Southbank proposed cultural and entertainment facilities along the waterfront as well residential, arts and commercial redevelopment of the 1000 hectares to the south. This generated a struggle for control between state and local government which delayed the project for 2 years until the state government used its legislative powers to take over the redevelopment (Dovey, 2005). The Darling Harbour scheme resulted in a similar victory for state over local government. The city council, reflecting concerted professional and community opposition, threatened to refuse consent for the monorail. Seeing the whole Darling Harbour project threatened, the state government legislated to exempt the monorail from the provisions of the planning act and a number of other acts (Ashton, 1993), removing it from the possibility of council refusal or any legal challenge.

Key Actors

In the interplay of various stakeholders attempting to influence the outcome of tourism precinct development, key individuals can play a decisive role. In general, this role will draw on existing underlying conditions for or against development as the basis for individual action. In five of the six case studies used for this chapter, the leading politician involved in the project had a decisive role in making the development happen and thus generating potential conflict with the community and other stakeholders. In the other case, Covent Garden, the leadership of two or three locals was critical in effectively mobilizing community resistance against redevelopment plans.

Of the key pro-development actors in the other five cases, two were mayors of Baltimore and Boston. In Baltimore Mayor Schaefer, who was elected in 1971, revived stalled plans to redevelop the waterfront area. Under his leadership Harborplace and other downtown projects were developed using a full array of tools available for local development in partnership with the private sector (Barnekov et al., 1989). In the case of Boston's historic Faneuil Hall area, the mayor had a decisive role in association with another key actor, developer James Rouse, who proposed a retail-based tourist precinct linking the CBD to the waterfront. Rouse's proposal was pitted against a rival proposal for offices and apartments. According to O'Connor (1993), the mayor's decision to go with Rouse's scheme was determined solely by the creative imagination and personal charisma of Rouse himself; his ideas 'captivated' the mayor.

More generally, Rouse illustrates one way in which the development politics of different urban tourism precincts can be interrelated. Rouse's involvement in such projects started with the Baltimore Harborplace development (Sudjic, 1993). The success of that development paved the way for his involvement in the Faneuil Hall redevelopment, and then for his consultancy in the Darling Harbour scheme. While the resulting development at Darling Harbour has been criticized as having a 'grim familiarity' and being 'monotonous and inevitable' (Sudjic, 1993: 300), it is likely that the successful precedent of Baltimore allowed Rouse's precepts for the festival marketplace and other elements of Darling Harbour to be quickly accepted without undue conflict and dispute.

In the waterfront-based tourism precincts developed in Melbourne, Sydney and Brisbane, the role of the respective State Premiers was decisive at various stages. In Melbourne, the election in 1992 of a pro-development government under a strong, authoritarian Premier, Jeff Kennett, caused Southbank's development to be steered to meeting global city competition. The part-finished museum was revamped as an exhibition centre, and the casino was pushed through. Darling Harbour's redevelopment owed much to the vision of Premier Wran, a highly popular leader who saw major tourism infrastructure as one of Sydney's key priorities for economic development (along with the finance and information technology industries), and Darling Harbour as the centrepiece of such infrastructure. The decision to redevelop Brisbane's South Bank for Expo 88 exemplified a deep-seated pro-development bias by Premier Bjelke-Peterson, who was the populist head of a dominant, long-serving National Party government (but which lost much of its legitimacy around the time of the Expo as a corruption inquiry took effect).

Tourism Precincts as Special Cases of Major Development

To what extent is the framework presented in this chapter applicable to major developments outside the tourism sector? The main elements of the framework, such as the importance of urban regimes and their market context, and the significance of discourse 'agenda-setting' and of key actors/agents, are common to most major urban development projects. The basic process of development of major tourism precinct is similar to that of other major urban projects.

Nevertheless, there is one critical difference in the nature of development in tourism precincts. This difference concerns the increased recreation and leisure opportunities for the local community that are generated by urban tourism schemes. A tourism project's parks, plazas, shops, markets, casinos and so forth become available to the local population as well as tourists. This local 'public good' aspect means that local communities are more likely to give support to project proposals. The Darling Harbour scheme, for example, was 'sold' to Sydneysiders as a major new recreation and leisure destination for the local population. At the same time, major tourist projects providing leisure facilities available to the community generate popular legitimation for governments, making government support for proposed projects even more likely. Thus, the supply of local public goods that come with major tourism projects will tend to result in less conflicted development.

Summary

This chapter has used six international examples of urban tourism precinct development to analyse the nature and resolution of conflict between stakeholders in such developments. The outcomes of development are seen to be the product of stakeholder interaction in which differential ability to exercise power is critical. This exercise of power includes the ability to 'set the agenda' via public discourses, while for public agencies the exercise of power has to take account of the need to retain legitimacy with the electorate.

The international examples show that conflict is minimized if there is a strong local need for economic development, especially if there is an urban growth regime involving close government-business coordination. Opposition to development is also reduced if the public development agencies can be given strong legal powers, and/or if the legitimacy of the development is actively constructed via rhetoric and other discourse. The effectiveness of community opposition depends to a significant extent on the size and socio-economic status of the resident population, which strongly influences the potential leadership and other community resources that can be generated to mount a fight. Local government is likely to support local community opinion where it is not unduly dependent on business development taxes (as it is in the USA). Wider public opposition can be generated if there are very negative impacts on adjacent areas valued by the population. Public opposition can change outcomes where government has become weakened. Professional opinion is able to empower communities by adding expert knowledge and legitimation for community positions. But professional views, like community views, can be ignored in the face of strong pro-development discourses and governments willing to exercise their powers in an authoritarian manner. Government leaders (mayors, premiers, etc.) can have a decisive influence in bringing about development where the underlying conditions favour this, while visionary, articulate developers in the James Rouse mould may also have a decisive role.

Discussion Questions and Exercises

(1) The notion that the exercise of differential power can 'explain' the variety of outcomes in conflicted tourism precinct developments has been used in this chapter. Can all of the factors that influence such outcomes really be reduced to such an explanatory framework?

(2) The importance of business taxes for the operation of city government in the USA means that such governments need to take a much more pro-business attitude to development proposals than in other countries. Does this suggest that we need to develop a fundamentally different model of tourism precinct development for US cities, or can we see development in US cities as part of a single development spectrum that embodies varying power exercisable by different stakeholders?

(3) The Covent Garden example is the only case in this chapter where the initial redevelopment plans were scrapped due to opposition to those plans. Does this reflect an earlier time when global city competition was much less significant, or could a similar outcome happen today?

(4) Community opinion had relatively limited influence on the precinct outcomes discussed here except in the Covent Garden example. Are we able to deduce, from the examples in this chapter, what circumstances will cause community opinion to be influential in determining development outcomes?

References

Ashton, P. (1993). *The Accidental City: Planning Sydney since 1788.* Sydney: Hale and Iremonger.

Barnekov, T., Boyle, R., & Rich, D. (1989). *Privatism and Urban Policy in Britain and the United States.* Oxford: Oxford University Press.

Burnett, A.D. (1984). The application of alternative theories in political geography: the case of political participation. In P. Taylor, & J. House (Eds.), *Political Geography: Recent Advances and Future Directions* (pp. 25–49). London and Totowa, NJ: Croom Helm and Barnes and Noble Books.

Castells, M. (1983). *The City and the Grassroots.* London: Edward Arnold.

Christensen, T. (1979). Covent Garden: a struggle for survival. *Political Quarterly,* 50(3), 336–348.

Craik, J. (1992). Expo 88: fashions of sight and politics of site. In T. Bennett, P. Buckridge, D. Carter, & C. Mercer (Eds.), *Celebrating the Nation: A Critical Study of Australia's Bicentenary* (pp. 142–159). St Leonards, NSW: Allen & Unwin.

Daly, M., & Malone, P. (1996). Sydney: the economic and political roots of Darling Harbour. In P. Malone (Ed.), *City, Capital and Water* (pp. 90–108). London: Routledge.

Day, P. (1988). *The Big Party Syndrome: A Study of the Impact of Special Events and Inner Urban Change in Brisbane.* St Lucia, Qld: Department of Social Work, University of Queensland.

Dovey, K. (2005). *Fluid City: Transforming Melbourne's Urban Waterfront.* Sydney and Abingdon: UNSW Press and Routledge.

Esher, L. (1981). *A Broken Wave: The Rebuilding of England 1940–1980.* London: Allen Lane.

Fagence, M. (1995). Episodic progress toward a grand design: waterside redevelopment of Brisbane's South Bank. In S.J. Craig-Smith, & M. Fagence (Eds.), *Recreation and Tourism as a Catalyst for Urban Waterfront Redevelopment* (pp. 71–87). Westport, CT: Praeger.

Flyvbjerg, B. (1998). *Rationality and Power: Democracy in Practice* Chicago, IL: University of Chicago Press.

Hall, P. (1988). *Cities of Tomorrow.* Blackwell: Oxford.

Hoyle, B. (2000). Global and local change on the port-city waterfront. *Geographical Review,* 90(3), 395–417.

Kilmartin, L., & Thorns, D.C. (1978). *Cities Unlimited: The Sociology of Urban Development in Australia and New Zealand.* Sydney: George Allen & Unwin.

Logan, J., & Molotch, H.L. (1987). *Urban Fortunes: The Political Economy of Place.* Berkeley, CA: University of California Press.

Mollenkopf, J.H. (1983). *The Contested City.* Princeton, NJ: Princeton University Press.

Mollenkopf, J.H. (1994). How to study urban power. Reprinted in E.A. Strom, & J.H. Mollenkopf (Eds.) (2007), *The Urban Politics Reader* (pp. 99–109). London: Routledge.

Noble, L. (2001). South Bank dreaming. *Architecture Australia*, 90(5), 86–93.

O'Connor, T.H. (1993). *Building a New Boston: Politics and Urban Renewal 1950–1970.* Boston, MA: Northeastern University Press.

Pickvance, C.G. (1976). *Urban Sociology: Critical Essays.* London: Tavistock.

Sandercock, L., & Dovey, K. (2002). Pleasure, politics and the 'public interest': Melbourne's riverscape revitalization. *Journal of the American Planning Association*, 68(2), 151–164.

Savage, M., & Warde, A. (1993). *Urban Sociology, Capitalism and Modernity.* Basingstoke: Macmillan.

Savitch, H.V., & Kantor, P. (2002). *Cities in the International Marketplace.* Princeton, NJ: Princeton University Press.

Stone, C.N. (1993). Urban regimes and the capacity to govern: a political economy approach. *Journal of Urban Affairs*, 15, 1–28.

Sudjic, D. (1993). *The 100 Mile City.* London: Flamingo.

11

Visitor–Host Relationships: Conviviality Between Visitors and Host Communities

Robert Maitland and Peter Newman

Introduction

This chapter explores the development of new, unplanned tourism areas close to established tourist zones in central London. We argue that the process of change in these areas draws on the preferences and resources of both hosts and visitors. The research findings discussed in the third section of the chapter suggest strong links and overlaps between host and tourist experience of place, and that at least in the cosmopolitan, gentrified areas we examine, the story may be one of conviviality rather than conflict. The London research took place in Islington and in Bankside, both areas close to the City and the West End with their historic sites, established cultural quarters and newer mixed-use precincts. Neither of our two study areas was planned as a tourist precinct although Bankside is contiguous with established tourist areas in central London, with well-signed pedestrian routes to and from the City and West End. In both areas, urban renewal has brought up-market housing, studios and offices, restaurants, bars and shopping to fringe locations. We argue that their development as tourism areas is closely related to other urban processes and in particular to the residential gentrification that has had profound impacts on London in recent decades.

In the first section of the chapter we aim to set the idea of conviviality between visitor and host community into wider debates about tourists and the city. We examine understandings of what visitors want from the city. Despite recent research exploring the characteristics and experience of visitors to particular areas in cities (Maitland, 2003; Maitland & Newman, 2004; Hayllar & Griffin, 2005; Maitland, 2006b) there is still 'limited research material … focussing on the experience of tourist within [tourism precincts and] … an understanding from the tourist's perspective has been a neglected dimension' (Hayllar & Griffin, 2005: 518). Lack of attention to relationships between visitors and the host community are part of that neglect. In the second section of the chapter we move beyond debates about tourism to wider discussions in contemporary urban studies about consumption and in particular about the preferences expressed in the gentrification of inner city areas. We suggest that the urban preferences of some groups of residents overlap substantially with those of some visitors. Gentrification studies help us focus these issues on the emergence of city neighbourhoods that can be desirable objects for resident and visitor alike. The gentrification literature allows us to develop general assumptions about conviviality into a finer grain of analysis of how distinctive places are made.

In the third section, we review experiences in London and refer to similar studies of the preferences of visitors undertaken in New York City (NCY). The final section of the chapter draws together conclusions from the studies of these new tourism areas and we suggest that shared interests help both visitor and resident to jointly produce desired environments and drive change in the city. Rather than conflict between visitor and host, we argue that more attention needs to be paid to the processes leading to conviviality as new tourism areas open up alongside established precincts.

Tourists and the City

Analysis of tourism in major cities has been strongly focused on the supply side. A considerable literature has developed examining the role of tourism in reconfiguring cities (Jansen-Verbeke, 1986; Law, 1993; Judd, 1995; Judd & Fainstein, 1999; Law, 2000; Law, 2002; Hoffman et al., 2003; Page & Hall 2003), often drawing on the way wider processes of change have impacts on the 'converted city' (Harvey, 1989; Zukin, 1995; Fainstein & Gladstone, 1999). There has been particular attention to tourism's role in economic development and regeneration (Beioley et al., 1990; Smales, 1994; Judd, 1995; Porter, 1995; Maitland, 1997; Porter, 1998; Smith, 2003; Church & Frost, 2004), how it can affect particular localities (Gordon & Goodall, 2000) and its role as cities become sites for consumption (Judd & Fainstein, 1999; Sassen & Roost, 1999). Development for tourism has tended to be organized around planned zones or precincts – tourist bubbles (Judd, 1999) or urban entertainment districts (Hannigan, 1998), cultural quarters (Montgomery, 2003; Montgomery, 2004) or new iconic attractions, like the Guggenheim, Bilbao, now ubiquitous in accounts of culture and regeneration. These approaches have been so widely emulated by cities across the world that serial reproduction of similar areas has undermined city distinctiveness (Richards & Wilson, 2006). Although there are differences between these models and their target visitor markets, they all rely on the city exploiting and revalorizing its cultural and heritage resources, developing new attractions, and reconfiguring places to attract visitors to zones or precincts that have been planned for tourism. From this perspective, tourism is still seen as a separate activity, physically or symbolically apart from the rest of the city.

We suggest that these accounts offer only a partial understanding of the role of tourism in city development and the interaction between visitors and other city users. As Selby (2004) argues, since so many studies look at the production of places rather than their consumption, questions and enquiry are framed from a producer's point of view, rather than that of the consumer. Thus visitors' experience of cities is neglected. From a visitor perspective, major cities – and especially polycentric world cities – do not simply comprise a series of well-defined and planned tourist zones or precincts. Rather, they are multifunctional places that offer a range of resources and raw materials from which visitors with different demands can create their own, different, 'cities' (Burtenshaw et al., 1991) – visitors wanting a nightlife city will focus on bars, clubs, cinemas, theatres and restaurants, for example. Whilst some of these 'cities' will include conventional tourism attractions, others may not; many visitors will not wish to spend their time only in planned tourism zones. As they pursue their consumption demands and preferences, we need to appreciate how tourists contribute to the dynamics of urban change.

To do so, we must also acknowledge that tourism is not a separate activity that occurs only in particular defined locations at particular times (Franklin & Crang, 2001); it is much more pervasive, and part of the very fabric of the city (Deben et al., 2000). Equally, the boundaries which have traditionally been seen to separate 'tourists' and 'locals' are dissolving – 'although their cultural references may be different, their consumption and spatial connections with cities and attractions are increasingly similar' (Richards, 2004: 10). Residents behave in a touristic manner (Franklin, 2003) and visitors may share the same consumption demands as residents (Maitland, 2007b). The consequence is that there is limited analytical value in trying to differentiate 'hosts' or 'locals' from 'guests' or 'tourists'. Rather, we need to recognize the widely differing power and urban preferences amongst the host 'community' on the one hand, and amongst visitors on the other. Both city residents and visitors can be considered as city users (Martinotti, 1999) with shared interests in (different patterns of) consumption.

Just as it is helpful to see visitors as one amongst several groups of city users, in much of the city we can see tourism as interacting with other forces that are reconfiguring places to meet the demands of city users. We suggest that in some places residents and visitors may have shared interests. Typically in upscale neighbourhoods that offer high amenity and opportunities for consumption we can see visitors as co-producers of new urban landscapes. The roles of residents in neighbourhoods of this type have been extensively examined in studies of gentrification and we now turn to look at how some of the insights of this work on the urban preferences of dominant groups link to the demands of some city tourists.

Gentrification and the City

Over the past 10 or so years cities have been increasingly understood as sites of consumption. During the 1990s the resurgence of cities generally and revival of central cities and return of a middle class became a major concern of urban studies in North America. Though with very different urban traditions, European cities were to be understood through consumption. 'For example, London, Paris, and Barcelona are also examples of high human capital cities that offer stunning consumption advantages to their residents' (Glaeser et al., 2000: 46).

Glaeser et al. (2000: 28) identify four critical urban amenities. First, the 'rich variety of services and consumer goods'; second 'aesthetics and physical setting'; third 'good public services' and fourth the 'ability to move around quickly'. Visitors may be less concerned with some public services – education for example – but this emphasis on cities as sites of consumption clearly includes residents and visitors. As Clark argues, 'locational decisions that emphasize taste and quality of life, and the rise of leisure and concern about the arts' (2003: 497–498) bring the interests of residents and workers close to the concerns of visitors. In his study of the success of Santa Barbara, Nevarez (2003) argued that 'spaces of lifestyle' are determined by residential preferences rather than company location preferences, and these urban preferences also match the representations of tourism businesses. Consumer cities match the desires of residents and others as the visitor as space consumer becomes a significant social identity. We can understand urban neighbourhoods through shared issues of aesthetics, consumption and services. Whilst this direction in urban studies seems to reflect trends in the central and inner areas of many cities we need to understand more about how such resident–visitor relations may be created in particular places.

In recent years gentrification research has offered a rich source of understanding the expression of urban preferences and the importance of consumption in processes of neighbourhood change. Gentrification has a strong economic dynamic, seen for example in the economic power of the 'financifiers' and 'super-gentrifiers' in big cities identified by Lees (2000). But equally gentrification is about the expression of cultural preferences through consumption and it is this dimension of gentrification studies that seems to offer a useful base for understanding resident–visitor relationships.

We look in turn at three issues that relate the urban preferences of (some) residents to those of (some) visitors to cities. First, the emphasis in gentrifying neighbourhoods on consumption; second, the aspiration among some gentrifiers to create a non-local, global identity; and third, differences within neighbourhoods and public policy implications.

Consumption

In his work on the strategies that middle-class households develop for urban living in inner London, Butler (2005) emphasizes the importance of market-based solutions. Whereas some earlier pioneering gentrifiers may have invested in neighbourhood preservation, environmental improvements and local politics, new gentrifiers manage life in inner London through the market by buying desired services. In addition to their environmental qualities gentrified neighbourhoods need to offer well-developed local consumption opportunities. Butler (2001) captures this strategy in the phrase 'eating out as opposed to joining in'. The transformation of commercial spaces to meet the consumption demands of a new middle class is feature of many neighbourhoods. Other city users can also enjoy such amenities.

Delocalizing Neighbourhoods: Translocal Aspirations

This transformation of urban neighbourhoods takes them out of local cultural traditions, and newly gentrified neighbourhoods in the 'high human capital' cities which '… have become global spaces, serving the international service class diaspora in a safe environment that acknowledges the cultural capital of the consumer, …' (Butler, 2005: 184).

Gentrification research has always emphasized the significance of cultural capital and the ability of middle-class residents to display distinctions of taste. This cultural orientation identified in an inner London middle class is echoed in other cities. In the case of Sydney, Rofe (2003) connects theories about gentrifiers and those about transnational elites in order to understand transforming neighbourhoods where residents self-identify as being 'global' and where the urban preferences of Australian global citizens means that they 'need and *want* to be at the heart of the action' (emphasis in original) in certain neighbourhoods in the city. What this cosmopolitan orientation demands is restaurants and galleries where distinctions of taste can be displayed. If in large cities gentrifying areas respond to the expressed demands of a self-defined translocal class then we should expect overlap with the desires of some visitors.

Cosmopolitanism, Conviviality and Tensions in Gentrified Neighbourhoods

The cosmopolitan orientation may be one strategy through which residents impose new consumption demands. In other big city cases, and other phases of gentrification, different strategies emerge for managing urban life. For example, in Belleville in Paris, Simon (2005) examines the different attitudes taken by the new middle class to other groups in the quarter with a class of 'multiculturals' looking for 'atmosphere' and sharing the 'social order' of the district as others seek but fail to find the consumption landscape they desire. In London we can see different periods of gentrification capturing these types of distinction. Whereas earlier pioneer gentrifiers may have invested time in the neighbourhood, now an exclusive landscape of consumption is desired. In looking at Battersea and Barnsbury:

> *'There is no sense here of the middle classes being embedded in a more "authentic", volatile or rounded London' (Butler, 2005: 183).*

Similarly in Brooklyn Heights, Lees (2000) finds a new generation of gentrifiers with less time for the neighbourhood and less interest in neighbourhood affairs.

In some cases we may find shared demand for neighbourhood amenity, consumption and 'character' which can coincide with what visitors may be drawn to. Elsewhere exclusive residential landscapes or volatile neighbourhoods demand different residential strategies and may discourage visitors. Residents and visitors are linked in complex ways with the range of elements that create the distinctive character of places. Understanding gentrification involves understanding the narrative strategies that residents develop to manage city life. Understanding the role of tourism in urban change involves understanding what visitors want from and how they perceive different parts of the city – particularly those not planned as tourism zones – and how they construct narratives to meet their preferences. Together, these understandings can give us an insight into complementarities between residents and visitors.

Visitor Demands and the City

Research in London and NYC has explored the characteristics, attitudes and perceptions of visitors to 'new tourism areas' – that is, areas that were known to attract considerable numbers of overseas visitors (London) or overseas and out of State visitors (NYC) but which had not been planned as tourism precincts or zones and did not form part of traditional tourist itineraries. In both London and NYC, visitor surveys have been used to explore visitor characteristics and attitudes. In London, qualitative research using semi-structured interviews with visitors has been used to explore visitor perceptions, motivations and narratives in more depth.

In London, the research took place in Islington and Bankside. Neither area has been planned as a tourist precinct, but Bankside is contiguous with established tourist zones in central London. Both have been subject to a process of regeneration and gentrification that involves up-market housing, studios and offices, restaurants, bars and shopping. Islington is physically separated from central London tourism zones (although it has excellent public transport connections) and has no substantial conventional tourist attractions, though it has a wide range of cultural facilities, from theatres through restaurants to bars and nightclubs. Bankside lies between well-established tourism precincts (Westminster and the South Bank Centre, and the London Bridge/Tower Bridge area) and includes two new flagship (or iconic) attractions – Shakespeare's Globe Theatre and the Tate Modern gallery along with bars, restaurants and speciality food shops. Whilst tourism has been a significant element in its development, it has been just one part of a wider process of regeneration including major office and residential building, and can be seen as an image based and opportunist response to a process of property speculation (Newman & Smith, 2000).

In NYC tourism has long been considered important to the central city but more recently its role in neighbourhoods outside the central city has been considered, particularly in inner city areas such as Harlem. In 2001, for example, the Ford Foundation spearheaded a citywide initiative to encourage community tourism in New York neighbourhoods outside the central tourist attractions to promote existing culture and heritage in non-traditional tourist destinations such as Harlem (Manhattan), Fort Greene (Brooklyn), Jamaica (Queens) and Richmond (Staten Island). However, there has been almost no analysis of the impacts of tourism upon these non-traditional tourist destinations or of the characteristics and motivations of tourists who visit the areas.

Overseas visitors to Islington and Bankside were surveyed in 2003 and 2004 to investigate their characteristics and the appeal of the area to them. The work has been fully reported elsewhere (Maitland, 2003; Maitland & Newman, 2004; Maitland, 2007a). It turned out that visitors in the surveys differed from overseas visitors to London as a whole. They were much more likely to be repeat visitors to London, were older and made use of friendship networks in deciding on the areas they wanted to visit. These characteristics were more pronounced in Islington than in Bankside. This is as one would expect, since Bankside now has good connections to established tourism beats and is more accessible – physically and symbolically – to visitors to established tourism zones. Visitors were asked what they liked most about their visit. In both areas, the appeal proved to be a distinctive built environment, sense of place or 'leisure setting' (Jansen-Verbeke, 1986), rather particular attractions. In Islington, visitors liked physical and cultural elements (e.g. architecture and the cosmopolitan atmosphere) but also the landscape of consumption – the range of shops, bars, cafes, restaurants and clubs. In Bankside, visitors referred to the architecture, the river, views, sense of history and atmosphere, and these aspects of sense of place were more important than the major attractions of Tate Modern and Shakespeare's Globe. It seemed that for these visitors at least, the appeal of the area lay in qualities that made it a distinctive place, and that apparently mundane elements of vernacular architecture, and shops and cafes could constitute attractions.

In NYC, surveys were undertaken in 2004 and 2005, employing substantially the same questionnaire, in Brooklyn's Grand Army Plaza and Harlem in Manhattan, both acknowledged to be 'off-the-beaten-path' city attractions by NYC and Company (the official tourism office for NYC).

231

The findings were consistent with the London surveys. Compared to visitors to NYC as a whole, survey respondents were more likely to be repeat visitors to the city, to be older, to have arranged their visit independently, to have obtained information from friends and relatives and guide books, and to be visiting friends or relatives as the main purpose of their visit. As in London, they were not drawn primarily by individual attractions but by qualities of place and culture – 'architecture', 'people', 'food', 'culture' and 'diversity' (Genoves et al., 2004; Gross, 2006).

It was clear from the surveys that areas that were off established tourist routes and had not been planned for tourism were attractive to some types of visitor, and also that place characteristics and consumption opportunities were central. Exploring visitors' experience further required qualitative research since that can yield data that are rich and holistic, locally grounded and focused on ordinary events, with an emphasis on lived experience (Miles & Huberman, 1994). Semi-structured interviews were undertaken with visitors to Bankside and Islington and this allowed investigation of the complexities of visitors' perceptions and motivations. The interviews were with overseas visitors whose ages ranged from early 20s to mid-60s, and took place in 2005. Visitors came from a wide range of countries from around the world including western, central and eastern Europe, North and South America, Australasia, India and Africa, but interviews were conducted in English. Most were in professional occupations – for example architect, doctor, teacher, management consultant – so could be seen as current or future members of the cosmopolitan consuming/creative class. They were often from or had spent considerable time living in cities. Fuller accounts of the interviews have been published elsewhere (Maitland, 2006; Maitland, 2007).

Visitors' accounts of their experience and perceptions of the areas are revealing and show that many are sophisticated users of places, conscious of switching between more or less 'touristy' activities. (In the discussion that follows, quotations from interviews are shown in *italics*.) Many relished Bankside or Islington as *quieter, less crowded, more off the beaten path* but had often enjoyed, or were planning, visits to other parts of London that are firmly on the tourist trail – tourism attractions and familiar landmarks like Buckingham Palace, the Tower of London, Covent Garden, Oxford Street, the British Museum, the

London Eye, Piccadilly Circus and St Paul's – *things you can't really come to London and not go to see*. Others behaved differently on different trips visiting *big places* like the British Museum on their first visit, subsequently enjoying an area that *not many people know*. Visitors enjoyed and were conscious of different experiences – *sometimes it's nice to be in a touristy area but I like to change venues every day*. In effect, they constructed not a uniform experience of 'London', but a series of different 'cities'. This allows us to explore how tourist experiences overlap or converge with those of residents and workers.

First, whilst some interviewees saw the areas mainly as another part of London's tourist landscape, most seemed to be discriminating users of the city, with tastes and preferences that converge with those of other users. For these interviewees, the quality of place was more important than major tourism attractions like Tate Modern – although they might well visit such attractions during their stay. Even though Bankside has been developed, cleaned up and had consistent urban design polices applied – *modernized* – it has not been designed as a tourism zone, and that was not how interviewees perceived it. For them, it was *off the beaten track, quieter* and more out of the way than the tourist spots they had visited. We might see them as visiting 'different cities' when they go to Bankside or Islington and when they go to Buckingham Palace or Covent Garden. They shift readily from visiting such primary attractions to the different experience of spending time in the gentrified areas of Bankside or Islington.

Second, buildings, space and the physical character of the place were of great importance, both because they offered distinctive elements – the detailed design of shop fronts in Islington, for example – and because they were seen as embedding the history of the area:

> *This part of the city, well, they're doing construction to make it more modern but it looks like there's older buildings from the late 19th Century, early 20th Century … Some of the buildings seem like they're about a hundred years old. They haven't renamed them at all or tried to keep them in a current state. They're just trying to upkeep the brick and the whatnot from a lot of years ago which is nice.*

233

These area characteristics were seen as contributing to a distinct sense of place, whereas some tourist attractions were what you would expect to find in any city. The way in which visitors experienced the areas was also important, with the opportunity to explore on foot frequently mentioned. *'take your time, you can walk for quite a walk'*, *'just walk and [decide what to do] at the moment'*; *'I have been here one month and I have been walking and really for me it is not boring, every time I find different things'* were typical comments. One interviewee felt that *if you want to know London, you have to walk the streets where the tourists don't go.*

Third, whilst the areas do have conventional tourist attractions, the facilities that interviewees mentioned were much more likely to part of a landscape of everyday consumption – pubs, cafes, clubs, shops and good transport facilities – made interesting because they had unfamiliar elements or were seen as a real part of life in the city. Bankside was described as *really more like kind of off the beaten path. Not the big touristy attractions.* The interviewee felt that it told her about the city, in a way that visits to conventional attractions would not. *Museums are museums and they're all interesting but museums are anywhere and I like to see more what the city is actually about ... The London Eye looks cool but it's just a big tourist attraction as well ... you get to know a city more by seeing the little, not so touristy things.*

These attitudes of interviewees are consistent with the Glaeser et al. (2000) discussion of the amenities that matter to city residents. The 'rich variety of services and consumer goods' and the 'aesthetics and physical setting' of the areas were central to what visitors liked about the area. They also valued accessibility and 'the ability to move around quickly' – in terms of public transport links, but also through the opportunities that walking created to access and explore areas as they pleased. They could explore the area and construct their own narratives and interpretations, rather than follow ones devised by the tourism industry.

Fourth, visitors' attitudes and perceptions also prove to fit well with Butler's discussion of the urban preferences of middle-class households in inner London. There is a shared desire for consumption opportunities, within an aesthetically appealing environment. Cafés, bars, places to eat and interesting shops were mentioned frequently, and many of the interviewees were staying in branded hotels. But it is the context within which the consumption takes place which is perhaps most interesting. Butler (2005) and Rofe (2003) emphasize the way in which residents of gentrified neighbourhoods value them as specifically global spaces, in which they can see themselves as 'at the heart of the action' and build cultural capital from cosmopolitan experiences. For them, the global connections displayed in restaurants, galleries and the cosmopolitan people who use them mark out the appeal of the areas. For our interviewees, other users of the areas were also important. They recognized that the areas they visited were also used by local residents and workers, and this was an important part of the experience. The chance to see everyday life at close quarters or to take part in it was important. One interviewee enjoyed Islington because *people are more relaxed, they sit down, drink coffee, and they talk a lot because it is more relaxed they have a little conversation with you.* Of course, tourists often say they like to meet local people. But interviewees seemed to want to go beyond that and were interested in the mundane details of everyday life: *I remember I went to Tesco to buy things, well it was an incredible experience because how people buy their food, the people wear different type of clothes.* Another interviewee pointed to her enjoyment of the everyday – *people going about their daily tasks ... I just see how people go about their day, as they would.*

Visitors liked Bankside because *people were just out and about, normal Londoners just doing their thing, as opposed to where all the tourists go.* Routine details of ordinary life became interesting as part of visitors' experience. *You can actually see the real London and see how people work. You can see their offices, them working in there. So you can't miss this ... you can walk by ... and see them typing on their computers ... It's kind of cool'.* Even the irritating aspects of daily life in Islington could be seen as part of an experience that *is rich, is good ... I haven't found anything bad about here yet [even though] ... the parking is diabolical and they are dynamite on fines!*

Visitors were realistic about the areas they visited, conscious that they were gentrified and comparatively up-market, like many of the affluent and cosmopolitan locals they were seeing and mixing with – *yuppies, maybe.* The presence of these locals was crucial, both adding to the

235

distinctive character of the areas, and serving to mark them out as places that was not just a tourist zone. For visitors, it showed that they were enjoying an experience created by them, not by the tourist industry, and everyday life and the presence of local people was a crucial element in the experience. As (Richards, 2004: 234) says 'the exotic ... is in the eye of the observer ... [and] can be manufactured from the mundane'.

Conclusions

The research suggests that there are strong links and overlaps between host and tourist experience of place, and that at least in the gentrified, cosmopolitan areas we have examined, the story may be one of conviviality rather than conflict. Both visitors and locals are city users with similar demands for amenity, consumption and the opportunity to display and enhance cultural capital. Changing processes of globalization and economic and visitor flows help account for this, for example through the emergence of a 'cosmopolitan consuming class' (Fainstein et al., 2003: 243) which includes tourists (including business travellers), locals and mobile professionals, resident in the city but not likely to stay for long. Indeed, the sorts of global forces shaping urban tourism identified by Fainstein et al. (2003: 243) suggest new perspectives on the roles of visitors who 'belong' to the cities they visit as much as cities of primary residence. In polycentric cities like London or New York there may be substantial overlap in the demands and tastes of [some] visitors with [some of] a 'host' population characterized by high levels of mobility.

If residents prefer market-based solutions to create amenity and consumption opportunities, then these may be reinforced by the demands of visitors. 'Tourist activities are not so separate from the places that are visited ... places to play involve performances by various kinds of "host" and especially by "guests" ' (Sheller & Urry, 2004: 7). Processes of gentrification can cater for and be driven by visitors as well as locals. Recognition of such conviviality has implications for the future management of urban neighbourhoods. Where non-residents share the interests of residents then the political questions raised by Martinotti about the representation of 'city users' in public policy making are important. According to Webster (2003: 2610), an 'efficient neighbourhood' is 'one in which all those who have an influence on the total value of (or welfare derived from) a neighbourhood have a residual claim on the benefits created by the resources that they influence'. If the city is an object of desire for residents and visitors then non-residents who invest cultural value or support consumption advantages are associated with the prestige of the city and have a stake in its future. Such shared values and demands may make middle-class residents and visitors a powerful influence over public policy.

Conviviality between residents and visitors may be limited to certain cities and certain neighbourhoods. We would expect different places in different cities to offer different types of more or less desirable environments for visitors to explore. Gentrified areas can offer a mix of aesthetic value, local distinctiveness and consumption opportunities that are attractive to visitors. Nonetheless, the recently identified phenomenon of 'super-gentrification' may make some residential districts less attractive to other city users. A mono-cultural, globalized landscape where historic character is overwritten with celebrations of privilege is likely to prove unattractive. For example, the Ostozhenka district in central Moscow, on the Moscava river close to the Cathedral of Christ the Saviour, has undergone substantial reconstruction to become a high-value residential quarter but with a loss of character, historic value and architectural integrity which may limit its interest to visitors straying from nearby central landmarks (Badyina & Golubchikov, 2005). Exclusive residential districts and privatized public spaces have less attraction for other city users. On the other hand some neighbourhoods may offer too much of the 'volatile, authentic and rounded' city character available in the inner city. Many studies of gentrified neighbourhoods however emphasize the tolerance of different groups with often very different daily concerns. Thus in Notting Hill, Martin (2005) reveals shared middle-class concerns with aesthetics contrasting with a lack of interest on the part of working-class residents.

In studies of urban tourism, the experience of visitors has been relatively neglected. When visitors have been considered alongside other city users the focus has often been conflict with a corresponding policy concern about visitor management. We have argued that more attention needs to be given to the motivations and desires of visitors and that in some neighbourhoods in some cities we may find that the preferences of visitors match those of residents. Both groups contribute to the revalorization of urban landscapes and the demand for new opportunities for consumption that have characterized the fast changing areas close to the centre of large cities.

Discussion Questions and Exercises

(1) This chapter argues that there can be strong links and overlaps between how hosts and tourists experience place and in their consumption demands, and that means there is conviviality rather than conflict between host and visitor. Examples are drawn from large polycentric cities like London and New York. Would you expect similar relationships in smaller cities? What city characteristics are central to producing convivial host–visitor relationships?

(2) It seems that some visitors see the local community and 'everyday life' as an important and positive part of their experience of the city. Are the number of tourists who value this increasing – and if so, for what reasons?

(3) The chapter shows that tourists can be discriminating and subtle in their appreciation of place and its distinctive characteristics. Yet, as the chapter points out, the tourism literature has neglected the visitor experience of cities, and tourists are often treated as a unitary type confined to a tourist bubble. How can we account for this neglect in tourism studies?

References

Badyina, A., & Golubchikov, O. (2005). Gentrification in central Moscow – a market process or a deliberate policy? *Geografiska Annaler*, 87B(2), 113–130.

Beioley, S., Maitland, R. et al. (1990). *Tourism and the Inner City*, London: HMSO.

Burtenshaw, D., Bateman, M., & Ashworth, G.J. (1991). *The European City: A Western Perspective*. London: David Fulton Publishers.

Butler, T. (2001). *Cities Summary: The Middle Class and the Future of London*. Available at www.cwis.livjm.ac.uk/cities/fs.publications. htm.

Butler, T. (2005). Gentrification. In N. Buck, I. Gordon, A. Ahrding., & I. Turok (Eds.), *Changing Cities* (pp. 172–187). Basingstoke: Palgrave.

Church, A., & Frost, M. (2004). Tourism, the global city and the labour market in London. *Tourism Geographies*, 6(2), 208–228.

Clark, T.N. (2003). *The City as an Entertainment Machine*. San Diego, CA: Elsevier.

Deben, L., Terhorst, P., et al. (2000). Amsterdam's Inner City as a Tourist Center: it's all in the mix (Mimeo).

Fainstein, S.S., & Gladstone, D. (1999). Evaluating urban tourism. In D.R. Judd, & S.S. Fainstein (Eds.), *The Tourist City* (pp. 21–34), New Haven: Yale University Press.

Fainstein, S.S., Hoffman, L. et al. (2003). Making theoretical sense of tourism. In L.M. Hoffman, S.S. Fainstein, & D.R. Judd (Eds.), *Cities and Visitors. Regulating People, Markets and City Space* (pp. 239–253). Oxford: Blackwell.

Franklin, A. (2003). *Tourism. An Introduction*. London: Sage.

Franklin, A., & Crang, M. (2001). The trouble with tourism and travel theory? *Tourist Studies*, 1(1), 5–22.

Genoves, R., Hogan, M. et al. (2004). *The Real New York*. New York: City University. (unpublished)

Glaeser, E., Kolko, L. et al. (2000). *Consumer City* Harvard, MA: Harvard Institute of Economic Research.

Gordon, I., & Goodall, B. (2000). Localities and tourism. *Tourism Geographies*, 2(3), 290–311.

Gross, J. (2006). Non-traditional tourist destinations and the tourists they attract. *Urban Affairs Association 36th Annual Meeting: Neighbourhoods and Urban Transformation: the New Global Context*, Montreal, Canada.

Hannigan, J. (1998). *Fantasy City. Pleasure and Profit in the Post-modern Metropolis*. London: Routledge.

Harvey, D. (1989). *The Condition of Postmodernity*. Oxford: Blackwell.

Hayllar, B., & Griffin, T. (2005). The precinct experience: a phenomenological approach. *Tourism Management*, 26(4), 517–528.

Hoffman, L.M., Fainstein, S.S., & Judd, D.R. (Eds.) (2003). *Cities and Visitors. Regulating People, Markets and City Space*. Oxford: Blackwell.

Jansen-Verbeke, M. (1986). Inner city tourism, resources, tourists and promoters. *Annals of Tourism Research*, 13, 79–100.

Judd, D.R. (1995). Promoting tourism in US cities. *Tourism Management*, 16(3), 175.

Judd, D.R., & Fainstein, S.S. (Eds.) (1999). *The Tourist City*. New Haven: Yale University.

Law, C.M. (1993). *Urban Tourism: Attracting Visitors to Large Cities*. New York: Mansell.

Law, C.M. (2000). Regenerating the city centre through leisure and tourism. *Built Environment*, 26(2), 117–129.

Law, C.M. (2002). *Urban Tourism*. London: Continuum.

Lees, L. (2000). A re-appraisal of gentrification: towards a geography of gentrification. *Progress in Human Geography*, 24, 389–408.

Maitland, R. (1997). Tourism and mixed use development in town centres. In A. Coupland (Ed.), *Reclaiming the City*. London: E & FN Spon.

Maitland, R. (2003). Cultural tourism and new tourism areas. *Cultural Tourism: Globalising the Local – Localising the Global*. Tilburg, Barcelona: ATLAS.

Maitland, R. (2006a). Culture, city users and the creation of new tourism areas in cities. In M.K. Smith (Ed.), *Tourism, Culture and Regeneration*. London: CABI.

Maitland, R. (2006b). Tourists, conviviality and distinctive tourism areas in London. Presented at *Cutting Edge Research in Tourism – New Directions, Challenges and Applications* (CD-ROM). University of Surrey, UK, 6–9 June.

Maitland, R. (2007a). Cultural tourism and the development of new tourism areas in London. In G. Richards (Ed.), *Cultural Tourism – Global and Local Perspectives*. Binghampton, NY: Haworth Press.

Maitland, R. (2007b). Tourists, the creative class, and distinctive areas in major cities. In G. Richards, & J. Wilson (Eds.), *Tourism, Creativity and Development*. London: Routledge.

Maitland, R., & Newman, P. (2004). Developing metropolitan tourism on the fringe of central London. *International Journal of Tourism Research*, 6(5), 339–348.

Martin, G.P. (2005). Narratives great and small: neighbourhood change, place and identity in Notting Hill. *International Journal of Urban and Regional Research*, 29(1), 67–88.

Martinotti, G. (1999). A city for whom? Transients and public life in the second-generation metropolis. In R. Beauregard, & S. Body-Gendrot (Eds.), *The Urban Moment* (pp. 155–184). London: Sage.

Miles, M.B., & Huberman, A.M. (1994). *Qualitative Data Analysis – an Expanded Sourcebook.* Thousand Oaks: Sage.

Montgomery, J. (2003). Cultural quarters as mechanisms for urban regeneration. Part 1: Conceptualising cultural quarters. *Planning, Practice and Research*, 18(4), 293–306.

Montgomery, J. (2004). Cultural quarters as mechanisms for urban regeneration. Part 2: A review of four cultural quarters in the UK, Ireland and Australia. *Planning, Practice and Research*, 19(1), 3–31.

Nevarez, L. (2003). *New Money, Nice Town.* New York: Routledge.

Newman, P., & Smith, I. (2000). Cultural production, place and politics on the South Bank of the Thames. *International Journal of Urban and Regional Research*, 24(1), 9–24.

Page, S., & Hall, C.M. (2003). *Managing Urban Tourism.* Harlow: Prentice-Hall.

Porter, M.E. (1995). Competitive advantage of the inner city. *Harvard Business Review*, 73(3), 55–71.

Porter, M.E. (1998). Clusters and the new economics of competition. *Harvard Business Review*, 76(6), 77–90.

Richards, G. (2004). Mallrats – harbingers of globalization or creators of the new locality? In Richards, G. (Ed.), *Cultural Tourism: Globalizing the local – localising the Global* (pp. 7–11). Tilburg: ATLAS.

Richards, G., & Wilson, J. (2006). Developing creativity in tourist experiences: a solution to the serial reproduction of culture? *Tourism Management*, 27, 1209–1223.

Rofe, M. (2003). 'I want to be global': theorising the gentrifying class as an emergent elite global community. *Urban Studies*, 40(12), 2511–2526.

Sassen, S., & Roost, F. (1999). The city: strategic site for the global entertainment industry, In D.R. Judd, & S.S. Fainstein, (Eds.), *The Tourist City*. (pp. 143–154), New Haven: Yale University Press.

Selby, M. (2004). *Understanding Urban Tourism*. London: I.B. Taurus.

Sheller, M., & Urry, J. (2004). Places to play, places in play. In M. Sheller, & J. Urry (Eds.), *Tourism Mobilities: Places to Play, Places in Play*. London: Routledge.

Simon, P. (2005). Gentrification of old neighbourhoods and social integration in Europe. In Y. Kazepov (Ed.), *Cities of Europe* (pp. 210–232). Oxford: Blackwell.

Smales, L. (1994). Desperate pragmatism or shrewd optimism? The image and selling of West Yorkshire. In G. Haughton, & D. Whitney (Eds.), *Reinventing a Region: Restructuring in West Yorkshire*. Aldershot: Avebury Press.

Smith, M.K. (2003). *Issues in Cultural Tourism Studies*. London: Routledge.

Webster, C. (2003). The nature of the neighbourhood. *Urban Studies*, 40(13), 2591–2612.

Zukin, S. (1995). *Cultures of Cities*. Oxford: Blackwell.

III

Precincts in Practice

12

Precinct Planning and Design, Management and Marketing: An Overview

Tony Griffin, Bruce Hayllar and
Deborah Edwards

Introduction

One of the principal aims of writing this book was to provide a base
for improving practices associated with the development and ongoing
governance of urban tourism precincts. Such an improvement is
predicated upon an understanding of what precincts are, how they
have evolved and what functions they perform in terms of satisfying
the tourist's needs and contributing to the city's role as a tourist destination. Section I of this book dealt with these foundational matters.
Just as vital, however, is an understanding of key issues associated
with urban tourism precincts, particularly from the perspectives of
the various stakeholders with interests in these areas, such as tourists,
tourism enterprises and host communities. Appropriate governance of
precincts needs to be informed by an understanding of: how tourists
experience precincts; factors that affect the quality of those experiences; how precincts contribute to the urban economy and to the city's

overall appeal and functionality as a tourist destination; what potential conflicts can arise between stakeholders in precinct development; and what costs and benefits the emergence of tourism precincts can generate for the host community. Such issues need to be recognized, addressed and appropriately dealt with if a precinct is to form a truly sustainable part of a city's touristic base. These issues, amongst others, have been raised and discussed in Section II of this book, while also drawing some implications for governance.

Section III focuses specifically on the practice of governance by presenting a range of international case studies. These case studies are intended to reflect exemplary practices as well as other situations where important lessons about precinct governance can be drawn from the experience. As a set, the case studies also attempt to provide an idea of the diversity of the challenges involved in developing and presenting urban tourism precincts. The main purpose of this chapter is to set the foundation for these case studies by defining the range of precinct governance activities and discussing some of the key associated challenges.

The Scope of Precinct Governance

The notion of governance is generally about control. When applied to urban tourism precincts this implies that it involves some deliberate effort on the part of a 'governing' organization, or set of organizations working collaboratively, to dictate certain events and outcomes associated with tourism in the precinct. Governance implies that there are stewards in charge who are seeking to get the best possible outcomes from the tourist use of the precinct for a variety of stakeholders. Rather than the precinct's development and ongoing use being dictated purely by market forces, reflecting the preferences and interests of individual consumers and producers, the notion of governance implies that there are mechanisms in existence for effecting collective decisions in the broader public interest.

Governance may be required at a number of different stages of a precinct's development. As discussed in Chapter 2 of this volume, tourism precincts in cities can evolve in a variety of ways. Some have been deliberately created through the major redevelopment of blighted, redundant industrial or waterfront land, where the old slate is wiped clean. Others have involved tourism uses being incorporated within an existing urban fabric, where that original fabric is a major part of the area's appeal to tourists and hence the changes introduced by tourism need to be controlled so that they conserve the attraction. In both situations conscious decisions need to be made about the desired future state of the precinct and deliberate actions taken to realize that state. As the precinct evolves, new issues continually emerge: tourism businesses come and go; tourist numbers grow and congestion needs to be managed; parts of the precinct show signs of wear and tear; and some local residents feel alienated from their own leisure spaces and places by the influx of tourists. The mix of activities and supporting infrastructure may need to be continuously adjusted to maintain the precinct's appeal and functionality. Initially, and from time to time thereafter, a precinct may need to be promoted so that prospective visitors are made aware of the experiences it offers, and new markets are sought to replace those that might be on the wane.

Generally speaking, the governance activities associated with urban tourism precincts can be divided into three broad categories:

(1) Planning and design
(2) Management
(3) Marketing

The nature of each of these activities, along with some of the key issues and challenges involved, is discussed below. As will be noted, there is considerable overlap between these activities.

Precinct Planning and Design

Fundamentally, planning is about deciding how a precinct should develop in the future. It involves having a vision about the precinct and then putting in place mechanisms that are intended to realize that vision. In some cases, this involves creating a new place by replacing the existing, often degraded fabric. The vision in this instance may involve formulating a grand design for the new precinct, accompanied by mechanisms that will facilitate development in the desired direction and at the appropriate pace. Implementing a grand design for a new precinct generally requires a high degree of control over the development process, hence this is often overseen by a special purpose authority that has both planning and development powers.

Most urban tourism precincts, however, do not involve the creation of a totally new place, where the pre-existing physical fabric has been razed and replaced by something markedly different. Rather they have involved introducing tourism-related land uses and activities into an existing fabric, most of which will be maintained. Indeed, in some cases it is the distinctiveness of the original physical fabric that has attracted tourists' interest, and the emergence of the area as a tourism precinct has been gradual and largely unintentional. In such precincts, planning is fundamentally about guiding or regulating future development so that the qualities of the place are at least maintained and if possible enhanced. Planners may establish controls over such things as: the design of new buildings so that they are compatible with the current architectural style; the types of land uses that are permitted so that they contribute to rather than detract from the appeal or activity base of the place; the height and bulk of buildings so that the human scale of the place is maintained; and the setback of buildings from public spaces so that their access to sunlight is preserved or the movement of visitors is not impeded. Planning in these situations involves being mindful of the quality of public spaces and places within the precinct, which are influenced by both the physical fabric of the buildings and the social atmosphere generated by the activities within the precinct. The influx of tourists to the area also places additional burdens on the precinct's supporting infrastructure, such as transport and parking facilities, and hence planning is needed to ensure that the capacity of this infrastructure can cope with the demands placed upon it.

Planning of tourism precincts within urban environments also needs to recognize other interests, issues and stakeholders beyond those associated with tourism. Cities, by their nature, have large resident populations, the vast majority of whom will have little or no direct interest in tourism. Their quality of life may, however, be impacted by tourism.

Tourism precincts may effectively evolve from local residents' leisure spaces and places, and tourists may represent an intrusion into those spaces and places, reducing both the quality and quantity of leisure opportunities available to locals. The resident population may lose a sense of ownership of these valuable spaces for communal social interaction. Local infrastructure may be overburdened by tourism, with consequent diminution of service adequacy for locals. Tourist activities may further intrude upon and reduce the amenity of residential neighbourhoods that surround tourist precincts. Even with major redevelopment projects where there is not an existing resident population to be concerned about, there are choices that must be made about broad land uses and dominant activities. The decision to encourage tourism as the dominant economic activity in such a precinct involves negating the possibility of the land being used for other activities such as commercial, industrial or residential, unless they are compatible with the tourism uses. Such planning decisions must consider the relative merits of various alternative land uses and determine what is best for the urban economy and community. In this sense, planning for tourism precincts involves resolving a series of questions of balance, sometimes seeking compromise between competing and conflicting interests, but on other occasions determining that a particular set of interests is paramount. This means that many planning decisions are fundamentally political in nature, and a key role for precinct planners may be the anticipating and resolving conflicts before they arise.

Precinct Management

While planning is primarily concerned with setting and then putting in place mechanisms to realize a vision for a precinct, management is more concerned with overseeing and maintaining its ongoing functionality, including its appeal as a place for tourist activities. Tourism precinct management is effectively a particular form of place management, which seeks to ensure that the area is appropriately serviced and both its condition and activity base are maintained.

The specific activities of precinct management may, however, vary significantly depending on the circumstances, in particular the degree of control that the precinct management authority possesses. The range of possibilities extends from the virtually absolute control of the landlord to the very weak control of an organization which relies on the powers of persuasion to elicit cooperation between a diverse array of stakeholders within a tourism precinct. In the former case, management can embrace such issues as the tenant mix, which in turn affects the range of activities within the precinct. Moreover, leasing conditions imposed on tenants can include performance clauses, which might impact on the quality of service provided to tourists, and also obligations that reflect the interdependency of tenants in the precinct situation. Individual commercial interests can be subjugated to the collective interest of maximizing the overall performance of the precinct, and micro-management of the precinct is possible in such situations. Where the management structure is reliant on voluntary and cooperative behaviour, much more effort needs to be put into maintaining good relationships with stakeholders and demonstrating the benefits of working together to achieve common goals. This is particularly problematic where some stakeholders within a precinct do not see themselves as being directly connected to or benefiting from tourism, and may in fact see their interests as being in conflict with it. Consultative processes and relationship-building are inherent parts of precinct management in such situations.

In tourism precincts, there is a particular focus on managing the public domain, because that is where tourists often spend the bulk of their time and where impressions of and feelings for the place are formed. The quality of the public domain is thus a prime determinant of the quality of a tourist's experience. Management of the public domain may include ensuring that it is safe, both during the day and the night, clean and maintained in good physical condition. Management also entails ensuring that tourists from diverse backgrounds and with a range of personal capabilities can find their way around the precinct with both ease and comfort. The public domain must also be engaging and interesting, and hence the activities that take place within it must be managed or at least enabled by management practices. Controlling the tenant mix around public spaces so that, for example, there is a concentration of outdoor cafes which generate a sense of vitality as well as afford opportunities to people-watch is one way of achieving this.

Another might relate to managing street entertainment and busking, or choosing not to control these activities if the desire is to allow the public space to develop its own character in this regard. The art of precinct management may thus include recognizing when it is best not to manage a particular feature. Tight adherence to management formulae, *a la* McDonalds, may lead to standardized, less distinctive places.

An increasingly important aspect of precinct management is related to the function that they may perform as a venue for events of various kinds. Indeed the recognition of the value of creating such venues has been part of the motivation behind major redevelopments of redundant urban sites into tourism precincts. The relationship between events and urban tourism precincts, however, could be characterized as a symbiotic one. While the desire to facilitate the staging of events may be a *raison d'etre* for developing precincts, events may also play a significant role in maintaining their long-term appeal and viability. Events can generate vitality in a precinct and attract visitors who may not otherwise have visited. Hence establishing, maintaining and operating a programme of events may be an important function of precinct management.

Precinct Marketing

The staging of events within precincts may, in fact, represent a particular marketing initiative. The marketing of tourism precincts is akin to the marketing of tourist destinations, in that the essential product that is being offered is an experience or amalgam of experiences within a particular geographic space. Unlike most 'product' marketing there is not necessarily a direct exchange process whereby a supplier provides a good or service to a consumer who pays money for same. In precinct marketing the 'product' is disparate and rarely will the marketer directly control, distribute or receive a direct payment from the visitor who 'consumes' the experiences of the precinct. The principal focus is thus on the promotional component of the marketing mix, with the prime object being to attract visitors who will then spend money in the various establishments within the precinct. The marketer is thus an intermediary rather than a direct beneficiary. There may be some exceptions to this, for instance where the precinct marketing authority is also the landlord, which will thus derive income from rents that are often tied to the turnover of commercial tenants.

In most cases the objective of precinct marketing will be to maximize the number of visitors coming to the precinct. In some instances marketing initiatives may further focus on attracting particular types of visitors who are most likely to spend money within the precinct. Occasionally, there may be an additional need to increase the volume of visitors at normally low periods of the year, which is often a motivation for the staging of events at particular times. The marketing of urban tourism precincts may, however, follow a distinctly non-traditional path if the popularity of the precinct exceeds either the capacity of the local infrastructure to support it, or the tolerance of the local community. In such cases, 'demarketing', involving deterring visitation in general or at particular times of the day or the year, may be an appropriate strategy.

Key Issues and Challenges

As has been noted earlier, some precincts have developed in an ad hoc manner largely in the absence of any formal planning or management. However, as Page observed, 'the long-term consequences of failing to plan for the future development of urban tourism has often led to insurmountable problems for some localities' (1995: 155). Pearce has argued that what is needed is a 'more explicit recognition of tourism as a distinctive land-use and a more proactive stance rather than reactive stance taken with regard to this sector' (1998: 63). There is hence a long-recognized need for appropriate planning and management of tourism development in urban areas, including within the specific manifestation of tourism precincts.

The practice of precinct planning and management, however, is complicated by the diverse organizational structures and contexts which support it. Occasionally, an authority is empowered to solely control most aspects of a precinct's planning, development, management and marketing. Such is the case in Sydney's Darling Harbour, one of the case studies presented later in this volume (Chapter 14). More typically, though, the responsibility for a tourism precinct is shared by several organizations with different, occasionally overlapping functions. Planning, management and marketing functions may be carried out by different organizations with varying and sometimes conflicting aims. These can include local and even higher level government organizations, chambers of commerce, business associations and tourism marketing bodies. The case study of London's south bank precinct clearly exemplifies this complexity and the challenges it presents for achieving effective planning and management (see Chapter 15). Even within the one type of governance organization there may be wide variations. For example, Page observed that 'identifying the archetypal local government organization [within any given country] ... is almost an impossible task' (1995: 162), in spite of them possessing a fairly common range of statutory functions and responsibilities.

Regardless of these variations in structure and organizational responsibility, some major, common challenges and issues are evident, which the responsible authorities must address. A selection of these key issues and challenges is discussed below. A number of these reflect key themes that have been discussed in previous chapters of this volume.

Understanding the Wider Context

Tourism precincts are inextricably linked to their surrounding urban environments. As such, the intensity and nature of the impact of tourism upon the city is determined largely by its spatial and temporal concentration and by its functional associations with other urban attributes. It is these two conditions rather than the absolute numbers of tourists or the locations of individual tourism facilities that present most of the opportunities and problems that challenge local planning and management. Thus, an understanding of the locational patterns of tourists and tourism facilities within the city in relation to the form and function of the city as a whole is critical.

Locals Are Just as Important as the Tourists

Common negative impacts in tourism precincts typically affect residents more than tourists, with effects such as inflated real estate prices and rents, traffic congestion, pollution, prostitution, crime and loss of leisure opportunities for locals high on the list of concerns (Getz, 1993). Pearce (1998) found that the major sources of tourist/local conflict in Parisian tourism precincts centred on parking and tour coach circulation. However, the role of local residents as contributors of tourism precinct experiences should also be carefully considered. Hayllar and Griffin (2005) highlighted the importance to tourists of The Rocks precinct in Sydney being a place where local residents and city workers engaged in everyday, mundane activities, as this created a feeling of authenticity about the place. In a similar study by the same authors in Fremantle, Western Australia, the existence of a working port provided a welcome element of gritty reality to this historic waterfront precinct, while the presence of children at play was a reassurance that this was not a contrived place created and managed just for tourists (Griffin & Hayllar, 2006). Pearce (1998) discussed how authorities have acted to protect the residential function of the Montmartre precinct in Paris. There was an overt objective to preserve the urban fabric of the area while establishing a balance between the residential and tourist functions. Hence, the strategy aimed to 'prevent the further intrusion of tourism into residential areas' by 'manipulating access between points of arrival and major tourist attractions' and thereby managing visitor flow (Pearce, 1998: 63).

Recognize the Importance of the Tourist's Experience

In an early study of inner-city tourism precincts, Jansen-Verbeke (1986) hinted at the gap between what tourism marketers and tourists consider important. The dilemma for marketers was whether to focus on the tourism services (attractions, accommodation, transport) or the actual experience of the place. The contemporary consensus on the appropriate answer to this question, as evidenced by tourist destination marketing practice and the recognition of the so-called 'experience economy', is that the tourists' experiences should be paramount. Understanding and responding appropriately to the desired experiences of tourists should thus be a fundamental basis for precinct planning, management and marketing. In this regard, there are some rudimentary matters that need to be addressed that enable or facilitate an experience without necessarily shaping it. In a study of Federation Square in Melbourne, Griffin and Hayllar (2006) found that visitors' experiences of the precinct were constrained by its lack of legibility; visitors had difficulty finding their way, understanding how to use the public space and knowing how to access the internal spaces and whether indeed it would be worthwhile to do so. Weaver (1993) observed a successful Caribbean historic precinct model where basic issues such as pedestrian convenience and safety were addressed by limiting vehicular access and providing good directional signage, lighting, litter removal and police services. This effectively enabled visitors to comfortably and securely enjoy the atmosphere and experience provided by musicians and vendors, who had been allowed to circulate among the precinct's restored buildings in order to give it an aura of authenticity. Understanding the experiences that tourists seek in precincts can also inform promotional messages that are intended to motivate tourists to visit.

Take a Long-Term Approach

Tourism precincts generally have a fairly substantial life-cycle. However, to achieve this longevity they often must undergo periods of rejuvenation. This is particularly true of precincts that have been created as a result of major urban redevelopment projects – see, for example, the cases of Navy Pier and Albert Dock presented in Chapter 2 of this volume. Ultimately, as Gibson and Hardman (1998) contend, the attractiveness to visitors and hence the marketability of the areas is best ensured by the relevant organizations working together and taking a long-term approach to maintenance and management, although this may be easier said than done given the fragmented nature of planning and management responsibilities in many precincts.

The Benefits of Diversity

A diversity of functions may be appropriate to ensure the long-term viability and success of tourism precincts. Gibson and Hardman (1998), for example, suggested that precincts that have encouraged other income generating uses such as shops and offices face a more secure future than those which rely predominantly on tourism and leisure. Getz (1993) also observed that some governing authorities have deliberately blended traditional central business functions with visitor-oriented attractions and services based on water frontages or natural or heritage attractions to form tourism precincts. Providing a diverse array of land uses within a tourism precinct may also be a major contributor to the quality of tourism experiences. Maitland (2006) observed how the tourist appeal of two emerging precincts in London relied partly on 'the everyday, and an appreciation of the conviviality of the ordinary' (p. 10). Visitors appreciated the experience of seeing Londoners doing everyday things, such as working on computers in offices. Hayllar and Griffin (2005) discussed the notion of 'layering experiences' (p. 526) within a precinct, thereby enabling different people to experience the precinct in different ways. This latter strategy may be facilitated not only by a diversity of land uses but also by a range of public spaces and routes that provide opportunities for exploration and discovery.

The Case Studies

The case studies presented in the following five chapters have been drawn from a number of countries around the world, and reflect a range of other contrasting contextual circumstances. There is a diversity of governance structures in evidence, the fundamental character of the precincts varies, and they represent different stages in the process of tourism precinct development or evolution. What they share is the ability to shed light on some key governance issues associated with urban tourism precincts and how these might be effectively dealt with. Each chapter is intended to focus on a particular set of governance practices – planning and design, management or marketing – but the reality is that the line between these sets is often blurred, particularly when a governing organization has multiple responsibilities and powers. The case studies vary in their focus but they all offer an opportunity to learn valuable lessons from the successes, and some of the failures, of governance practices in these precincts.

Each of the case studies is introduced below, with a brief indication of the principal focus and the key governance issues that the case illustrates and addresses.

Grote Markt, Groningen, The Netherlands

The case of the Grote Markt in the northern Dutch city of Groningen serves to illustrate the complexities inherent in precinct planning. In particular, it emphasizes the importance of developing a strategic vision to guide the planning process, and the challenges associated with arriving at a consensus amongst stakeholders on that vision. In a broader context, it highlights how leisure and tourism have changed the way we view central city areas and how these activities are increasingly forming a significant part of an overall multifunctional vision for the city.

Darling Harbour, Sydney, Australia

Darling Harbour represents an exemplary precinct development in a number of ways. It has been extraordinarily successful in terms of attracting visitors over a long period, yet it has been heavily criticized. It was planned, developed and continues to be owned, managed and marketed by a single statutory authority, which broke many of the 'normal' planning rules, like allowing community participation, to carry out this major redevelopment relatively quickly. Its consequent success from a users' perspective challenges the conventional wisdom about how such places should be planned. It further demonstrates the links between the planning, management and marketing of precincts, and the evolutionary and necessarily flexible nature of place making.

London's South Bank, United Kingdom

In contrast to Darling Harbour, London's south bank precinct illustrates the complexity of precinct management where responsibilities are heavily fragmented. In this situation, a range of private and public sector groups have had to find a way of collaborating for the common good, a challenging task in itself. There have been some reluctant participants in this process, most notably one of the area's local government authorities, but the case study points to some means by which effective collaboration may be achieved. Ultimately, the case demonstrates that it is preferable to meet these challenges and to manage tourism in a precinct than to let it occur 'naturally'.

257

Sheffield City Centre, United Kingdom

While the London example was primarily concerned with precinct management structures, the Sheffield City Centre case deals with more day-to-day management issues. In particular, it points to the importance of managing the public realm and some of the key dilemmas that this presents, for example maintaining a 'light touch' when it comes to controlling visitor behaviour. It reinforces themes from the London study about the need for collaboration between public and private sector interests, but raises some concerns about the extent to which the private sector will contribute to the common good. More generally, it emphasizes that planning must be followed up by effective management and marketing if a precinct is to be sustainably successful.

Evora, Portugal and Hoi An, Vietnam

The final chapter in this section presents two case studies, linked by the common thread of being World Heritage listed places: Evora in Portugal and Hoi An in Vietnam. Generally the chapter highlights the challenges of managing and marketing such places for tourism while at the same time considering locals' needs. The Evora case study emphasizes the need to link the governance of this precinct with broader objectives relating to the overall planning and development of the city, and improving the quality of life for the residents. The experience in Hoi An demonstrates the need to consider how the benefits of tourism promotion might spread to the local community through the creation of linkages with the tourism sector.

References

Getz, D. (1993). Planning for tourism business districts. *Annals of Tourism Research*, 20(3), 583–600.

Gibson, C., & Hardman, D. (1998). Regenerating urban heritage for tourism. *Managing Leisure*, 3(1), 37–54.

Griffin, T., & Hayllar, B. (2006). Historic waterfronts as tourism precincts: an experiential perspective. *Tourism and Hospitality Research*, 7(1), 3–16.

Hayllar, B., & Griffin, T. (2005). The precinct experience: a phenom-enological approach. *Tourism Management*, 26(4), 517–528.

Jansen-Verbeke, M. (1986). Inner city tourism: resources, tourists, promoters. *Annals of Tourism Research*, 13(1), 79–100.

Maitland, R. (2006). Tourists, conviviality and distinctive tourism areas in London. Presented at *Cutting Edge Research in Tourism – New Directions, Challenges and Applications* (CD-ROM). University of Surrey, UK, 6–9 June.

Page, S. (1995). *Urban Tourism*. London: Routledge.

Pearce, D. (1998). Tourist districts in Paris: structure and functions. *Tourism Management*, 19(1), 49–66.

Weaver, D.B. (1993). A model of urban tourism space in small Caribbean islands. *Geographical Review*, 83(2), 134–140.

13

Grote Markt Groningen: The Re-heritagization of the Public Realm

Gregory J. Ashworth

Introduction

The *Grote Markt* has been for 1000 years the 'living room' of the Northern Dutch city of Groningen. The space, one of the largest market squares in Europe, and its surrounding buildings have been, and remain today the focus of commercial, political, cultural and social life in the city. Groningen, like cities in general, has experienced constant change and has been in a permanent state of growth or decline throughout its 1000 years of existence. Neither change nor the active responsive management of such change by local government agencies are recent phenomena. The city has been in an almost constant state of renewal, retrenchment or repositioning in response to the expectations placed upon it. The stimulus has often been external trends while the response in the shaping of strategic vision as well as its manifestation and application in detailed, and often quite routine, spatial management has been dominantly local.

Strategic thinking for the city as a whole has become focused on the restructuring of the central city and ultimately upon its central space, the *Grote Markt* and surroundings. This space, small in area, came to represent, not least symbolically, perceptions and aspirations of what the city is for, what it should represent and in whose interests does it exist. The original version of the planning ideas for this area was entitled 'A new heart for Groningen', intentionally suggesting the *double entendre* of both a particular space to be physically arranged and a core belief and vision for the city as a whole. 'The creation of strategic visions implies the design of shared futures' (Albrechts, 2003: 1). The difficulty lies both in conceiving a consensual future and actually managing it.

Unlike many of the cases discussed elsewhere in this book, there is in Groningen no single strategic planning document expressing unambiguously a clear consensual vision. Instead, there is a collection of loosely related sector and area plans, and a battery of policy decisions, which in aggregate, and through a process of 'logical incrementalism' (Quinn, 1980) have radically transformed the Grote Markt in response to changes in the expectations that citizens have of it.

The Contexts

The National and International Context

Cities exist and interact within wider national and international contexts and local urban planning and management actions are necessarily inextricably entangled in much wider concerns. The Netherlands has experienced a number of relevant trends, which form the social context to change. These reflect even wider trends within Western societies and it is this very embedding, as contributory cause, amplifier and equally potential solution that complicates discussion and decision. These trends can be summarized as the individualization of society and consequent collapse of social and political corporatism; the decline in popular participation in the formal democratic procedures of government together with a rise in ad hoc and single interest activism; changes in life style that have led to changes in the use of space, specifically urban space both public and private; a redefinition and revaluation of urban environments, reflected in concerns for environmental safety, amenity, aesthetic beauty, historicity and the like, manifested in the rise of the environmental and heritage consensus. All of the above are reflected in change in the public expectations of cities, their service delivery and government, which is amplified in the Netherlands by its high population densities and limited physical space.

The Local Context

National and international trends are filtered through, and modified by, the distinctive characteristics of the city of Groningen. The 'city' (*stad*) is the decisive governmental and legal entity (the *gemeente*), and has a population of just under 200,000, a figure which has not changed much in the past 30 years. It is the city with its directly elected council, its nationally appointed *burgermeester* and large planning department that makes and executes policies and plans. However, the inner city, the subject of this discussion, has a resident population of less than 10,000 and no separate political representation. In addition, the contiguous suburbs and functional hinterland of Groningen extends far wider, encompassing parts of three provinces and a population of close to half a million. This city region is managed by only a loose and largely informal cooperation of the constituent local authorities. The city has experienced quite radical demographic and social change in the past 30 years. While its total population has changed little, the age group 20–35 has grown substantially and the city has been transformed from a staid culturally homogeneous northern market town to a much livelier, hedonistic and culturally diverse city. The city and the northern region it serves have suffered from a long-term structural decline in its traditional manufacturing and agricultural processing economic base resulting in a lag in most economic indicators of around 20–30 per cent behind national averages (Kooij & Pellenbarg, 1994). The city has traditionally experienced strong political government (by left of centre parties) together with strong personal government (aided by the party-dominated electoral system). This has resulted in notably stable social democrat led coalitions often dominated by powerful individuals. A certain tradition of top-down 'revolution by decree' has been noted

(Tsubohara, 2003). The continuing perceived relative national spatial peripherality and deterioration in the traditional economic base, together with the perceived failure of long-standing regional economic policies and increased inter-regional and international competition, have all combined to encourage a search for new directions. There has been a shift from a political–economic dependency model, where the national core, known here as 'the west', supported the north with financial subsidies in return for political support. Success in Groningen politics was measured by success in extracting such support from 'The Hague'. A range of factors operating in combination over the past 30 years have encouraged a redefinition of the city, physically, economically and perceptually, and a central role for public planning and management agencies in executing such a redefinition. The 'old' identity of the Northern Netherlands was defined by its peripheral spatially but also its marginal and by extension 'backwardness' economically and even culturally.

There was an imposed and accepted collective inferiority complex, which is now being replaced by a new self-consciousness, which rejects the former imposed role and asserts an, as yet vaguely defined, new identity (Cusveller, 1994). An indicator of the new confident élan was unexpectedly but dramatically revealed in 2007 when an EU study of citizen satisfaction with their cities and their governments placed Groningen in the first position among 75 European towns (European Commission, 2007).

Tourism plays a somewhat muted role in the city. Groningen is not one of Europe's major heritage and cultural tourism centres. It is relatively inaccessible, has only a weakly developed image as a tourism destination on national and international tourism markets, and has never regarded the development of tourism as a major policy goal. Like many, if not most, European medium-sized, regional market centres with 1000 years of historical development, it exists to serve principally its own citizens and those of its surrounding region. Tourism is regarded in part as marginal windfall gain and in part as an inevitable inflow that is neither particularly welcomed nor resisted. The approximately 1 million day visitors are dominantly shoppers from neighbouring Germany and the approximately 200,000 overnight stays are business visitors and conference delegates, especially connected to the university, holidaymakers in transit from Scandinavia to Southern Europe, and short stay cultural tourists attracted by the museum and cultural events. The policies and actions described below were not designed to serve the tourist and tourism is normally mentioned only as an assumed additional benefit. This situation is, I believe, quite typical of the European city outside the handful of cultural tourism honey-pots.

The Grote Markt in the Context of the City

Groningen has, even by comparable European standards, a remarkably compact and physically distinctive inner city. It accommodates in a very restricted area most of the retailing, city and provincial administrations, and entertainment facilities serving the greater city region of around half a million inhabitants. In addition, it houses the major symbolic buildings of culture, the arts, the university and more generally the major structures of the city's built environmental heritage. Thus, the tourism function is also strongly focused on the Grote Markt, around which are located a number of major historic buildings (Town Hall, Cathedral Church) but also the city tourism information office. It is also the location for events whether regular, such as the food market, or sporadic such as festivals and performances. The inner city has also, it should be remembered, a resident population of around 10,000 people, dominantly in small households and there is a general absence of the vacancy above city centre commercial premises that is so prevalent in many comparable Western cities. The competitive pressures for space and the possibilities for conflict between functions are endemic and to an extent exacerbated by the idea of the multifunctional inner city, which has long been a mantra of government at all levels.

Dutch cities differ in some important respects from most other Western cities (Faludi & v.d.Valk, 1994). Since the Second World War there has been a public acceptance of strong expert-driven, top-down regulatory land-use planning. This has been largely successful in containing urban sprawl, preventing urban periphery commercial development, notably shopping or office centres, and severely limiting new urban road building. All of this has intensified land-use demands in the inner cities, which still accommodate most commercial, governmental and recreational functions for the entire urban region. Physical compactness and high densities are reflected in accessibility dominated by public transport and bicycles. In Groningen, notably, 52 per cent of all journeys within the urban area are made by bicycle.

The perceived necessity for radical restructuring of the whole of the central area of the inner city was motivated in large part by the increasingly evident changes in life style and spatial behaviour outlined above but was rendered more compelling and visually intrusive by the physical and aesthetic condition of the *Grote Markt* area that had resulted from a particular historical episode. The 3-day liberation battle in April 1945 resulted in the destruction of the north and east sides of the *Grote Markt*, the neighbouring *Waagstraat* and *Walburgerstraat* (Ashworth, 1995). In the immediate post-war period of 1945–1965 the economic and psychological imperative led to rapid reconstruction which favoured 'international' style minimalist modernist buildings with dominantly public and private office functions and large-scale retailing, then viewed as the two main future functions of the central city. Destruction had opened up a number of new routes and vistas, which were at that time welcomed and maintained for new road accessibility and motor vehicle circulation.

By 1990, these post-1945 developments were generally regarded as aesthetically and functionally unsuitable for the contemporary city as it then viewed itself. The city core had acquired additional functions, especially in culture, entertainment and leisure shopping, while previously dominant back office and traffic parking and circulation functions were viewed as less desirable land uses. There was, in addition, a renewed consciousness of the semiotic function of urban form and thus significance of urban design. In short, the city core, and notably the Grote Markt, no longer accommodated or expressed the vision of the city held by a dominant consensus of governors and citizens. That something should be done had become obvious: what this 'something' should be, was less clear and has resulted in sharp debate and two referendums.

Discussions and Decisions

No single plan or policy document expresses a clear strategic vision at a specific moment. Instead, there is a plethora of plans and policies over some 30 years, which taken together amount to a strategic change in direction and reformulation of the functions and forms of the Grote Markt.

The Role of Local Plans

In 1972 a short, general and non-specific policy document was approved by the city council as a statement of the perceived functions of the inner city within the goals of the city as a whole (*Doelstellingennota*/report on the establishment of objectives). It gave little indication of how these goals were to be attained but introduced many of the 'multi' ideas that have dominated discussion ever since. It now seems a statement of the self-evidently obvious that the inner city should be multifunctional, multifaceted, multicultural and the like, which only indicates how successfully these ideas were propagated by the city authorities as a counter to the much narrower post-war conception of the role of inner cities as car accessible monofunctional office and shopping centres.

One of the first major applications of these ideas was the Groningen Traffic Circulation Plan (*Verkeerscirculatieplan*) adopted in 1977. Although not completely original (cities such as Norwich and Göteborg had implemented versions earlier), it was seen then and now as revolutionary in Groningen and in the Netherlands (see Tsubohara, 2003). A 'ring and sector' plan pedestrianized the Grote Markt and surroundings, which had become little more than a three-lane traffic island, and removed all inner city through traffic, except public transport and bicycles. Peripheral paid parking, improved bus and bicycle accessibility, service delivery controls and the like created not only a new traffic circulation pattern but also a new approach to urban accessibility that has survived with only minor amendments to the present. More profoundly it initiated the redefinition of the purpose and functions of the inner city: a process that is continuing.

In 1990, a document appeared from the city planning department summarizing the projects executed through the previous decade and outlining the topics and sites for attention in the immediate future. This had the somewhat contradictory title of 'Plan of action for the inner city: a development strategy' (*Plan van aanpak voor de binnenstad: een ontwikkelingstrategie*), which restated the key ideas introduced almost 20 years earlier but also identifying what and where action should be taken. It could thus be seen as an intermediate statement attempting to move strategy towards application and provide a framework for the more detailed implementation plans to follow.

As part of the legally required *gemeente* (district) planning process the inner city has received specific attention as befits the significance of its recognized role in the city as a whole. A long-term and multifaceted plan, named 'Inner city improvement' (*Binnenstad Beter*) began in 1992 and is still continuing to evolve. It includes many sector plans for inner city functions, such as for retailing, cultural facilities, and entertainment, and also separate planning documents for topics such as accessibility, public open space and 'green' space. One notable aspect of this set of plans is the manner of their publication and communication. As well as the usual publication of the official planning documents and maps, considerable effort has been made to communicate with citizens and users in a less formal way. A broadsheet multi-coloured news bulletin is published regularly and delivered to all households and even a noted local cartoonist has been commissioned to produce and publicly display a humorous visual commentary on progress.

The Entry of the Italians

The 'Italianisation of Groningen' that began to be evident from around 1995 (Ashworth, 2005) is in part the result of the work of a handful of imported Italian designers, but more widely a reassertion of the role of design in general coupled with a somewhat romanticized view of a preferred life style. It is of course an expression of a Groningen idea of being Italian, that is more relaxed, hedonistic and engaged with the public realm of side-walk terraces and squares, rather than any attempt to replicate actual aspects of the contemporary Italian city. Design was seen as not only a reflection of function but also an instrument for the expression of urban aspirations and ultimately an urban identity.

The past was to be evoked and reflected in the design but the past so selected was freely eclectic in time and space.

As part of the redefinition of the city the 'City marking project' attempted to imitate a supposedly medieval idea of urban enclosure by 'marking' the city boundaries with visibly notable art-works and a few visibly notable buildings (especially the *Gasunie* building on the southern city boundary). In addition, a unified design schema for public open space, roads, street furniture and place name and directional marking was introduced into the city centre (the 'yellow brick roads' in popular parlance).

In Groningen, as elsewhere, 'hallmark' public buildings were seen as playing a major role in not only 'putting the city on the map' but also by determining through association which map, in practice which network of similar cities, Groningen had now joined. Even more significantly perhaps, is that such buildings by their physical obtrusiveness demonstrate unambiguously to local residents that something serious is happening to the city. Again as elsewhere reliance was placed upon the architects' 'star system' whereby the international fame of particular architects is used to endorse the new status and values of the city. Ultimately, the functioning of such buildings in terms of what they contain is of minor relevance, as is their intrinsic aesthetic quality, compared to their simple existence as a creative product of the master enhancing the city. Whether such hallmark buildings in themselves actually stimulate cultural or economic activities through some trickle down effect, or remain 'cathedrals in the desert' is arguable: the importance of their promotional impact, particularly on the inhabitants of the city itself, is not.

The most important of these city centre hallmark developments include:

- The new central public library in the *Oude Boteringestraat* (designed by Grassi).
- The new Groningen Museum, a highly visible eclectically postmodern structure (designed by, inter alia, Stark, the Himmelb(l)au co-operative, and, as coordinator, Mendini). Its location on an artificial island between the railway station and the city centre, together with the spectacular restoration in 1999 of the 1896 constructed central

station (architect Gottschalk) created a new entry to the city and altered the whole pedestrian and bicycle circulation pattern (Dijkstra & Akkerman, 1999). This in turn created a daily confrontation of large numbers of passing citizens with the building and thus disseminated and reinforced the clear statement of change. This signature building was so noticeable as to partially replace the 17th century *Martinitoren* as the main physical symbol of the city on a number of publicity documents (Ennen, 1997).

■ The *Waagstraat* complex on the west side of the Grote Markt, designed by Natalini, was opened in 1994. This involved the demolition of the local authority offices built in 1962, the recreation of a pre-1945 street, the creation of a new public open *piazza* (*Waagplein*), and the replacement of back office functions by street-level shops and cafes and upper-level housing. The 'Bolognaisation of Groningen' was further reinforced by open-air opera in the *Grote Markt* (Kuipers & Ashworth, 2002: 90).

Conflict and Decision on the North and East Sides of the Grote Markt

It was a short and logical step to shift attention to the final unreconstructed areas, the north and east sides of the *Grote Markt*. Destroyed in 1945 and hurriedly rebuilt in modernist style, the streetscape now appeared visually incongruous, functionally outdated and somewhat tawdry. In addition, the back lots behind both north and east façades had been left to an untidy piecemeal development of storage, delivery and car parking functions.

Initially, the north side was to be treated with a plan involving demolition of the existing 1950s to 1960s north side and adjacent lots. The rebuilding in a style yet to be detailed, but assumed to be historicist, would be compatible with the conserved south side and *Martini* church. Retailing and counter function offices would be strengthened and extended into new semi-subterranean shopping terraces and undercover boulevards. The existing bus station and open-air market would be re-sited and the existing public open space redesigned, enhanced and extended, including again the creation of a new *piazza*. This was to be dominantly privately financed and a broad-based coalition of support was assembled from all the main political parties across the political spectrum, the main commercial interests of the city and the national government. This plan was opposed by an ad hoc coalition of environmentalists (opposing the underground car parking), urban conservationists (fearful of damage to the historic buildings), market traders (fearing disruption and displacement), radical socialists (opposing the private financing) and citizens (uneasy over the apparent distant arrogance of the city government who had failed to consult them). The only common element was in the persistent posing, not answering, of the question, 'whose city is it?' In 2001, a city wide referendum on the plan resulted in a remarkably high 57 per cent turnout and an 81 per cent 'no' vote (Ashworth, 2001). The plan was immediately shelved.

A crisis of planning and more widely of city government was immediately evident in the wake of the referendum result. A dangerous and at the time largely unappreciated gap had opened up between governors and the governed. Traditional expert-driven, top-down planning had been rejected but public participation resulted in, as could have been expected, a myriad of conflicting opinions, ideas and plans about the Grote Markt which covered the full spectrum from 'do nothing' to 'do everything' and from public spaces and functions to private commercial development. There is also a wide gap in aesthetic taste between the *avant garde* 'experts' favouring experimental design and conservative *vox populi* who favoured historicist facsimile reconstruction of 17th century façades. The three interrelated stumbling blocks to all the proposals remained finance, accessibility and selection between functions: who should pay for it, how do you get there and what (and who) is the city centre for? The urgent necessity for restructuring the north and east sides of the *Grote Markt* remained as did the inherent contradictions of the necessity for private funding and the desire for collective public uses.

By 2004, a broad consensus had emerged that favoured representative, symbolic, publicly accessible and 'cultural' functions on the Grote Markt. However, public finance is not limitless and private investment requires profit making commercial functions and is fixated by car accessibility. There is also a consensus that the quality of the design of forms and spaces should be a more central concern than it had been 50 years ago. The proposed plan for the east side involved a complete demolition of the existing buildings and a restructuring of the building lots behind. Into this space would be inserted a multifunctional cultural centre, combining a relocated existing public library, new historical museum, a relocated Arts cinema and various public exhibition spaces. This 'Forum' is seen as a central meeting place for the city and major tourism attraction and is to be housed in a new and, hopefully signature building of architectural allure. This plan was put to a referendum in 2005. Despite the, probably intentional, vagueness in the detailing of the scheme, the turnout failed to reach the 30 per cent threshold and the plan, if not enthusiastically endorsed by citizens, at least was not passionately opposed by them.

Construction is expected to commence next year and be completed in 2010.

Lessons and Warnings

This single case, severely bounded in space and time, focused attention on three questions about how the city of Groningen sees itself, wishes to express itself and ultimately be planned and governed. In all three, the Grote Markt has been the arena and touchstone for discussion, conflict and decision. The questions may have remained the same since 1945 but the answers have changed radically in response to changes in life style, land-use requirements, political participation and attitudes towards the built environment. The succession of plans for the Grote Markt has reflected these changes.

Whether the plans described above form a body of 'best practice' for elsewhere to imitate, examples of errors and delays to be avoided or a set of unique outcomes stemming from a unique experience, is for other cities to evaluate. The ultimate lessons of more than 50 years of planning for this one small space are dominantly for governance. Firstly, academic commentators tend towards an evolutionary explanation of change in planning approaches. They envisage logical trajectories in planning philosophies, techniques and processes. However, organizations and notably those composed of elected representatives have a very limited and short collective memory. Secondly, much traditional planning is based on the assumption of the existence of definable interest groups, the 'actors' or 'stakeholders', which casts the planner in the role either of 'director' or representative of a 'public interest'. If everyone is an actor, playing simultaneously or sequentially in a number of different roles, reading from a unique script and performing in an individual play, sometimes on the same stage as others, then the role of the planner becomes very indeterminate. Finally, if ideology and its collective expression have been replaced by individualism and single issue temporary coalition then planning, which since its inception has been 'ism' driven, is left with only 'ad hocism' as its strategic guide and driving force.

Discussion Questions and Exercises

(1) It has been argued that the changes to the way we consider cities are reflective of larger changes in Western democratic societies. What are these changes and how do you see them being played out in Groningen's broader development and the Grote Markt in particular.

(2) What makes Dutch cities significantly different from most other Western cities and how does that impact upon the establishment of city spaces?

(3) What are the roles of hallmark buildings in a city and its precincts? Does it matter if they are 'successful' in terms of their functional roles? Why or why not?

(4) Discuss the following:

If everyone is an actor, playing simultaneously or sequentially in a number of different roles, reading from a unique script and performing in an individual play, sometimes on the same stage as others, then the role of the planner becomes very indeterminate.

(5) Groningen has been undergoing processes of regeneration for many years. In what ways might ongoing change to a precinct enhance or undermine the experience of both visitors and locals?

References

Albrechts, L. (2003). *Strategic Spatial Planning Revisited.* Hanoi: APSA Congress.

Ashworth, G.J. (1995). The city as battlefield: the liberation of Groningen, April 1945, Groningen Studies 61.

Ashworth, G.J. (2001). Planning by referendum: empowerment or anarchy in Groningen, The Netherlands. *Local Environment*, 6(3), 367–372.

Ashworth, G.J. (2005). Puo una citta olandese divertare italiana? Il cambiamento strategico del cuore di Groningen. In F. Martinelli (Ed.), *La Plianificazione Strategica in Italia e in Europa* (pp. 181–202). Milano: Francoangeli.

Cusveller, S. (Ed.) (1994). *Stad! De stad en haar identiteit.* Hoogezand: Molior.

Dijkstra, J., & Akkerman, H. (1999). *Groningen Hoofdstation Centraal.* Groningen: Regio-Projekt uitgevers.

Ennen, E. (1997). The Groningen museum: urban heritage in fragments. *International Journal of Heritage Studies*, 3, 144–156.

European Commission (2007). *Survey on the Perceptions of Quality if Life in 75 European Cities.* Brussels: Eurobarometer, DG Regional Policy.

Faludi, A., & v.d.Valk, A. (1994). *Rule and Order: Dutch Planning Doctrine in the 20th Century.* Amsterdam: Kluwer.

Kuipers, M.J., & Ashworth, G.J. (2002). Waagstraatcomplex and Hoofdstation, Groningen: Consequence or cause of place identity?. In A. Phelps, G.J. Ashworth, & B. Johansson (Eds.), *The Construction of Built Heritage* (pp. 87–99). Aldershot: Ashgate.

Kooij, P., & Pellenbarg, P. (Eds.) (1994). *Regional Capitals: Past, Present, Prospects.* Assen: Van Gorcum.

Quinn, J.B. (1980). *Strategies for Change: Logical Incrementalism.* Homewood, IL: Down-Jones Irwin.

Tsubohara, S. (2003). Politicisation, polarisation and public participation: planning history of Groningen in the 1970s. *URSI Onderzoekverslagen* 302/303.

14

Darling Harbour: Looking Back and Moving Forward

Deborah Edwards, Tony Griffin and Bruce Hayllar

Introduction

Sydney Harbour is a defining element for the city and features prominently in national and international tourism marketing campaigns (Marshall, 2001). It is not surprising, then, that so much tourist activity is focused on the harbour and around its foreshores. In some ways the international tourism boom which Australia experienced in the 1980s focused the attention of both Sydneysiders and their government representatives on the harbour and the poor condition of much of its foreshore area, particularly on its industrialized southern side. Since that time substantial areas of harbourside land, formerly occupied by industry and shipping activities, have been opened up and transformed, many into significant places and spaces for leisure activities. No single area more typifies this pattern of development than Darling Harbour.

Occupying a prime harbourside location adjacent to the Sydney Central Business District (CBD), Darling Harbour represents a major concentration of leisure activities designed to service the needs of the local community as well as domestic and international tourists. Annual visitor numbers exceed 26 million people (Sydney Harbour Foreshore Authority, 2006b) and the site plays host to an extensive array of festivals, events and conventions such that it could be considered a 'global playground'. Conceived as one of a number of projects to celebrate the Australian Bicentennial in 1988, Darling Harbour occupies 54 hectares of redeveloped harbour land. The precinct encompasses large footprint facilities including the Sydney Aquarium, Sydney Entertainment Centre, Sydney Convention and Exhibition Centre, the Australian National Maritime Museum and the Chinese Gardens. The Star City Casino is also within close proximity.

Darling Harbour has had a chequered history, being at various times cited as a major success story (Breen & Rigby, 1996) or, within the wider urban context, accused of failing to integrate with the fabric of the city (Marshall, 2001). With these conflicting views in mind, this case study examines the key planning and design issues associated with Darling Harbour, strategies used to deal with those issues, and the lessons that arise for precinct development and management in general.

A Brief History of the Precinct

Darling Harbour was named after Lieutenant-General Darling, who was Governor of New South Wales (NSW) from 1825 to 1831. The precinct itself is situated between the Sydney CBD and the remaining shipping container wharves of East Darling Harbour to the east and north, and the gentrifying suburbs of Ultimo and Pyrmont to the south and west.

Its 'central' location is the result of its historical role as a sea and transport hub for industrial goods from 1826 to 1945. From World War II onwards its importance slowly diminished as Port Botany, to the south of the city, was progressively established as Sydney's major port. The changes in shipping technology towards containerization, and a decline in rail transport in favour of road, left massive warehouses and rail infrastructure substantially underutilized and in decline. By the 1970s it was a largely derelict, unutilized space, separated from the physical, social and economic activity of the city. In a metaphorical portent of its industrial future, the last freight train left Darling Harbour to the strains of a funeral march played by the NSW Transport

Workers Union Band in 1984. Soon after, the NSW Government announced its decision to redevelop Darling Harbour and 'return it to the people' after 150 years of industrial use (Picture 14.1).

From that time, Darling Harbour has been totally transformed in a number of development stages. In the early 1980s, some development had already been undertaken at the southern end of the site incorporating the Sydney Entertainment Centre, the Institute of Technology and the conversion of the Ultimo power station into the Powerhouse Museum. The advent of the 'Festival Market' model of the 1980s (Marshall, 2001), however, was the turning point for the large-scale redevelopment of Darling Harbour. In 1984, a decision was taken to develop the site into a tourism, leisure and recreational precinct for the community and visitor: an emphasis on consumption rather than transportation and warehousing (Holmes, 2001).

According to Waitt (2001), imaging a city through the organization of spectacular urban space is a mechanism for attracting capital and people during times of intense urban competition. The redevelopment of Darling Harbour was a logical progression and would incorporate all the usual activities of a tourist city, subsequently identified by Ashworth and Tunbridge (1990), such as restaurants, museums, nightclubs, casinos, hotels and shopping. The new site included a Chinese landscaped garden

Picture 14.1 Darling Harbour c1884–1917 Kerry and Co., Sydney, Australia (http://www.sydneyarchitecture.com/PYR/PYR.htm)

(paid entry) on the edge of Chinatown, a semi-circular focal green space, a boating lake and a green axis and walkway linking these spaces with a Convention and Exhibition Centre, Harbourside Restaurant and Shopping complex, the National Maritime Museum and Sydney Aquarium. Some original planned inclusions in the redeveloped site, primarily on the eastern side of the precinct, never eventuated due to the commercial failure of the private developer. The 'new' Darling Harbour was reopened in 1988 by Queen Elizabeth II.

Ten years later, in anticipation of the 2000 Sydney Olympics, the eastern side of Darling Harbour, including Cockle Bay and King Street Wharves, was redeveloped into broader entertainment areas encompassing bars, restaurants and cafes with outside seating that lined the harbour, and moorings for private and public boats. During the Olympic Games, Darling Harbour became a hub for social activity as well as hosting five Olympic sports (Picture 14.2). In 2003, it fulfilled a similar function as a 'live site' for the Rugby World Cup.

The Star City Casino complex opened in 1997 on the western periphery of Darling Harbour. The casino was established to both increase state revenues and contribute to the tourism landscape of Darling Harbour (Searle & Bounds, 1999). Star City includes a 480-room hotel and apartment complex, two theatres, a large banquet and convention facility, seven restaurants and a nightclub. Although not strictly within the Darling Harbour precinct, Star City does form an extension of it and contributes to people's perceptions of the area as a whole.

Picture 14.2 Cockle Bay Wharf looking towards Harbourside Shopping Complex (http://www.darlingharbour.com.au/sydney-Discover-Heritage_History-The_ Convict_Town_to_Port_City.htm)

Management Structure

The Sydney Harbour Foreshore Authority (SHFA) was established in 1998 to operate as a place manager for a number of Sydney's significant waterfront precincts. Upon its creation, it replaced the Sydney Cove Authority as the responsible authority for the historic Rocks precinct and in 2001 SHFA became landlord and custodian of Darling Harbour. Prior to this, Darling Harbour had been under the control of another special purpose statutory authority, the Darling Harbour Authority (DHA), which had been created by an Act of the NSW Parliament in 1984. SHFA owns over 400 hectares of land within the central city (Sydney Harbour Foreshore Authority, 2003).

SHFA is subject to the control and direction of the NSW Minister for Planning. Diagram 14.1 represents the management structure of SHFA. A board comprising the Chief Executive Officer, the Director-General of the NSW Department of Planning and a maximum of five people appointed by the Minister set strategic direction for SHFA, ensures compliance with statutory requirements and oversees the organization's policies, management and performance.

The Chief Executive Officer is responsible for the day-to-day management of the Foreshore Authority's affairs. SHFA funds its own operations principally from rental and other property income. Each year SHFA invests extensively in community service obligations and on property/heritage-related capital works as part of its responsibilities to meet community, cultural, tourism, heritage and commercial objectives (see Table 14.1).

Darling Harbour was initially marketed as a 'fun place' which has evolved to its current branding of 'Play Darling Harbour', a theme aimed at highlighting the shopping, attractions, events, festivals and cultural experiences offered by the precinct.

Issues and Problems in Planning and Design

The issues and problems associated with Darling Harbour predominantly stem from its planning and design processes. During its initial development and subsequent evolution, these processes were challenged

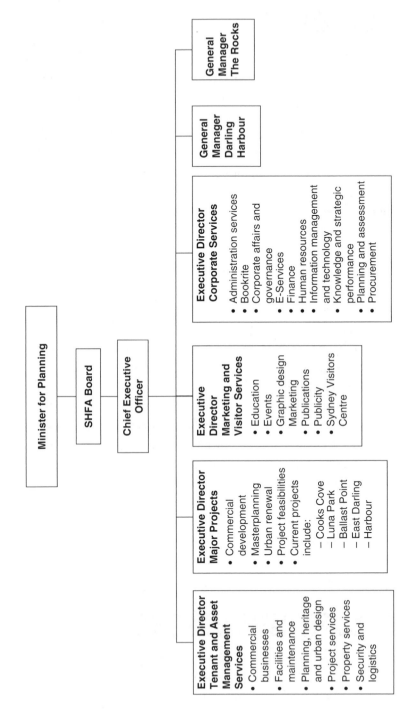

Diagram 14.1 SHFA organization chart (Sydney Harbour Foreshore Authority, 2006a)

Table 14.1 SHFA community service obligations

■ Support of community events	– New Years Eve
	– Australia Day
	– ANZAC Day
	– St Patrick's Day
	– Egyptian, Malaysian, Thai, Lebanese, Brazilian, Indian, Armenian and Chinese festivals
	– Community Aid Abroad's Walk Against Want
■ Sponsorship of community organizations and events	– Sydney Festival
	– NSW Wheelchair Sports Association Oz Day 10-kilometre Wheelchair Race in The Rocks
	– New South Wales Tourism Awards
	– Pyrmont/Ultimo Festival
	– Mustard Seed Church at Pyrmont
	– UNICEF United Buddy Bear Exhibition
■ In-kind contributions	– Venue hire and other services to community groups and charities
	– Crowd control, security, waste management and logistics to the city of Sydney
■ Facility provision, upgrading and maintenance	– Roads, bridges, parks, and public domain areas, open space, foreshore promenades, signage and lighting within precincts and non-commercial capital works projects cleaning and waste management, security and public domain maintenance
	– Security and cleaning services in the precincts under SHFA's care
■ Interactive web sites	– To increase awareness of events, as well as provide an interactive communication tool for the community
	– To assist public consultation
■ Funding and manning of two visitor information centres	

by competing tensions in terms of political control and the incorporation of its various design elements.

Political Tensions

It has been argued that much of Sydney's physical history has been shaped by commercial and political motives above any sense of a public realm (Marshall, 2001), an historic legacy shared by Darling Harbour. In part, these motives are a consequence of Australia's three-tiered system of government (local, state and national) which is plagued by competition, and a lack of coordination and cooperation between each tier. A lack of coordination between government agencies and other stakeholders is a significant problem perceived by the tourism sector in NSW (Griffin et al., 2007), which regards inter-level coordination as critical to the appropriate planning of urban development.

In Australia, state governments have passed Acts to extend their direct authority over particular urban developments that reduce the ability of local authorities to decide the quality or form of development of their areas (Searle & Bounds, 1999; Stilwell & Troy, 2000; Punter, 2005). This was the case with both the decision to redevelop Darling Harbour area as an entertainment and recreation complex for the NSW bicentennial celebrations in 1988 and the development of Star City Casino. Both Darling Harbour and Star City received intensive community opposition as a response to what the local community perceived as a lack of consultation in the planning process and the way the developments were exempted from any (local) Council control (Searle & Byrne, 2002; Punter, 2005).

To 'fast-track' the process, the DHA was established as both the landowner and planning consent authority to oversee development and construction of Darling Harbour. To ensure that development occurred on time, exemption from normal statutory planning and development control requirements under both State and local government jurisdictions was granted to the Authority (Marshall, 2001). This had the effect of enabling the authority to isolate itself administratively by minimizing communication with other agencies in the city. Normal rights of community participation in planning decisions were also denied under the Darling Harbour Authority Act.

In respect of Star City Casino, the winning development proposal was opposed by the Sydney City Council and a number of community groups (Searle & Bounds, 1999). The council objected to the proposal and the selected site, arguing that it would compromise the existing residential character of the neighbouring suburb of Pyrmont and would negatively influence the potential for high quality residential development (Searle & Bounds, 1999). Community groups opposed the development for two reasons. Firstly, they argued that the 'height, scale and intensity of the casino would dominate the Pyrmont precinct and detrimentally affect existing and future residential amenity' (p. 169). Secondly, it was believed that commercial developments and tourist activities would favour those who could afford it. Various protest groups formed and were marginally successful in retaining some older style housing in Pyrmont for heritage conservation. However, the State Government owned the site and the authority to approve the development. Thus, to avoid the implications of negative reactions and any delay in the State receiving a $376 million casino licence fee, the Minister for Planning assumed the authority to approve the development of the project (Searle & Byrne, 2002). This served to centralize the planning process and ensured the project's timely completion.

The issues discussed here represent the contest that can exist between a powerful State Government and an disempowered city council for public space (Marshall, 2001). Both lay claim to the space of the city in different ways, with different agendas. Unfortunately, this lack of unity can contribute to disjointed urban development, a continuing lack of coordination and cooperation, and a general distrust between the various stakeholders. Both Darling Harbour and Star City received intensive community opposition in terms of the lack of consultation in the planning process and the way the developments were exempted from any Council control (Searle & Byrne, 2002; Punter, 2005).

Design Tensions

There are three aspects of design on which Darling Harbour has been criticized:
(1) its boundedness;
(2) its lack of accessibility to other urban locations;
(3) its inability to attract a broader (non-tourist) shopping clientele.

An early criticism was that Darling Harbour was hampered by conspicuous roadways constructed in the 1950s and 1960s to meet the earlier industrial needs of the site. The Western Distributor encircles and cuts through the site, essentially separating south Darling Harbour from the north and East Darling Harbour from the CBD. These roadways, Marshall (2001) argues, act to alienate the site from the waterfront strip and the rest of the city. Although this design issue is a legacy from earlier city planning it is a separation that is reinforced by Darling Harbour's larger facilities. The exhibition and convention buildings, hotels, Star City Casino complex, and a bounded campus development at the southern end act as a wall around the site, closing it off from the surrounding city (Marshall, 2001). While the design aims to capitalize on land use, Searle and Byrne (2002: 23) argue that it has resulted in:

> *a shift in place identity from industrial and working class to high-tech and upper income, from a habitus of production – a manufacturing and freight enclave, to that of consumption – decontextualised domiciles, and ultimately from a neighbourhood to a commodity.*

A second major criticism of Darling Harbour has been its poor and awkward accessibility into and from the city. Punter (2005) argues that the project is not linked into the city in the way it should be. It was not a fluid relationship and the awkward transitions between other spaces and Darling Harbour has exacerbated the difficulties experienced by the shopping complex which was designed for retail and entertainment activities without due consideration to residential or commercial space (Marshall, 2001). The precinct therefore relies solely on visitors.

Strategies for Dealing with the Issues

Planning and Design Solutions

In an attempt to avoid the expressway viaducts impinging on the pedestrian experience within Darling Harbour, the viaduct pillars were treated as sculptural elements and the space below was landscaped with 'tall cabbage-tree palms, creating a cathedral like quality' and lining the walkway and 'urban stream that links the harbour' (Morrison, 1997: 108).

Steps taken to deal with Darling Harbour's isolation from the city have included a circular monorail linking the site to the CBD and the retail core; laneways and pathways leading into the site; foot bridges over major roadways; and steps down from the upper levels to the lower levels of Darling Harbour (Punter, 2005). To address the lack of residential and commercial complexes, in the past six years there has been increasing residential and commercial redevelopment of Pyrmont and the wharves located on the eastern side of the harbour.

A large project is currently underway to redevelop Darling Harbour East, a promontory that is currently occupied by commercial docks and container terminal. Darling Harbour East is planned as an extension of Sydney's commercial business core and will incorporate an 11 hectare foreshore park, commercial space, and some retail, hotel, residential and community uses. The addition of a park and harbourfront promenade will enable people to walk 14 kilometres along the Sydney foreshore from Anzac Bridge to the west of Sydney through to Woolloomooloo in the east. Between these two locations, the walk will take in Star City Casino, Darling Harbour, Darling Harbour East, the Sydney Harbour Bridge, Circular Quay, the Opera House and the Botanical Gardens. It will function as a visually appealing and welcoming environment adding to the perception of Sydney as a pedestrian-friendly city whilst enhancing the restaurants and attractions that currently exist.

Management Practices

SHFA sees sound corporate governance as central to its responsibilities as a management agency. Their vision, purpose and charter (see Table 14.2) focus on effective precinct management, community engagement and long-term viability. The strategies they have employed to realize these objectives are set out below.

Table 14.2 SHFA corporate vision and charter

Vision
To make unique places in Sydney that the world talks about.
Our precincts are unique Sydney icons – The Rocks is renowned for its historical and cultural significance and Darling Harbour is one of the world's best waterfront entertainment destinations.

Purpose
Creating and sustaining living places and great experiences.
Our key role is to be an expert place maker by managing places profitably and sociably, promoting places effectively, developing places responsibly and managing our organization efficiently.

Charter
■ Community
Enhance the Foreshore Authority's areas as accessible, rich and diverse environments for all communities, while protecting their natural and cultural heritage.
■ Visitor
Increase visitation and yield while exceeding stakeholder expectations and maintaining accessibility.
■ Commercial – core and growth
  – Generate agreed rates of return from existing business activities to fund operating costs.
  – Meet community service obligations, dividend obligations and basic capital investment requirements.
  – Within a capital and risk-constrained environment, seek and exploit opportunities to generate future revenue streams.
■ Economic development
  – Recognize and encourage the generation of economic benefits to the State and balance these with the need to produce direct financial returns so as to sustain long-term financial viability.

Our brand – what we stand for
The Foreshore Authority uniquely adds value to precincts and provides outstanding customer service to stakeholders, including:
■ Partnering with tenants to enable business and precinct success.
■ Making living places and great experiences for visitors.
■ Delivering community service by caring for the foreshore at the heart of Sydney – past, present and future.
■ Proudly working with employees to make a difference in our precincts.

Source: Sydney Harbour Foreshore Authority (2006a: 3).

Over the past three years, SHFA has been developing a 'way finding' strategy. As part of this strategy entry markers have been installed around Darling Harbour to alert visitors that they have 'arrived' and to denote the precinct as a destination. The new entry markers are 7 metres tall and are situated around the outskirts of the precinct. They are branded in the Darling Harbour colours, and are now part of the overall 'family' of signs used by SHFA. To further improve ease of movement around Darling Harbour, a water-taxi style shuttle was recently introduced to link the Harbourside Shopping Centre, Cockle Bay, King Street Wharf and the National Maritime Museum.

To improve accessibility for all people SHFA set up the Disability Access Advisory Group (DAAG), a committee comprising SHFA representatives from all its Divisions and precincts. This group formulated the Action Plan for People with Disabilities 2003/2005 (Sydney Harbour Foreshore Authority, 2003). The Plan includes the appointment of a Disability Contact Officer, whose role is to provide a single point of contact for external enquiries. The DAAG has also undertaken a number of projects to improve facilities and customer service for the benefit of people with disabilities. These projects include:

- a disability access audit for Darling Harbour with an improvement works programme;
- capital and maintenance projects to improve physical accessibility such as the widening of footpaths; and
- training that focuses on increasing the knowledge of staff in areas of disability issues and legislation.

To counter the economic difficulties experienced by Darling Harbour's shopping, accommodation and attraction complexes, SHFA introduced Club Darling and the Sydney Visitor Pass. Club Darling, specifically targeted to regular Darling Harbour visitors, is a privilege programme that provides special offers across a range of attractions, dining, shopping and accommodation establishments. Members are sent regular e-mails on special offers, competitions and upcoming events at Darling Harbour. The Sydney Visitor Pass offers discounts to holders on a range of leisure, dining and shopping benefits, and is offered to any new visitor to Darling Harbour.

Key Ingredients for Success: Satisfying Visitors

Darling Harbour has been cited as both a waterfront success story and a planning disaster (Breen & Rigby, 1996). It has been likened to a global playground with images of the ideal, international cosmopolitan globetrotter where everyone becomes a tourist, a voyeur and a symbolic consumer all mingling, gazing, to find their own piece of mass-produced memorabilia to say that they were there (Parker, 2003). Parker argues that it exists as a largely impersonal and homogenous space placing it in the same category as Auckland's American Express Viaduct Harbour, South Bank in Brisbane and Melbourne. Recently Professor Jan Gehl, considered to be one of the world's eminent urban designers, referred to Darling Harbour as 'too much of a theme park' (Gilmore, 2007).

However, there are a number of factors that suggest that Darling Harbour is more a success than a disaster. As a tourist destination, Darling Harbour has added value to Sydney. On weekends, it is heavily used by local people as well as tourists. Visitors to Darling Harbour have increased from one million in 1988 to approximately 26 million in June 2006 (Sydney Harbour Foreshore Authority, 2006b). The site provides much-needed large indoor venues and public open space that is adjacent to the waterfront, within close proximity to a variety of facilities and developments, and high-density housing and urban parks (Marshall, 2001). Darling Harbour hosts numerous ongoing festival and event activities throughout the year, making use of its varied park space, entertainment areas and water spaces. The events themselves are made more festive and global because they include international music and often booths sell food prepared by restaurants from around the city. These activities in combination with the major attractions that border the precinct make Darling Harbour an attractive convention destination (Punter, 2005), enabling Sydney to compete at an international level.

The criticism that Darling Harbour rarely feels like a piece of the city, can also be considered an asset as this very aspect makes one feel that they are in a refuge from the city (Morrison, 1991). In an unpublished study on visitors to Darling Harbour the authors asked both domestic and international visitors about their experiences of Darling Harbour. They found that the vast majority of respondents enjoyed visiting Darling Harbour, would visit Darling Harbour on a future visit to Sydney and would recommend Darling Harbour to anyone visiting Sydney. Significantly, visitors indicated that, in their view, Darling Harbour:

- is a good place to interact with Sydney people;
- is a good place to interact with other tourists;
- is a good place for people watching;
- has a relaxing atmosphere;
- has a lively/vibrant atmosphere;
- offers different and interesting sounds;
- offers something for everyone;
- is a good place to start exploring Sydney;
- has interesting things to see;
- is easy to find one's way around;
- is a place in which a visitor can wander around for hours; and
- is a place that visitors feel safe.

Darling Harbour, moreover, appears to have added considerable value to the visitor's general experience of Sydney as a tourist destination. Respondents felt that being in Darling Harbour was more distinctive than being in other parts of Sydney, and it was how they imagined Sydney to be. It thus not only possessed a strong sense of place in its own right but also contributed substantially to Sydney's sense of place. They felt that their visit to Darling Harbour enabled them to feel more connected to Sydney as they could see how Sydneysiders enjoy themselves. It was these elements which provided respondents with an understanding of the city that they otherwise would not have had.

The strategies adopted by SHFA purposefully sought to fix and control place meanings and identity, and 'design' a sense of place (Cosgrove, 2000). These strategies seem to have worked in a number of ways. Improvements in signage and walkways have enabled people to move more freely to, from and within Darling Harbour. With its open spaces, attractions, restaurants and festival activities Darling

Harbour embodies what Hayllar and Griffin (2005: 525) refer to as a 'more human scale'; 'a situational and social counterpoint to the nearby city'. SHFA sought to construct a sense of place for both those who live there, and for the tourists who come to see, experience and to consume. Visitor responses indicate that the strategies have been successful in creating the right 'atmosphere' and a sense of 'difference' (Hayllar & Griffin, 2005) which in the minds of visitors has set Darling Harbour apart from other precincts in the city. Visitor perceptions such as these enable Sydney to compete nationally and globally with other urban precincts for capital and visitors.

Lessons for Practice in Precinct Development

Searle and Byrne (2002) argue that a major lesson in the redevelopment of urban precincts is that planners cannot be relied upon to give primacy to the interests of the marginalized and/or underrepresented, particularly in the provision of affordable housing and representing the interests of communities and nature. From their perspective, planning for the Darling Harbour precinct was: lacking in accountability and community consultation in its formative phase; represented a tendency towards creating places for wealthy professional residents at the expense of existing residents; and demonstrated the need for continued research into planners' roles as place entrepreneurs (Searle & Byrne, 2002).

Few would disagree that urban precinct redevelopment programmes should be integrated into the fabric of the host city through effective cooperation and collaboration between the community and various government stakeholders. However, this case study demonstrates that with ongoing management practices precincts can evolve both physically and socially, to compensate for past mistakes and to appeal to a diverse mix of audiences. Consultation and communication can be embraced at any time and although it has been argued that these elements were lacking early in the development of Darling Harbour they are elements that have subsequently been incorporated into the management practices of SHFA.

The case study has highlighted a number of conflicting perspectives in relation to the design and function of Darling Harbour and subsequently its success as a precinct. Despite Darling Harbour's chequered history, planning agencies have worked with the precinct's design limitations and SHFA has focused on creating a bright and lively, interactive space that sits comfortably against other urban uses. SHFA has positioned Darling Harbour in the minds and hearts of the local community and tourists as a place to play and enjoy. Ultimately, it must be to those who use the precinct that we should turn for confirmation of its success, and in this regard it is enjoyed by both tourists and locals alike.

Conclusion

In developing urban spaces it can help to look back to move forward. City spaces are in a constant circulatory movement where that movement views mixing, variety or diversity as integral to the city. City spaces everywhere are constantly faced with unprecedented upsurges in tourism development directed to an ongoing succession of projects and intensities that constantly make problematic the question of who controls the means of interpretation of the city and the power to define it as a space of participation. For Darling Harbour it has been a difficult journey where a number of tensions existed early in the process of its redevelopment and the venue it was to become. Numerous consent bodies, government agencies and community stakeholders all competed for control which compromised the long-term planning efforts of Darling Harbour. Subsequently, Darling Harbour was developed somewhat separately from the city.

However Darling Harbour has evolved from an industrialized site to a recreational and entertainment precinct that is enjoyed by both the people of Sydney and tourists. Planners and agencies have learnt from past mistakes and are continually designing new ways for Darling Harbour to reconnect with the city and to strengthen its relationship with the water. The new waterfront promenade represents a will to redress past mistakes and to assist Darling Harbour to fully connect with the water and the city beyond; it will be one of the most engaging waterfront promenades in the world.

Discussion Questions and Exercises

(1) In thinking about the governance of precincts, what would you consider to be the major points of potential conflict between the various stakeholders? As a way of working through this question in relation to the Darling Harbour precinct: firstly identify the stakeholders; then list what each stakeholder stands to gain or lose from increased tourism activity in a precinct; and finally, from your list identify key areas where a gain for one stakeholder represents losses for others.

(2) There was strong criticism of the way in which Darling Harbour was developed that is at odds with the current popularity of the site. Is it possible that effective communication can be used to avoid critical public commentary? Discuss your response.

(3) SHFA has employed a number of strategies to create a recreational and entertainment precinct that is enjoyed by visitors and locals. Suggest ways in which tourist businesses that operate within this precinct can play a role in co-creating an attractive space.

(4) 'If a thing is worth doing it is worth doing badly.' This statement was made by an Australian State Minister for Planning and referred to the difficulties inherent in planning and developing major urban infrastructure projects. Discuss how the planning and development of Darling Harbour provides evidence to support this statement.

(5) Based on the evidence presented in this chapter, is Darling Harbour reflective of serial planning practices?

References

Ashworth, G.J., & Tunbridge, J.E. (1990). *The Tourist-Historic City*. London: Belhaven.

Breen, A., & Rigby, D. (1996). *The New Waterfront: A Worldwide Urban Success Story*. New York: McGraw-Hill.

Cosgrove, D. (2000). Sense of place. In R.J. Johnston, D. Gregory, G. Pratt, & M. Watts (Eds.), *The Dictionary of Human Geography* (4th edn). Oxford: Blackwell.

Gilmore, H. (2007, 16, 2002). Meet the New Mr Sydney. *The Sun-Herald*, p. 7.

Griffin, T., Edwards, D.C., & Hayllar, B. (2007). Urban tourism research priorities: contrasting perspectives of industry and academia. Paper presented at the *Tourism – Past Achievements, Future Challenges*, 11–14 February, Sydney, Australia.

Hayllar, B., & Griffin, T. (2005). The precinct experience: a phenomenological approach. *Tourism Management*, 26, 517–528.

Holmes, D. (2001). *Virtual Globalization: Virtual Spaces/Tourist Spaces*. London, GBR: Routledge.

Marshall, R. (2001). Connection to the waterfront: Vancouver and Sydney. In R. Marshall (Ed.), *Waterfronts in Post-industrial Cities*. London, Spon Press.

Morrison, F. (1991). Sydney! Sydney!. *Urban Design Quarterly*, 39, 3–5.

Morrison, F. (1997). *Sydney: A Guide to Recent Architecture*. London: Ellipsis, Könemann.

Parker, K.W. (2003). Two visions of globalisation: an account of the America's Cup Harbour and South Auckland. *Creating Spaces Conference: Interdisciplinary Writings in the Social Science*, Canberra.

Punter, J. (2005). Urban design in central Sydney 1945–2002: Laissez-Faire and discretionary traditions in the accidental city. *Progress in Planning*, 63(1), 11–160.

Searle, G., & Bounds, M. (1999). State powers, state land and competition for global entertainment: the case of Sydney. *Events and Debates*, 166–172.

Searle, G., & Byrne, J. (2002). Selective memories, sanitised futures: constructing visions of future place in Sydney. *Urban Policy and Research*, 20(1), 7–25.

Stilwell, F., & Troy, P. (2000). Multilevel governance and urban development in Australia. *Urban Studies*, 37(5–6), 909–930.

Sydney Harbour Foreshore Authority (2003). *Sydney Harbour Foreshore Authority Annual Report 2002/2003* Sydney: Sydney Harbour Foreshore Authority.

Sydney Harbour Foreshore Authority (2006a). *Sydney Harbour Foreshore Authority Annual Report 2005/2006* Sydney: Sydney Harbour Foreshore Authority.

Sydney Harbour Foreshore Authority (2006b). *Visitor Snapshot Darling Harbour July 2005–June 2006.* Retrieved 25 January 2007, from http://www.shfa.nsw.gov.au/uploads/documents/ Factsheet%20FY05-06%20Darling%20Harbour.pdf

Waitt, G. (2001). The city as tourist spectacle: marketing Sydney for the 2000 Olympics. In D. Holmes (Ed.), *Virtual Globalization: Virtual Spaces/Tourist Spaces.* London, GBR: Routledge, 220–244.

15

London's 'South Bank'[1] Precinct: From Post-industrial Wasteland to Managed Precinct

Duncan Tyler and Munir Morad

Introduction

The chapter examines the evolution of one of London's newest tourism precincts that had suffered historically as a post-industrial zone, but is now one of London's top precinct destinations–ranking alongside other iconic precincts such as Covent Garden and Leicester Square. The chapter focuses on the management structures that have evolved over the past two decades, and links these to the different stages of

---

[1] There are major problems in identity with this precinct. It is comprised of three distinct sub-areas known historically as South Bank, Bankside and the Pool of London. There is no formal or recognized collective name, although here we refer to it as south bank (uncapitalized) for the collective precinct and South Bank (capitalized) for the area known, historically, by this name.

its development. It highlights success factors, noticeably in leadership, the adoption of new governance techniques, the ability to access new resources and a pragmatic and opportunistic approach to management structures.

The data and quotes for this study were taken from the unpublished PhD thesis of Duncan Tyler completed June 2007. The survey was of 180 local authority tourism officers in England seeking information about the influences they come under when developing local tourism policy. The quotes are from councillors and officers of the London Borough of Southwark (LBS) and the partners mentioned in the chapter.

The Precinct and Key Management Issues

The south bank of the River Thames has become the newest and one of the most popular visitor precincts in London. It stretches from Westminster Bridge in the west to the Pool of London, just downstream from Tower Bridge, in the east. It is some 3.5 km in length and

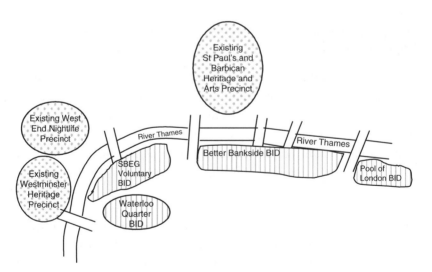

Map 15.1 London's south bank precinct with BID areas and London's traditional tourism precincts north of the River

merely 200 m at its widest point. The precinct winds its way through three historically distinct sub-areas (see Map 15.1):

(1) The South Bank – located in the London Borough of Lambeth (LBL) and home to the London Eye, Royal Festival Hall (RFH) and the South Bank Arts Centre (Europe's largest).
(2) Bankside – in which are located the new and vastly successful Shakespeare's Globe theatre and education complex, the Tate Gallery of Modern Art housed in a former power station and the Borough Market (London's largest farmers' market).
(3) The Pool of London – site of the up-market gastrodome at Butler's Wharf, Southwark Cathedral and Tower Bridge.

The management of such a precinct gives rise to several key issues. These are:

(1) Generating an identity out of three historically separate locations.
(2) Managing a precinct in which a sub-area is located in a separate administrative area where the local authority has been purpose-fully non-active.
(3) Creating a management structure that can help attract resources to the precinct and engage the local tourism industry in taking a broader than self-interested stance on the precincts future.
(4) Integrating the precinct into London's tourism infrastructure.

The following section provides a contextual background to the precinct's development.

The History of the Precincts' Development

The South Bank was traditionally an area of mud flats, timber yards, wharves and industry, what Mullins (2007) called a 'ramshackle medley of pontoons, wooden piles and floating decks. With tapering mud banks revealed at low tide'.

The South Bank finally got its own embankment after the Second World War when the 27 acre site was home to the temporary South Bank Exhibition. The South Bank Exhibition along with the pleasure gardens in Battersea Park (some two miles up river) and the science exhibition at South Kensington, formed the backbone of the Festival of Britain which was billed as a 'tonic for the nation' after the deprivation of the war and post-war rationing. The South Bank Exhibition comprised the Dome of Discovery, Skylon, RFH, flags, fountains and dancing areas and open-air restaurants. Of these only the RFH was maintained after the exhibition concluded, to be joined in the 1960s by the architecturally controversial South Bank Centre (the Centre) comprising the national theatre, Purcell Rooms, Hayward Gallery and Queen Elizabeth Hall.

In 2005 the RFH closed for major refurbishment of its interior, increasing its public space by 35 per cent. More importantly, from the precinct's point of view, the Southbank Centre that owns the buildings and public realm of the South Bank developed a new active public frontage with shops, restaurants, public art, outdoor seating and improved access to the buildings and embraced to more liminal aspects of local culture such as the graffiti covered skateboarder adopted areas under the Centre's walkways. The RFH reopened in 2007.

This recent process effectively democratized the space within and around what had previously been an elite cultural indoor facility. It was, however, not a process without its problems. The local council (Lambeth) did not engage with RFH development, and failed to give any policy support in any of its strategic planning documentation. There were also tensions with the Mayor of London who sought to take control of the Centre in 2002 and then robustly criticized its management over a rent issue between the Centre and the London Eye – its tenant. Nonetheless, after several aborted attempts through the 1980s and 1990s to masterplan the future of the South Bank, a more pragmatic plan evolved to enable works to be done to its buildings and the public realm and is bearing results.

Downstream of the South Bank is Bankside. Located in a different London Borough (Southwark), its political history is reviewed in Tyler (1998) but bears some recapping here. Like South Bank it, too, was badly bombed in Second World War and little development took place alongside the waterfront, other than light industry and the building of the Bankside Power Station. Bankside also had a chequered planning history. Throughout the 1980s the local authority was generally viewed as hard left wing and antagonistic to the prevailing right wing national government. Its anti-development manifesto of 1982 was supported by some very strident local residents' groups that did not wish to see the riverside dominated by office blocks that would, it felt, render the neighbourhood sterile, particularly, in the evenings. It wished to retain the residential nature of the area yet see its improvement by providing local jobs for local people. Tourism was seen as a 'candy floss' industry providing low paid part-time work that was no substitute for the head-of-household jobs that had been lost from the light manufacturing and distribution sectors during the economic depression of the 1970s.

However, champions for the tourism cause emerged in the late 1980s when the local Chamber of Commerce commissioned a report on the potential of tourism which concluded that whether the local council liked it or not the tourism industry was beginning to develop significantly and that it was best to manage tourism rather than leave it to market forces. In 1987, the Southwark Heritage Association (SHA), a voluntary group, took up tourism's case under the banner of 'Historic Southwark Alive Today'. It organized 'swap-shops' to bring together parties interested in tourism and began the task of networking between key attractions including Tower Bridge, the London Dungeon and Imperial War Museum. By 1988 they had "reached a critical point and could make a case for potential tourism development in Southwark" (Peter Challen Chairman SHA) having achieved funding from the government's new partnership funding mechanism called The City Action Team.

In 1988 a Southwark Council Officer concluded that:

> *Tourism is not a panacea for Southwark's economic and unemployment problems. It could, however, be a key strand in a development strategy for the borough. Market-led developments are now so well established and Southwark so natural a venue that tourism will expand irrespective of the Council's wishes. The Council should, therefore, take the opportunity to influence and manage tourism in ways it finds acceptable for the residents of the borough (London Borough of Southwark, 1988a: 3).*

However, little progress was made, other than some small-scale projects such as self-guided leaflets, until 1992 when Southwark's hard-left council was replaced by a new soft-left administration. The latter recognized the need to work with central government, and that the strategy of trying to attract manufacturing jobs back to the north of the borough was doomed to fail. Tourism thus became the new tool for economic development. This new mind-set would see three key changes:

(1) Bankside and the Pool of London were strategically re-aligned to the centre of London rather than with the more working class, deprived areas to the south.
(2) The Council entered into the new multi-sector urban governance mechanisms thus accessing new sources of knowledge, interest and finance.
(3) The Council re-organized its own administrative structure to realize a new proactive, enabling role for itself. Significantly, the old confrontational style of officer was replaced with a new positive proactive senior team.

SHA's wish for the council to take the lead on tourism was soon realized. The council swiftly gave permission of the development of Shakespeare's Globe after 20 years of negativity towards it and funded the £2 million feasibility study for the conversion of a derelict power station into a gallery of modern art. With such a new impetus Bankside and the Pool of London started a period of sustained tourism and arts growth, not directed by a masterplan, but by a series of flexible, tourism and economic development strategies aimed at encouraging inward investment from both the public and private sectors.

Developing Management Networks and Structures

From the mid-1990s, the LBS whole-heartedly adopted the new governance mechanisms promoted by the central government. In association with other riparian councils, Southwark set up the strategic Cross River Partnership that attracted £319 million of public sector money to leverage an extra £31 million from the private sector. Much of this was to be invested directly into the 'new cultural quarter' by developing the general infrastructure and urbanscape (e.g. completing the pedestrianization of the waterfront and eventually major foot bridges linking the north and south banks).

The cultural quarter model is now widely held by tourism researchers as a successful 'means of achieving regeneration outcomes. Such strategies have been followed particularly by cities with perceived problems in relation to image and identity, linked to the need to promote inward investment and tourism' (McCarthy, 2005: 280).

The strategic partnerships between the four riparian local authorities, the Central Government, the Government Office for London and the Cross River Partnership are represented in Fig. 15.1. Underneath these partnerships three local partnerships were developed for each historic area:

(1) The *Pool of London Partnership (PLP)* was instigated by the Government Office for London to address urbanscape issues around the key attractions of the Tower of London and Tower Bridge. It subsequently addressed a wide range of issues including the improvement of the public realm, attracting inward investment and promoting training schemes for local people.

(2) The *Bankside Marketing Partnership (BMP)* was more closely targeted at tourism and comprised just the tourism operators from Bankside. It took a broad view of marketing concentrating on

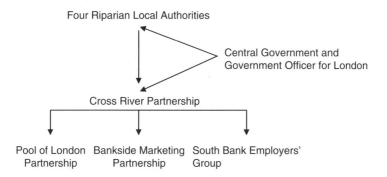

Figure 15.1 Early precinct management structure

improvements to the basic tourism infrastructure (e.g. signposting, road surfacing) and soft marketing via guide leaflets and an events programme.

(3) The *South Bank Employers Group (SBEG)*, set up in the South Bank area where the LBL paid, and still do pay, little attention to tourism. This area was not politically important for the borough, its population was falling and employment was in large office blocks, generally not providing jobs for local people. This lack of interest resulted in the decay of the public realm and so the major employers formed the partnership, putting in their own money to attract national government monies to help fund improvements to the public realm and undertake city marketing activities. Although outside its constituency, LBS did contribute some funding to SBEG as it recognized the synergies with its own partnerships and efforts to develop the precinct as a whole.

However, even with a local partnership structure in place, progress in developing the precinct was slow. In Bankside and the Pool of London, SHA was dominant but it focused on small-scale projects and its internal politics took up much council officer time. The arrival of a new Tourism Officer in the LBS presented an opportunity for change:

[my predecessor] spent a lot of time on small projects [forwarded by SHA]. I didn't want to go down that track because I felt there were so many things happening with big players – the big organ-isations, the new hotels, etc. – we couldn't spend too much time dealing with small projects – [my predecessor] got into a hole, I went in brash, the council's steering group saw it as a chance to sever links with those. SHA [the heritage group] were too niche, too small, too low key – tourism had moved on a scale (Southwark Tourism Officer).

Part of this "moving on" was to develop the partnerships and give them resources to achieve more significant results. Picking up on the new governance regimes the council set up a high-level officer group to oversee the development of tourism and its management structures:

> *Everyone was talking about joined up thinking and joined up government ... we took the view [that] we had to kick-start things and put some money into groups like the Bankside Marketing Group and the Pool of London Partnership to show willing and, therefore, some of the big players may come in as well ... I think the Council leaders were quite effective figures because they gave the Directors [of Depts] freedom to work and make decisions (Southwark Tourism Officer).*

What emerged was a local management network. This can be conceived as two distinct but related sub-networks and a series of consultee groups (see Fig. 15.2).

Strategic guidance sub-network

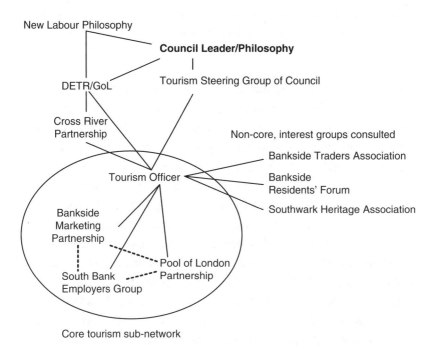

Figure 15.2 Tourism network structure in London's south bank precinct

The Core Tourism Sub-Network comprised the local council tourism officer and the three key partnerships within the precinct. The partners in the sub-network were people who were looking at policy with the council providing the delivery mechanism. All members signed up to the Council's tourism strategy that was written in 2000 (London Borough of Southwark, 2000) and updated in 2005. The Council sought to play an active role in partnerships which would support and encourage the formation of associations and consortia. In this way the core sub-network was guided by the strategy and addressed detailed rather than strategic policy, and focused on improving the public realm and more recently marketing and implementation.

The core sub-network was steered by a Strategic Guidance Sub-Network which comprised two main elements. First a political/philosophical element where:

> *politics were involved in it. We're a Labour local government and Labour administration, so we were following what government was telling us to do as a local authority (Tourism Officer).*

These key management messages came from both the Department for the Environment, Transport and the Regions (DETR) and the Government Office for London, which were promoting new governance mechanisms of partnerships and joined up thinking. This central government guidance was further compounded by strategic project guidance from the Cross River Partnership and political guidance from the Council Leadership and a specially commissioned Tourism Steering Group. The partnerships were, therefore, very aware of the context within which they worked.

The second element of this structure is too loose to be conceived as a sub-network. It comprised stand-alone groups that might be impacted by the development of tourism, but were outside the process of policy development and implementation. These were the local traders' groups, small firms, the residents' group and the SHA – the former tourism champion that could not adjust as the pace and scale of tourism development grew.

304

Local traders and small firms appear to be far less directly involved in tourism planning processes than might have been expected. This pattern is, however, broadly consistent with recent research focusing on understanding urban-based tourism policy making, with particular reference to small firms. As Thomas and Thomas (2005: 121) observed: '... existing understanding of tourism policy formulation at a local level is deficient. Small firms ... [need] ... particular attention [in future research agendas] because of their incidence and their proximity to the tourist experience'.

The area's traditional working class residents remained sceptical of tourism's ability to deliver a better quality of life and pointed to the lack of community facilities, local shops and leisure facilities even though over half a billion pounds of investment had been put into the area. New residents, who have bought up and gentrified property in the area or bought new up-market flats, do not seem to have adopted this attitude and so have diluted the anti-development voice.

The hub of this structure is the Council's tourism officer who played the role of network manager and tourism champion and whose management style, skills and experience closely steered the Core Tourism Sub-Network.

This structure was based around Bankside and the Pool of London, although the SBEG represented interests in the South Bank. Nonetheless, changes to the South Bank were also taking place although in an ad hoc manner. These brought with them tourism management problems. The London Eye was developed alongside the County Hall complex of hotels, aquarium, restaurants and games arcades, yet the public realm, especially Jubilee Gardens, remained in poor condition despite several masterplans. Queues at the Eye made use of the river walkway difficult for those wishing to stroll along the river. In 2005, a new Artistic Director for the Centre sought to reinvigorate not just the buildings but the public realm also, including the commissioning of lighting, flags and canopies and a new design for Jubilee Gardens.

The level of cooperation between all parties on the precinct (excepting LBL) has worked so well that the precinct is seeking to become the Cultural Quarter for the 2012 Olympic Games.

Network Management

One can observe from the previous section that a complex network was steered and managed from above. In this way it was not self-organizing but required proactive management from the LBS, the SBEG and the Centre to enable solutions to be generated to emergent problems. This required the development of new skills to go with the new governance structures being imposed from central government. These skills included the management of negotiations, bargaining and consultation.

Kickert and Koppenjan (1997) observed that there had been no empirical studies of the conditions required for network management but suggest eight factors that may come into play. These are listed in Table 15.1 and relate to the case study.

Table 15.1 Conditions of network management in London Borough of Southwark tourism arena

Conditions	Evidence from local-level survey and case study
The Number of Actors: Involve only those groups that are indispensable.	Local heritage groups excluded when no longer considered important and residents' groups consulted but outside the main Council: industry network.
Diversity Within Networks: Requires targeted network management techniques and thus increased costs.	Core tourism sub-network is business dominated, largely a case of coordination skills.
	Management of non-tourism groups by negotiation and bargaining.
	Two sides kept apart to reduce negotiation and bargaining costs. Ultimate mediation by Tourism Steering Group of LBS and Governors' of Southbank Centre.
Closed Nature of Networks: Having opposing networks may bring creative tensions and mutual adjustments.	No evidence of creative tensions between tourism industry and other network types.
	Residents groups adjusting more than others, but able to exert some pressure on details of policy.

(continued)

Table 15.1 (Continued)

Conditions	Evidence from local-level survey and case study
Conflicts of Interests: Interests are socially constructed and therefore possible to negotiate.	LBS, but not LBL, re-constructed its conception and opinion of tourism. Residents remain sceptical of tourism's ability to deliver liveable neighbourhood, new local development frameworks being used to develop wider context for tourism development.
Cost of Network Management: Costs rise as move from facilitation to mediation to arbitration.	Keeping residents and industry separate reduces network management costs. Arbitration cost reduced by having clear tourism strategy to which all parties sign up to.
Political and Social Context: Changes in external environment affect network.	Major changes in political ethos of LBS facilitated tourism development and local tourism network to establish. Lack of LBL leadership means development of South Bank has been slower and more controversial. Changing social make-up of local population reduces tensions between developers and residents.
Leadership and Commitment Power: Network members must champion network when back in own organization.	LBS adopt strategic leadership role. Officers steered by senior management and councillors. Industry players high-up in organizations or have mandate to proceed as they think fit. Lack of LBL leadership means Southbank Centre has to re-think its role and move to work with public realm as well as with the cultural buildings.
Skills: Tactical and strategic know-how is important.	Well established in local network, partnership skills especially well developed.

Source: Based on Kickert and Koppenjan (1997).

Table 15.1 suggests that a strong public sector role is important in managing the tourism network. This requires the development of new skills around negotiation, arbitration, consultation and bargaining. In this way, the council, or a substitute organization (e.g. SBEG or the Centre), steers policy. The sub-networks manage out tensions between local amenity groups and the tourism partnerships by avoiding confrontation and coordinating their interests through the tourism officer or other network managers.

Figures 15.1 and 15.2 and Table 15.1 suggest that there is a well structured, managed and focused local tourism network. While this may be so, all parties need to remain both reactive and proactive. Much of the monies for the management of the network structure, and the partnerships within it, came from a central government source known as the Single Regeneration Budget (SRB). The three partnerships along with the Cross River Partnerships were highly successful in gaining hundreds of millions of pounds of public money for their projects. Yet, this source has now ceased to exist. It meant that the partnerships had to seek new sources of funds and consequently amend their aims and projects to fit. This they have done by evolving from an SRB funded partnership into Business Improvement Districts.

Business Improvement Districts

A *Business Improvement District* (BID) is a funding system designed to improve and manage a commercial area, financed by an additional levy on all defined (business) ratepayers following a majority vote. Once the vote is successful, which must achieve both a majority in terms of number of ratepayers and the proportion of their rateable value, the levy becomes mandatory on all defined ratepayers and is treated in the same way as the business rate becoming a statutory debt. BIDs have been established (Map 15.1) in each of the three historic areas of the south bank plus a neighbouring area based around Waterloo International Train Station and Business Area (London Development Agency, 2006). The details of these are:

(1) The PLP regeneration partnership successfully sponsored the 'London Bridge BID' which was announced in November 2005.

PLP had undertaken over 18 months of consultation on the BID concept with the business community, Southwark Council and other agencies operating in the area. According to PLP sources, the key tasks for the new BID will be:

- providing representation and advice on local development and planning issues for business rate-paying organizations around London Bridge;
- funding projects and services aimed at enhanced local security, extra street cleaning, and extra marketing and promotional support for the area.

(2) The BMP is to evolve into the 'Better Bankside BID'. It has worked as a shadow BID for 4 years alongside the BMP. It seeks to levy £650,000 from local businesses and to use this to lever in a total of £3 million over the next 5 years. Its three main aims are to:

- attract more customers and encourage them to stay longer;
- make staff, visitors and clients feel happier about being there;
- help businesses secure a real return in their investment in the area.

(3) The SBEG operates in a cross-boundary area across the LBL and LBS. The Group has acted as a 'voluntary BID' and will continue to do so. In addition to committing substantial private investment into the area, SBEG has also delivered the local regeneration programme on behalf of Waterloo Project Board, aimed at:

- marketing South Bank and its attractions as a major visitor precinct;
- facilitating capital improvements and enhanced area management;
- increasing the economic success of the area, particularly by developing local skills and increasing job opportunities;
- delivering social programmes by developing sports and leisure facilities for the use of local residents and employees.

(4) With encouragement from Lambeth Borough Council, Waterloo Quarter Business Alliance BID (WQBA) has become Lambeth's first BID after a successful local vote in February 2006. It like other BIDs will operate for 5 years, and seeks to leverage in £1.4

million of additional funding to be spent on four projects agreed during the course of consultations with local businesses:

- radio-link scheme for local businesses;
- environmental (including street furniture) improvements and a graffiti removal operations;
- retail Strategy Study for the shopping district and a Street Market Management Study;
- Christmas lights and hanging baskets around Waterloo.

Good Practice in Local Precinct Management

The above analysis suggests that local groups and councils need to be pragmatic, opportunistic and able to work collaboratively. In other words, groups must adapt to their changing environment in terms of both the political and funding regimes to which they are exposed but also to changes in the needs of the precinct itself as it evolves. If they are unable to adapt they risk being excluded from the local management of the precinct. The following four elements of good practice can be identified from the case study.

Local Groups Must be Locally Embedded and Address Economic Development Issues that Are Wider than the Self-interest of Their Members

Council can be strong players, steering interested groups and partnerships to help achieve strategic aims for tourism and economic development in general. Local groups in the form of partnerships are important to the Council because of their ability to present evidence, in the form of local knowledge, and their ability to present this such that they may take other segments, such as the wider business community and local residents with them. Representatives of each of the main tourism-related partnerships each spoke of the need to be locally embedded. Although there were early 'feuds' hard work at identifying common interests led to a partnership and voluntary BIDs that are accepted alternative voices to that of the uninterested local authority.

Resident groups were unprepared for the ongoing nature of tourism development and impacts and felt unprepared and unempowered for this [role]. But it was found through their work with local communities, residents' acceptance levels of tourism as a legitimate activity in the area rose from 54 per cent in 1997 to 65 per cent in 2001.

Therefore, the local embeddedness and cross-sectoral support for the activities of tourism groups and partnerships has been important in justifying the strategy to develop tourism and tourism partnerships. Central to this was the coordination and communication role of the partnerships and Council.

Local Groups Must Adapt to Key Public Sector Agendas and Processes

A key adaptation has been for local groups to realize the importance of new governance mechanisms, such as partnerships and the BIDs. Each group recognizes the importance of the Government Office for London in suggesting how and why the groups could come together, in particular to access public sector monies.

However, as new governance mechanisms can be opportunistic, groups have to be flexible and pragmatic. An officer of the PLP stated:

> *we are the result of new thinking, new governance. We were not originally part of the LBS strategy – we were opportunistic, there to help the area.*

Partnerships worked in the borough of Lambeth because the local authority was happy not to be involved in the 'dialogue for change, and evolution in the way that the area was managed and developed' (Marketing Officer SBEG).

The local partnerships in Southwark, on the other hand, worked because the local authority was very supportive and pragmatic after early reservations about the new governance mechanisms.

All the partnerships in the precinct arose out of adoption of the ideas, language and *modus operandi* of new governance. The groups were born of and into the new governance structures. In fact, no group other than tenants' associations existed prior to the decision to develop the riverside in 1992.

Groups Must be Able to Coordinate and Deliver Resources

The local heritage group (SHA) were the major drivers of tourism in Bankside and the Pool of London from 1990 to 1995. On behalf of the local chamber of commerce they were the local tourism champions running small-scale projects and lobbying to save historic buildings to demonstrate the value of the historic waterfront and the role tourism could play in this. However, once they had won their arguments and the majority of historic buildings had been saved and re-used, their role was limited. Although the local authority tourism officer spoke of having to move tourism up a scale the problem was that SHA's objectives did not readily fit into the new proactive, big budget, development focused tourism strategy, and SHA itself did not have the resources or interest to adapt.

The key players, therefore, were those that could bring, or help bring, resources to the table. For example, the PLP successfully coordinated four SRB bids (worth over £35 million) and the Cross River Partnership in association with the other local partnerships raised over £50 million from the same. Other partnerships raised money from local businesses, for example the BMP raised membership fees of between £500 and £3000 from local tourism businesses to help with urban environmental improvements and marketing campaigns. They used the money to directly fund campaigns or fund bids for regeneration money. LBS contributed resources, usually on a 50:50 basis with their partners. Their contribution was mostly made up of officer time rather than money per se; alternatively, the more distant LBL provided some money but no other resources.

The coordination of resources was mostly achieved through meetings and SRB bids. Here partners pooled their knowledge of tourism and contacts in order to forward policy ideas both in pursuit of the objectives of the tourism strategy or to take advantage of ad hoc government initiatives. Some resources were purely commercial in nature such as selling advertising space on walking tour leaflets, but the most important resource appears to be a 'unity of purpose'. This requires a certain value coincidence amongst partnership members, and it is perhaps for this reason that the successful partnerships were focused on economic development, and why SHA and Bankside Residents Forum were treated as separate.

Interested Parties Must be Able to Work Independently and in Collaboration

Collaboration, through partnership arrangements, is key to the development of tourism policy at the local level. The case study has shown the strength of these collaborations when bidding for resources from government initiatives.

However, groups need to identify their *raison d'etre* or the niche they will fill in the local tourism landscape. The three partnerships covered the main historic areas that formed the new precinct, with a further strategic partnership overarching them to source finance and undertake projects of wider significance.

The partnerships have been successful in filling in the policy gaps considered to be of mutual self-interest. But individual organizations, rather than groups, were also important players in guiding local policy and economic development. Using their lobbying skills and contacts at the national and local levels they sought to acquire resources for themselves and to smooth the way with residents and the councils in forwarding their own interests. For example, the Tate Gallery of Modern Art and the Globe Theatre used their public relations skills, even before they opened their doors to the public, to work with local residents and schools and allay fears regarding tourism development.

However, it is the partnerships themselves that are key to developing and managing the precinct. Partnerships that are able to work in this manner and show their relevance and ability to contribute to an agenda wider than their own self-interest put themselves in a position to influence the management of the precinct. The willingness of key cultural

313

players such as the Tate Modern, the Globe Theatre and increasingly the Southbank Centre to engage in collaborative activities has not been universal amongst all tourism operators. For example, Southwark Cathedral (a parish church which became a cathedral early in the 20th century) and one of the south bank's popular attractions for foreign tourists, has not featured prominently in any of the strategic plans. This is in stark contrast to evidence suggesting that major places of worship remain attractive urban tourism attractions (Woodward, 2004).

Conclusions

This case study demonstrates how management structures can evolve rapidly over time. Once LBS engaged with tourism in 1992 the aim was to harness and work with the enthusiasm of local heritage groups. Thus, a conservation-based policy existed. Subsequently, as the Council itself became more active and plugged into central government initiatives the emphasis turned to economic development and job creation. As economic development got underway, the local partnerships looked towards the management of the public realm to help ensure the quality of the precinct using central government monies from both the SRB and, when the funding regime changed, BIDs.

Similarly, in the South Bank sub-area the SBEG developed as a response to the lack of local government activity. This evolved into a major city marketing group and its activities, among other things, have encouraged the Southbank Centre to become active in the development and management of the precinct outside of the walls of its cultural buildings.

A key to enabling this transformation in Bankside and the Pool of London was the change in the local council from a purposeful 'non-participant' in tourism to a 'proactive leader'. It used its own resources – mostly time and knowledge of its officers – to steer the agenda. Its positional power, as the main coordinating body required for making SRB bids, and as overseer of the public realm, was used to bring together local tourism players and boost the profile of tourism. Crucially, however, the Council remained in this new governance role, happy to sit back and let the BIDs takeover the management of much of the public realm and economic development policy (e.g. training) that it would traditionally have done itself.

The adoption of the role of facilitator, enabler and leader has been vital in bringing together the support of local industry players and convincing the government to award SRB funds and BIDs status. It was the single most important factor in the development and management of the precinct.

However, that is not to say that everything is rosy on London's south bank precinct. Of the four key management issues highlighted at the beginning of this case study, two remain unresolved. First, the neighbouring Lambeth Council still do not appear to have any proactive interest in tourism management which is starting to have a negative effect on the area around the iconic London Eye attraction, despite the recent efforts of the Centre.

Secondly, as BIDs replicate the boundaries of the three historic areas of South Bank, Bankside and the Pool of London, the issue of identity for the composite precinct remains, and may become worse given the loss of the over-arching and strategic Cross River Partnership. Perhaps the three historic areas will survive, but one wonders if tourists and guide books will just collectively call it the South Bank, echoing Paris's Left Bank. If so the BIDs may find pressure to make more pragmatic, but strategic change and become a single precinct management partnership, possibly with the concomitant loss of historic and local identity.

Discussion Questions and Exercises

(1) Tourism precincts can encompass a number of local government areas or political jurisdictions. Discuss how barriers to cooperation in such situations can be overcome.

(2) In relation to this case study why have some stakeholders opted for involvement while others have not? Identify strategies which could more effectively engage broader stakeholder involvement.

(3) Compare this case study with the case study presented in Chapter 16. Why has it been more challenging to achieve precinct planning objectives in London's south bank than it has in Sheffield City Centre?

(4) This case study differs to others in the book in that the precinct actually comprises three distinct sub-areas. How does this issue of scale affect the planning and development of this precinct?

(5) Four elements of good practice were identified from this case study – local groups must address economic development issues, partnerships, coordinating and delivering resources, and independent and collaborative partnerships. Do you think these four elements could be applied to the planning of other urban destinations? Explain your answer.

References

Kickert, W.J.M., & Koppenjan, J. (1997). *Managing Complex Networks: Strategies for the Public Sector.* London: Sage.

London Development Agency (2006). *London Bids.* Available at www. londonbids.info (accessed 19 September 2006).

London Borough of Southwark (1988). *Towards a Strategy for Tourism*: Report of the Inter-departmental Working Party.

London Borough of Southwark (2000). *Southwark Tourism Plan. 2000–2005.* Department of Leisure Services.

London Borough of Southwark (2005). *Southwark Tourism Strategy. 2005–2010.* Department of Regeneration.

McCarthy, J. (2005). *Promoting image and identity in 'Cultural Quarters': the case of Dundee. Local Economy*, 20(3), 280–293.

Mullins, C. (2007). *The South Bank Centre: A Festival on the River.* London: Penguin.

Thomas, R., & Thomas, H. (2005). Understanding tourism policy-making in urban areas, with particular reference to small firms. *Tourism Geographies*, 7(2), 121–137.

Tyler, D. (1998). Getting tourism on the agenda: policy development in the London Borough of Southwark. In D. Tyler, Y. Guerrier, & M. Robertson (Eds.), *Managing Tourism in Cities: Policy Process and Practice.* Chichester: John Wiley & Sons.

Woodward, S.C. (2004). Faith and tourism: planning tourism in relation to places of worship. *Tourism and Hospitality: Planning and Development*, 1(2), 173–186. Discussion Questions and Exercises

16

Sheffield City Centre: The Heart of the City Precinct

Kirsten Holmes and Yasminah Beebeejaun

Introduction

The year is 1999; a couple has enjoyed an evening at Sheffield Theatres (the largest theatre complex in the UK outside of London's West End). Walking from the Crucible Theatre, which also stages the World Snooker Championships each year, they pass through Tudor Square, down Pinstone Street, the main shopping thoroughfare in Sheffield and onto Barkers Pool, where they take a taxi from outside the city hall. The city centre they have just passed through would have been almost entirely deserted after the shops had closed and people had gone home from work. People did not socialize in Sheffield City Centre after the shops closed, rather they returned home to the suburbs, where the best restaurants were found. Neither did Sheffield have a wealth of tourist attractions in the city centre to attract either business or leisure tourists, or any high quality hotels in which they could stay, although it is close to many attractions in the Peak District National Park.

Both tourist and local resident use of the city centre after dark was limited.

Less than a decade later the city centre has been transformed as part of a new masterplan, which is creating 10 new quarters within the city centre. The area linking Sheffield Theatres and the city hall is known as the Heart of the City. Gone is the ugly town hall extension, known locally as the 'eggbox'. In its place stand the award-winning Winter Garden and Millennium Galleries, linking Sheffield Theatres, the Graves Art Gallery, the Peace Gardens, Pinstone Street and the railway station. In amongst these are commercial developments, including a new four star hotel and No. 1 St Paul's Place, a mixed-use development that includes bars and restaurants. A surge in city centre residential developments mean that after dark the city centre is increasingly vibrant for both residents and tourists alike.

This chapter presents a case study of Sheffield's City Centre redevelopment, focusing on the *Heart of the City* civic core. In particular, we examine how this new precinct links key cultural venues within the city centre and provides cultural spaces for both residents and visitors. The Heart of the City is a planned precinct, designed to attract both residents and tourists into the city centre. We argue that the city council's continuing management of this space has been essential to the success of the regeneration strategy.

The Changing Role of Sheffield City Centre

Sheffield is a post-industrial city in the UK located approximately 170 miles north of London, within Yorkshire. The city's population stands at 516,100. Historically, Sheffield has been known for its paternalistic and interventionist local government, which has operated largely under the control of the Labour Party. The city council's interventionist approach can be observed within the local economy, with cultural policy actions traceable back to the early 1980s, in contrast to the national Conservative government's laissez-faire approach (Booth, 2005). There are tensions in this approach but this chapter illustrates how it has led to issues of social inclusion being part of any council led strategy.

Sheffield's economy was focused on the steel industry, with steel production and metalworking forming the main economic base and source of employment within the city. A number of factors, however, caused the decline in this traditional industry and by 1997, 75 per cent of jobs were in the service sector (Moss, 2002). Sheffield City Council continued their interventionist approach by taking a proactive role in shaping the future of the city, by looking to culture as an alternative economic base to the traditional manufacturing industries. From the mid-1980s, the city council began to fund one of the first urban cultural districts in the UK, by establishing the Cultural Industries Quarter (CIQ). The CIQ was established to stimulate employment, enhance cultural provision and attract tourism. This project was visionary but ultimately failed to create a vibrant public space as so little was known at the time about successful cultural regeneration (Moss, 2002). For example, although the location of the CIQ means that it is close to transport links it effectively stands at the edge of the city centre.

Sheffield's progressive planning process of the 1980s had identified the need to consult with a range of groups traditionally under-represented within planning. These groups included Black and Minority Ethnic (BME) groups, women and people in low paid work or currently unemployed. As far back as 1986 the draft central area plan:

> *stated that after very little development in the central area for over a decade the plan could act as a vehicle for promoting investment (especially on large parcels of land in council ownership). However the plan was also intended to ensure that commercial development did not over-rule community needs ... (Darke, 1990: 175).*

The process of engagement did have shortcomings but was able to reveal a number of concerns about safety in the city centre and the need for management and maintenance of public spaces. Furthermore, it identified the need for the city centre to make provision for those not engaging in consumer activity (Darke, 1990). These issues were taken forward into the planning policy of the time, but have re-emerged as issues in the current masterplan.

Sheffield City Council reassessed their cultural policy in the early 1990s and noted that their cultural venues were located around the city in a way that effectively segregated them and a more integrated approach to cultural planning was recommended (Betterton & Blanchard, 1992). The report also noted that Sheffield was suffering from a series of infrastructure problems, including transport links, which meant that the city struggled both to attract tourists and new businesses, in sharp contrast to nearby Meadowhall, an out-of-town shopping centre.

During the 1990s, Sheffield's traditional cultural facilities faced inadequate financing and were under threat of closure, not supported by the very real closure of the city council's Arts Department. Eventually all of the council's cultural facilities were externalized from the council's direct control into a series of charitable trusts (Roodhouse, 2000). This trust status enabled the independent Showroom cinema in the CIQ to reopen; the Millennium Galleries to be built and Sheffield Theatres to achieve financial stability and international acclaim for its productions.

Sheffield's cultural facilities also benefited from the introduction of a national lottery in the UK in 1994. Within the CIQ, two attractions: the Showroom cinema and the Site Gallery (a contemporary visual arts gallery) both received lottery funding. Subsequently, the Millennium Galleries, Sheffield Theatres and the Winter Garden have all received large lottery grants, which they may not have been eligible for had they remained under direct council control. These cultural attractions form the focus for Sheffield's new city centre masterplan, aspiring to a new era of regeneration and the Heart of the City precinct links these attractions together.

In 2000, Sheffield City Council launched an urban regeneration partnership, which would be responsible for implementing the city centre masterplan. The aim of the masterplan was to improve the city's economy, particularly by creating new jobs and improving the property market, the retail, leisure and cultural facilities in the city centre and the city's transport system. Cultural attractions would be only part of the

1996	Beginning of redevelopment of Sheffield City Centre
1998	Creation of city centre management team
2000	Creation of Sheffield One and launch of city centre masterplan
2000	Opening of the Millenium Galleries
2001	Opening of the Winter Garden
2005	Completion of the Peace Gardens
	Opening of No.1 St Paul's Place
2006	Opening of the hotel adjoining the Winter Garden
2010	Projected completion of the city centre redevelopment

Figure 16.1 A timeline of the Heart of the City precinct

masterplan but these would form the most visible changes to local residents and tourists alike. Sheffield's urban regeneration company (URC), Sheffield One, has responsibility for the new masterplan for the city, which divides the city centre into 10 different 'quarters', each with an individual but connected regeneration plan. The Heart of the City, one of these 10 quarters, is the lynchpin of the regeneration of Sheffield.

The Heart of the City redevelopment took place in two phases and began in 1996 (pre-dating the masterplan) through extensive landscaping and construction to redevelop the Peace Gardens, a new public space in the city centre, next to the Grade 1 listed (a building of outstanding or national architectural or historic interest) Town Hall. Two new cultural attractions were added to this, both supported by funding from the national lottery: the Millennium Galleries and the Winter Garden. The remaining works have now been completed and include the demolition of the town hall extension, the construction of a mixed-use development on this site and a hotel adjoining the Winter Garden. A number of privately owned developments including St Paul's Gardens incorporating retail, offices, apartments and bars, No. 1 St Paul's Place an office development, with ground-floor restaurant and bar space, and Howden House (Sheffield City Council office block) form the remainder of the precinct (Holmes & Beebeejaun, 2007). The timeline for the city centre precinct is set out in Fig. 16.1.

The Management of the Heart of the City

The city centre masterplan is the result of a series of partnerships between the public, commercial and voluntary sectors. These reflect central government's policy for partnership working within city planning, which seeks to limit the dominance of the public sector and also share responsibility with the private sector. Partnership working is, however, complicated. The URC responsible for the city centre masterplan is called Sheffield One. Sheffield One is a partnership between Sheffield City Council, Yorkshire Forward (the regional development agency) and English Partnerships (the UK Government's national regeneration agency). The redevelopment of the city centre is also a concern for Sheffield First, the Local Strategic Partnership (LSP), which is a forum for ensuring that a range of stakeholders are consulted about changes within the city centre. Sheffield First 'brings together the public, private, voluntary, community and faith sectors to collaborate in making Sheffield a successful city' (Sheffield One, 2005: 5). Two board members of the URC sit on the board for Sheffield First and the powers of the URC are determined through the LSP. Sheffield One is the delivery agent for specific strategic objectives within the city and its environs but it does not have the monopoly over policy decisions.

Sheffield First (Sheffield One, 2005:9) set out a number of key features that would define for them a successful city:

- Strong economy
- Vibrant city centre
- Well connected
- High employment and high skills in a learning city
- An exceptional cultural and sporting city
- Attractive, successful neighbourhoods
- Great place to grow up
- Good health and well-being for all communities
- Low crime
- Environmental excellence
- Inclusive and cosmopolitan city
- Well run and well regarded

The masterplan was the result of a series of partnerships between the public, commercial and voluntary sectors, but the Heart of the City is entirely managed by the city council. The exceptions to this are the individual cultural spaces (the Millennium Galleries, Sheffield Theatres), which are managed by charitable trusts that include council representatives on their Boards of Trustees and so are managed semi-independently of the council (Roodhouse, 2000).

A key aspect of the regeneration strategy has been the recognition of a commitment to safeguard and maintain the newly created public spaces within the Heart of the City precinct (Holmes & Beebeejaun, 2007). Sheffield City Council integrated city centre services through the creation of the city centre management team in 1998. This team is responsible for the maintenance of the public realm and ensuring safety through City Centre Ambassadors and partnership with South Yorkshire police, as well as marketing special events, designed to maximize use of the city centre. The city centre manager describes the bringing together of these services as:

a holistic approach, assets are people and places and we have a presence, safety on the street. All of the public realm in the city centre has 24-hour security (personal communication).

The team coordinate a range of activities around safety, maintaining a clean city centre and providing information to the public, as well as marketing (Sheffield City Council, undated). A key feature of this strategy is the paid employment of City Centre Ambassadors who work in the city centre area throughout the day. One of the duties of these ambassadors is to:

Keep a watchful eye over the award winning public realm areas including Peace Gardens, Winter Garden, Barkers Pool, St Paul's Square and Howard Street (Sheffield City Council, undated).

The City Centre Ambassadors also manage the tourist information desk in the Winter Garden and in their distinctive bright blue uniforms are clearly visible to tourists within the city centre. Good links between the city centre management team, Sheffield One and Sheffield First are necessary. The city centre manager reported positive relationships with Sheffield One who had consistently highlighted the value of the role they played in ensuring longevity of the new cultural spaces.

Key Issues and Problems

The redevelopment of Sheffield City Centre has transformed the city centre physically. Central government's expectation that the public sector consults and involves other stakeholders has meant a change in the council's working practices (Sullivan & Howard, 2005). Not only is the city council reliant on a broader range of agencies to provide funding, but they must also market the city centre to appeal to investors, potential residents and tourists. This process is initiated through regular meetings with the ward councillors, attendance at residents' fora, and partnerships with agencies including the local police force.

The changing context from a more interventionist style to a partnership approach, presents a number of challenges to maintain a coherent policy in the face of a fragmented range of interests. This is physically manifested in the differences between the quality of the public sector developments and the more mundane architecture of some of the private sector developments. For example, while the new public sector Millennium Galleries and Winter Garden have both won national awards, the design for No. 1 St Paul's Place, a commercial development and now the tallest building in Sheffield City Centre, was originally rejected by city councillors. In trying to implement the city council's partnership policy, the city centre management team is engaged in promoting their services to private sector interests. This has resulted in a comprehensive set of services such as security, cleansing operations and tourist information, which are delivered principally through a mixture of local, central and European government funding.

A concern of this partnership approach is, however, that as the city council strives to create a landscape which will encourage investor confidence, the commercial sector has become complacent in their contributions to the city centre. For example, in the late 1990s, Sheffield was known as the graffiti capital of Britain (Sheffield Star, 2007). In spite of their interventionist tradition, in the past the city council would seek a contribution from the owner of the affected building and if this was not forthcoming then the graffiti would remain in situ. The regeneration of the city centre has refocused the city council on issues, such as graffiti, which impact visually on the whole space. Where such concerns are not being dealt with by building owners, the city council has reverted to its traditional interventionist approach and taken full responsibility for graffiti removal. In addition, private sector financial contributions towards the city centre have typically been through project-based funding, for example, by funding city centre events such as the Winter Illuminations. The levels of commercial contributions to these events have continued to decline despite the increasing improvements to the city centre. It is not clear, therefore, how effective a broader, partnership approach to the development of the city centre has been.

Strategies for Dealing with Issues and Problems

A key feature of the management of the new city centre precincts has been the relationships the city council has established with the new commercial partners in Sheffield City Centre. This includes the city council managing the space outside St Paul's Gardens, a commercial development, which enables the mix of public and private activity to seamlessly appear as part of the public realm. This is an interesting reversal of the traditional viewpoint in the UK of the public sector as inefficient and needing to sub-contract to the commercial sector. The effective partnership strategy addresses some of the tensions which emerge from the Heart of the City development, with changing use of public space from public ownership, as the site of council offices, to its current use as a commercial sector development.

The council is now moving into a phase of more proactive marketing of Sheffield's new city centre and this has focused around four key events, which take place within the Heart of the City precinct at key times in the year. These include the World Snooker Championships, Sheffield on Show in the summer, Fright Night at Halloween and City Lights, when the Christmas Illuminations are switched on. These four key events see the Heart of the City precinct transformed into a public leisure space, with the World Snooker Championships featuring outdoor screens, Fright Night hosting a funfair and a variety of specialist markets on Pinstone Street, the shopping area adjacent to the Peace Gardens.

The ideal of the 24-hour city with a variety of users, however, brings with it a new set of interests which potentially give rise to conflicts, particularly regarding noise and visual impacts (Roberts & Turner, 2005). The intensification of users contributes to a shift from a city centre that is largely vacant after dark to one which has increasing numbers of leisure users. This presents new challenges to the city council, although they are not able to control all issues that arise. The principal concern focuses on the need to clean and maintain the public realm and how this impacts on the increasing number of city centre residents, along with tourists staying at the new hotel, adjoining the Winter Garden. Maintenance work starts at 5 a.m. each morning which impacts negatively on some residents, both temporary and permanent. Some measures have been taken including ensuring that sirens on cleansing machines do not sound in the early morning, but there is limited scope for change. The mix of uses also means that waste from the catering trade is readily visible to some city centre residents and tourists. This issue has been fairly easily resolved through liaison with the city centre planning team. It is now a standard condition for hot food takeaways to provide sheltered bin storage as part of achieving planning consent.

The city centre management team also recognizes the greater degree of citizen involvement and voice, particularly from more affluent residents and the team attends a number of the local residents' groups. There are continuing tensions, however, particularly over drunken behaviour late at night, which includes students from the city's two universities. The anti-social behaviour causes immediate tensions with other city centre users, especially visitors to the thriving theatre district on the edge of the Heart of the City. The problem of drunken behaviour is long-standing in cities with large student populations. Students were previously concentrated in university owned accommodation in the affluent western suburbs of Sheffield but a mixture of the change of ownership of student housing and the approval of development in land zoned for industrial use has contributed to students migrating to the city centre. Whilst some of the private landlords have contributed to the employment of City Centre Ambassadors to patrol the new student areas, this has been mixed with more punitive measures such as the creation of an alcohol exclusion zone in the city centre which bans on-street drinking (South Yorkshire Police, 2006) and the ability to make on the spot fines for anti-social behaviour.

Council officers are aware that there is some way to go before Sheffield is a true 24-hour city. As the city centre becomes more successful, tensions are starting to arise between various user groups such as those in the city principally to drink and those enjoying cultural facilities. As the city becomes enjoyed later and later into the evening there are also tensions between residents, tourists and the need to clean and maintain the urban environment. Whilst destinations such as London are recognized as busy throughout the day and night, Sheffield has never been such a city and there needs to be further dialogue about the impacts the city's many uses have on different stakeholders.

The Heart of the City: A Recipe for Success?

The Heart of the City precinct includes the Grade 1 listed Town Hall, the Peace Gardens and the two new flagship cultural attractions: the Winter Garden and the Millennium Galleries; and links these to the theatre square, the main shopping precinct and the railway station. The effectiveness of the Heart of the City precinct can be measured in three ways: public use, external recognition and by examining how far the actual precinct has met the principles of the original masterplan.

Public Use

Public use is evident in the way that the Peace Gardens have become a heavily used and popular pedestrian space. External recognition is particularly notable for the Millennium Galleries, which opened in 2001, providing high quality gallery exhibition space, attracting exhibitions from London and abroad. The gallery building has won several awards for its architecture. The Winter Garden, a temperate glasshouse completed in 2002, provides an undercover space in a building of architectural merit adjoining the Millennium Galleries and has also won several awards, including a joint award with the Millennium Galleries from the Royal Institute of British Architects.

The first principle of the city centre masterplan was to create 'a dynamic public and civic realm', and this has largely been achieved through the creation of the public spaces described above. The more recent commercial spaces, including the new office block and the hotel, which adjoins the Winter Garden, however, question how far the principle of 'a socially and economically accessible city centre' has been achieved. The construction of the hotel has been particularly controversial as it is physically attached to the Winter Garden (Holmes & Beebeejaun, 2007). The Winter Garden is described by Sheffield City Council as an example of stunning architecture; a place for people to relax and a venue which is accessible to everyone in Sheffield and as a free entry venue it is open to everyone. The national press in the UK described the Winter Garden and adjoining Millennium Galleries as 'bringing together clear-spirited, clean-cut architecture and high quality art of every sort' and a 'brave and popular new complex of permeable, public city centre buildings', which the author hopes will be replicated in other cities in the UK (Glancey, 2003). The Winter Garden has largely been seen as a success story and building a free, indoor attraction in a northern European city is clearly a sensible concept. The Garden also provides a covered public space which links the Peace Gardens to the Millennium Galleries and onwards to the CIQ and Sheffield's train and bus stations.

While the Winter Garden may have won a number of architectural awards, prominent views of it have been obscured by the hotel, as Fig. 16.2 illustrates (the Winter Garden can just be seen peeking out from behind the hotel). In the masterplan, the Winter Garden 'was intended to be partly hidden and "discovered" by catching glimpses of it from the Peace Gardens, thereby encouraging people to walk

Figure 16.2 The Winter Garden

through' (Sheffield One, undated). Yet, the cultural attractions were completed before the private sector developments, with everyone enjoying a full view of the Winter Garden for over 3 years, before the building was obscured. In addition, the Winter Garden closes at 6 p.m. and the only way visitors and residents can enjoy this attraction is by viewing it from the bar of the hotel, which can hardly be described as an inclusive space.

The Heart of the City redevelopment is a planned precinct, which links both new and older cultural attractions with transport nodes, hotels, bars, restaurants and shops (Ashworth & Tunbridge, 2000). The new attractions and the pedestrian precinct which links these together has created a clustering of cultural attractions within the city centre (Jansen-Verbeke & Lievois, 1999). Additionally, the design has sought to create a 'sense of place' connecting the new developments with the city's industrial past, an important feature of a tourist precinct (Smith, 2007). The Millennium Galleries contains a metalwork gallery, showcasing Sheffield's history; the precinct linking the Winter Garden

Figure 16.3 Relaxing in the Peace Gardens with the new hotel behind the fountain (No. 1 St Paul's Place is on the right, the tallest building in Sheffield City Centre)

and Peace Gardens features a series of large, stainless steel spheres (Fig. 16.3) and the Peace Gardens fountain is designed to represent flowing molten steel.

Has the Heart of the City Met the Principles of the Masterplan?

The new Heart of the City precinct includes award-winning public spaces but are these spaces open to all? The city centre management team ensures that these new public spaces are continually surveyed, with various guidelines about the types of behaviour that may or may not be acceptable. For example, a tradition has begun in the redeveloped Peace Gardens, whereby children run through the fountains on sunny days. Nearby stands a sign advising users that running in the fountains is not permitted. Yet, City Centre Ambassadors stand by and watch young children enjoy the water. However, when an older teenager joins in with the children they are politely tapped on the arm and asked to restrain their behaviour (personal observation).

The city centre management team offers a particular type of public space coterminous with the activities going on in the commercial spaces surrounding – restaurants, bars and shops. The space is managed, but with an apparently light touch. What is interesting, however, is the contracting of the management of the surrounding commercial spaces to the city centre management team, providing a revenue stream from the private to the public sector. The City Centre Ambassador programme, with its light touch and personal approach to public space management allows for a different type of relationship with socially excluded groups including homeless people in contrast to commercial security services or the police, as the city centre manager further explained:

> We've had a few success stories where they've directed people to services or gone out with outreach workers and helped them solve problems. The police aren't seen like that (personal communication).

Nonetheless the Heart of the City precinct occupies an area which was once wholly public space and as such the commercial sector's ownership of this space needs to be handled with sensitivity. These commercial businesses enjoy the benefits of the publicly funded public realm improvements, while potentially constraining public spaces and this should be a concern for any city authority which seeks to be inclusive. Furthermore, the City Centre Ambassadors only operate until 6 p.m. each day, and thereby have not replaced traditional security arrangements. As such it is difficult to assess whether these new, patrolled public spaces are perceived as safe and inclusive or exclusionary.

There is no doubt that Sheffield City Centre is a more aesthetically pleasing place to be. Both tourists and residents enjoy better quality cultural attractions. These attractions are better linked together with a vibrant precinct, which has received a high level of external recognition:

> *... the Peace Gardens became the first city centre park to win a Green Flag (a national award for parks and green spaces) and it managed to retain the award for a second year running. The Winter Garden is the first covered structure to win a Green Flag, whilst Sheffield is unique in having won two Green Flags for spaces within a city centre (Sheffield City Council, 2004).*

These developments have tried to redress the problems caused by the earlier phase of cultural planning, with the CIQ, which failed to provide good cultural spaces. These public spaces are also safer and their quality will be maintained, as they are patrolled by City Centre Ambassadors. If we compare the outcomes of the Heart of the City masterplan with Sheffield First's 12 features of a successful city, we can see that on most levels, Sheffield One has delivered. The Heart of the City precinct provides a well-connected, vibrant city centre, contributes to an exceptional cultural city, attractive neighbourhoods for city centre residents and is generally well-run and increasingly well-regarded outside the region.

There is also evidence that the Heart of the City precinct and its cultural attractions are having wider impacts on Sheffield's future. Sheffield is not Yorkshire's primary city and perceptions of Sheffield are still somewhat negative outside the region. Cultural attractions such as the Millennium Galleries and Winter Garden can make a city a more attractive place to live and work. This means that the public sector has to subsidize the private sector by creating a better environment, leading to higher property rents and yields, which will encourage the private sector to invest. There is evidence that this policy is at least achieving some success, as the first speculative office development in Sheffield for several years has begun on the edge of the city centre, close to transport links. Since the masterplan is being implemented over an extended timescale of 10–15 years, it seems that this current redevelopment is an organic process.

The Heart of the City precinct is also central to the city council's cultural strategy, recently launched and setting out the city's cultural direction up to 2016 (Gosse, 2006). The council's cultural vision for Sheffield is that it becomes 'a European centre for cultural excellence, where culture contributes to the development of success-ful individuals, thriving communities and a strong economy'. The council's strategy lists seven statements of intent, including strength-ening the 'reputation of Sheffield as a vibrant cultural centre for residents, visitors and tourists', through marketing Sheffield's cul-tural attractions and improving access between these 'cultural hubs'; enhancing the visitor experience by providing 'high quality environ-ments [and] first class venues'; and 'promoting culture as central to the thriving and vibrant city life including restaurants, bars, night-clubs and accommodation'. In addition, other statements are more explicit about promoting Sheffield as a destination for cultural tour-ism, which would involve 'celebrating Sheffield's industrial, architec-tural and green landscape heritage, celebrating a sense of place and important landmarks' (Gosse, 2006: 11). The city council intends to add to the cultural regeneration of the city centre by redeveloping the Graves Art Gallery, which stands opposite the Millennium Galleries and refurbishing the Crucible Theatre, which hosts the World Snooker Championships.

Lessons for Practice

This chapter has documented the long-running attempts to create a city centre that reflect both civic excellence and also a progressive set of city politics. The opportunities presented by both the changing politi-cal landscape (Booth, 2005) and the UK's strengthening economy have given the city council the chance to realize an ambitious rede-velopment programme. One of the key attributes of this programme has been the integration of day-to-day city management strategies to complement flagship cultural attractions. There has been attention to the needs of both residents and tourists as well as a realistic acknow-ledgement that even award-winning architecture and public space may be subjected to anti-social behaviour and vandalism. The story of Sheffield's Heart of the City precinct demonstrates that even within partnership approaches to city centre regeneration there needs to be a strong public sector presence, in this case the city council. The URC is seen as a successful venture by those within Sheffield but perhaps part-nership is a fluid concept (Booth, 2005), and the relationship between the different actors is not constant and indeed successful partnership working may depend on this flexibility.

The case study of Sheffield City Centre offers interesting lessons regarding redevelopment and the management of redeveloped spaces. The city council, whilst shedding its paternalistic role, has implemented a strong vision for the city centre. This vision is being driven by the city council but has required funding from both central government and investment from the commercial sector. Building relationships with commercial developers has been vital in filling the redesigned public spaces. The design quality of the commercial development, however, is disappointing in comparison and perhaps reflects the international-ization of companies, who no longer have strong roots within a locality and have less interest in the contribution they make to the visual amen-ity of the precinct.

Sheffield's masterplanning exercise was able to articulate a vision of a revitalized 'creative Sheffield' to bring about funding for a range of cultural attractions and infrastructure improvements. While the new city centre is busy and thriving with visitors and residents even after dark, it remains to be seen whether all residents are equally welcome within the new precinct. There are hints that undesirable users, such as the homeless, have simply been displaced to more marginal areas around the city centre. While we have focused on the Heart of the City project in this chapter, this is just one of 10 city centre quarters within the masterplan and the continuing redevelopment will feature more new precincts that connect the city centre together. We recom-mend that the issues raised in this chapter are revisited when the work is completed.

Discussion Questions and Exercises

(1) Think about and list what you would consider as the 'markers' of the Heart of the City precinct. What are some of the visual, physical, tactile and commercial markers of the space?

(2) The authors raise a number of issues that could arise in creating a 24-hour precinct. Identify these issues and discuss how they have been overcome. Can you suggest other ways to deal with these issues?

(3) The authors discuss whether the Heart of the City has met the principles of the masterplan. Using this case study as an example do you think planning has to achieve 100 per cent of its objectives in order to be regarded as successful? Why or why not?

(4) Identify the ways in which Sheffield City Council are planning for intergenerational equity?

(5) Identify the stakeholders involved in the redevelopment of the Heart of the City civic core. Map the relationships and their strength between the stakeholders. Identify which relationships require strengthening and the strategies you could use to strengthen those relationships.

References

Ashworth, G.J. & Tunbridge, J.E. (2000). *The Tourist-Historic City: Retrospect and Prospect of Managing the Heritage City* (2nd edn.) Amsterdam: Pergamon.

Betterton, R., & Blanchard, S. (1992). *Made in Sheffield: Towards a Cultural Plan for Sheffield in the 1990s.* Sheffield: Sheffield City Council.

Booth, P. (2005). Partnerships and networks: the governance of urban regeneration in Britain. *Journal of Housing and the Built Environment*, 20, 257–269.

Darke, R. (1990). A city centre for people: popular planning in Sheffield. In J. Montgomery, & A. Thronley (Eds.), *Radical Planning Initiatives: New Directions for Urban Planning in the 1990s.* Aldershot: Gower.

Glancey, J. (2003). Underneath the arches. *The Guardian*, 6 January.

Gosse, A. (2006). *Sheffield Culture: A Strategy for Inclusive Cultural and Sporting Development*. Sheffield: Sheffield City Council.

Holmes, K., & Beebeejaun, Y. (2007). City centre masterplanning and cultural spaces: a case study of Sheffield. *Journal of Retail and Leisure Property*, 6(9), 29–46.

Jansen-Verbeke, M., & Lievois, E. (1999). Analysing heritage resources for urban tourism in European cities. In D.G. Pearce, & R.W. Butler (Eds.), *Contemporary Issues in Tourism Development: Analysis and Applications*. London and New York: Routledge.

Moss, L. (2002). Sheffield's cultural industries quarter 20 years on: what can be learned from a pioneering example? *International Journal of Cultural Policy*, 8(2), 211–219.

Roberts, M., & Turner, C. (2005). Conflicts of liveability in the 24-hour city: learning from 48 hours in the life of London's Soho. *Journal of Urban Design*, 10(2), 171–193.

Roodhouse, S. (2000). The wheel of history – a relinquishing of city council cultural control and the freedom to Management: Sheffield Galleries and Museums Trust. *International Journal of Arts Management*, 3(1), 78–86.

Sheffield City Council (2004). *Sheffield to Fly Three Green Flags*. Press Release, 4 November 2004. Available at http://www.sccplugins.sheffield.gov.uk/press/news/aRelease.asp?akey=2387&Mon=01/11/2004 (accessed 19 March 2007).

Sheffield City Council (undated). *City Centre Management Team*. Available at http://www.sheffield.gov.uk/out--about/city-centre/city-centre-management (accessed 20 March 2007).

Sheffield City Council (undated). *City Centre Ambassadors*. Available at http://www.sheffield.gov.uk/out--about/city-centre/city-centre-ambassadors (accessed 20 March 2007).

Sheffield One (undated). *The Heart of the City*. Available at http://www.sheffield1.com/heart.html (accessed 26 March 2007).

Sheffield One (2005). *Creative Sheffield: Transforming Sheffield's Economy*. Sheffield: Sheffield First Partnership.

Sheffield Star (2007). Graffiti artist Simon now on gallery wall. *Sheffield Star*, 14 February.

Smith, M.K. (2007). *Tourism, Culture, and Regeneration.* Wallingford, Oxfordshire, UK: CAB International.

South Yorkshire Police (2006). *New Year Podcast.* Available at http://www.southyorks.police.uk/podcasts/transcripts/newyear.pdf (accessed 20 March 2007).

Sullivan, H., & Howard, J. (2005). *National Evaluation of Local Strategic Partnerships.* Issues Paper: Below the local strategic partnership. London: ODPM.

17

Exploiting the Benefits of World Heritage Listing: Evora, Portugal and Hoi An, Vietnam

Graham Brooks

Synopsis

Urban tourism is a well-known phenomenon in many historic towns and cities. Such places contribute strongly to a nation's cultural heritage identity and form a major component of the tourism resources of many countries around the world. This case study draws lessons from two very diverse places, Evora in Portugal and Hoi An in Vietnam. They are historic towns which are on the World Heritage List. Their sensitive development and successful long-term tourism management can inform planning of city spaces in other historic places.

World Heritage inscription usually brings increased tourism with both positive and negative impacts. Urban tourism can bring many benefits to a local economy but it can also disrupt the quality of life of the local inhabitants. If the social and physical nature of an historic town or city, including its urban spaces, is not well managed it may lose its attractiveness to visitors and suffer terminal decline as a tourism attraction.

Local politicians and city managers in Evora and Hoi An have cleverly exploited the inscription of their historic towns on the World Heritage List to successfully construct a holistic management model that has secured sustainable cultural heritage conservation, social development and urban tourism for their communities. Each has carefully developed the quality and character of their historic urban spaces to ensure that they attract visitors while remaining relevant to the contemporary life of the local people.

Both Evora and Hoi An have taken advantage of the increased international profile that comes with World Heritage inscription. They have captured external expertise and mobilized local community support to build a well-defined image of their town that guides development while ensuring that urban tourism provides a strong component of the local economy. In taking this route, many aspects of each town have been improved, a process that has benefited both the local people and visitors.

The author has personal experience of the urban spaces and tourist places in both towns. In 1997, he participated in an international seminar in Evora when the Organization of World Heritage Cities (OWHC) examined the issue of urban tourism. The symposium coincided with a workshop by the International Council on Monuments and Sites (ICOMOS), International Cultural Tourism Committee as part of the preparation of the ICOMOS International Cultural Tourism Charter. Between 1999 and 2002, he was a member of the international advisory group to the United Nations Educational, Scientific and Cultural Organization (UNESCO) in Bangkok that developed the so-called Lijiang Models for Cooperation among Stakeholders. Hoi An was one of nine historic cities throughout Asia that were examined as part of the process of identifying factors that could ensure local populations benefited from tourism activity. He visited Hoi An in 2003 and 2005.

Introduction

Historic towns and cities present a unique aspect in the overall nature of urban tourism, one that cannot be ignored given the huge increases in tourism to such places over recent decades. There are now over 200 historic towns and cities that are inscribed in the World Heritage List in recognition of their universal heritage values and distinctive cultural identities. They vary in nature from the old European centres such as Prague and Rome, former colonial centres such as Puebla in Mexico and Vigan in the Philippines, traditional settlements such as Djenne in Africa, to religious and pilgrimage places such as Kyoto in Japan, Santiago de Compostela in Spain and Kandy in Sri Lanka. Greatly increased tourism is an inevitable consequence of World Heritage Listing. It provides a boost to local pride and great opportunities to present the historic city to domestic and international visitors. Alternatively there is a substantial risk of negative outcomes arising from the imbalances of tourism congestion, loss of identity, loss of variety in local commercial and community services, and physical damage to heritage sites and monuments. It is often the direct presence of large numbers of visitors in the streets, plazas and squares of an historic centre, especially in peak seasons, that poses one of the greatest threats to the quality of life of local inhabitants.

In the September 1997, *Newsletter* of the OWHC, Mr Lakshman Ratnapala, President of the Pacific Asia Travel Association (PATA) commented that there was a symbiotic relationship between heritage and tourism one in which each enriches the other. He believes that it was important that not only tourists gain from experiencing heritage sites, but also that the local communities in the destinations being visited benefited from the development of tourism otherwise tourism would be meaningless.

There are a number of organizations that contribute to the coordination of the management of such cities, including the World Heritage Committee, the Organization of World Heritage Cities and the League of Historic Cities. The United Nations World Tourism Organization has actively cooperated with these organizations to identify and recommend ways to improve tourism management in historic cities. ICOMOS, the international professional organization that brings together those who work in the field of heritage conservation, and the ICOMOS International Cultural Tourism Committee also seek to develop best-practice models for managing the complex and dynamic relationships between tourism and historic urban ensembles.

While many historic cities have developed strategies and techniques for managing urban tourism, the experiences of two in particular, Evora in Portugal and Hoi An in Vietnam, provide an interesting perspective of how strong local leadership can embrace international recognition and support to ensure that urban tourism contributes to conservation of the cultural heritage, enhancement of urban spaces, improvement of livelihoods within local communities and a worthwhile tourism experience for visitors.

Two Distinctive Historic Towns

Evora, Portugal

The town of Evora is located 150 kilometres south east of Lisbon in the rich agricultural Alentejo plains. Originally established by the Romans to exploit not only wheat but also copper and iron mines, Evora was controlled by the Visigoths after 414 and the Moors between 713 and 1165, after which the town became an important centre of Portuguese political and religious life. It was chosen by the Jesuits as a seat of learning and hosted the courts of King Alfonso IV and Manuel 1 prior to 1511. In the 18th century, its influence waned when the University was forcefully closed with the expulsion of the Jesuits. Despite some conservation activity in the late 19th century, by the time of the Portuguese revolution in the mid-1970s, Evora was no more than a quiet rural town, much neglected in terms of its heritage and infrastructure.

The historic urban form of Evora is defined by encircling walls that effectively contain the historic town and form a distinctive separation from the surrounding modern neighbourhoods. Within the historic town the most prominent feature is without doubt the 2nd or 3rd century ruins of a Roman Temple dedicated to the Goddess Diana. Other attractive features are the 12th century Gothic Cathedral, a 15th century convent, several 15th century palaces, urban parks and the main square with its 16th century fountain. A dramatic 18-kilometre long

16th century aqueduct dominates the outskirts of the town. There are several museums, including the Museu de Évora, located in the former Bishop's Palace. Evora was inscribed on the World Heritage List in 1986 (United Nations Educational Scientific and Cultural Organisation, 2007). Its unique historic urban quality stems from the whitewashed houses decorated with *azulejos* and wrought-iron balconies dating from the 16th to the 18th century. Its monuments had a profound influence on Portuguese architecture in Brazil (Pictures 17.1 and 17.2).

Hoi An, Vietnam

Hoi An has become a special symbol for Vietnam. At its hiatus in the 17th and 18th centuries, it was an important river port for trade routes for the Cham Empire that stretched throughout South East Asia. Permanent Japanese and Chinese settlements existed and there is evidence that Dutch and other Europeans also frequented Hoi An. The deepest cultural impressions were, however, left by the Chinese.

The Old Quarter of Hoi An has been preserved in a manner that retained and upgraded many historic houses. More than 1000 privately

Picture 17.1 Historic centre of Evora

Picture 17.2 World Heritage symbol on an Evora bus

and collectively owned residential, commercial and community religious properties line its narrow streets. In addition to the architecture, many aspects of traditional life – food, festivals, occupations, crafts, religion – provide a strong, if less tangible traditional heritage and contemporary life. Hoi An was inscribed on the World Heritage List in 1999 (United Nations Educational Scientific and Cultural Organisation, 2007). The principal heritage values for which it was listed are that Hoi An is an out-standing material manifestation of the fusion of cultures over time in an international commercial port, and it is an exceptionally well-preserved example of a traditional Asian trading port (Pictures 17.3 and 17.4).

Evora: International Heritage Status Supports a Conceptual Framework for Development

When he delivered the Opening Address at the *4th International Symposium of the Organisation of World Heritage Cities*, in September 1997, Mr Abílio Dias Fernandes, the Mayor of Evora, spoke of the challenges and opportunities inherent in the positive and negative consequences of the tourism pressures that inevitably arise when

Picture 17.3 A back street in Hoi An

Picture 17.4 A café in Hoi An

an historic town or city attains World Heritage Listing. He spoke of the notion 'that sustainable tourism will provide for the harmonious coexistence of tourism and heritage, such that economic development is not allowed to proceed at the expense of fundamental values

347

and does not impede access to culture by the communities which have inherited it' (Fernandes, 1997: 3):

> *Thus, cultural tourism could in practice meet two different sets of needs: on the one hand the need for development, employment, and the improvement of quality of life, and on the other hand, the need for preserving the physical and environmental heritage and respect for the identities of the communities who produced it. Only in this way can tourism fulfil its cultural role and contribute towards attenuating differences, help promote peace and understanding, and reveal the multiplicity of forms and the perennial nature of the human condition.*

The future of Evora was deeply influenced by the social and political changes connected with the nation-wide Revolution of the Flowers on 25 April 1974 that led to the formation of a democratic system of local government. Two of the key challenges facing Evora were to meet the basic social and infrastructure needs of the people while capturing the potential for conservation and protection of the cultural heritage to constitute an important factor in promoting development.

The new Municipal Government in Evora inherited an extremely rich, if run-down urban heritage within the old city walls. However, it also inherited a growing suburban area outside the walls that was developing in a completely unplanned and unrestricted manner. Entire suburbs lacked public water supply, there was a serious housing shortage and a general lack of basic infrastructure and social facilities. The double-sided urban development strategy that emerged combined the retention, re-use and conservation of the urban architectural heritage of the city while at the same time carrying out a series of measures that met the most pressing social needs while imposing a carefully considered order on the urban development process. As a result, in the two decades since the mid-1970s, the City of Evora found a remarkable convergence and complementarity between urban heritage conservation and integrated development planning.

One of the key steps forward in this long-term strategy was to seek and obtain World Heritage Listing in 1986 for the historic town. The status of this international recognition gave the people of Evora a greater appreciation of their city and generated support for the Municipality's efforts to maintain and conserve the World Heritage character. It provided a strong conceptual basis for city planning whereby an overall cultural construct informed physical development, historic building conservation and new projects and improvements in the urban public spaces that gave the town its identity. Inscription on the World Heritage List also went some way to assist in raising funds and technical support both within Portugal and internationally. Detailed conservation and re-use projects for the urban fabric within the historic town proceeded at a similar pace with improvements in water supply and sewerage provision and the imposition of planning controls over the suburban spread outside the old walls. The City took a strong lead in controlling unregulated land speculation and real estate development while providing stimuli for private and cooperative housing development. Throughout there was a strong and continuous involvement of local citizens and interest groups to ensure that the planning process moved forward in a cooperative manner. In essence, improvements in the urban spaces and urban fabric took place simultaneously within the historic centre and throughout the surrounding suburbs.

The author during his attendance at the *1997 OWHC Symposium* observed local pride in the heritage status of the city in a number of ways: the World Heritage symbol adorned the sides of city buses; the Opening Ceremony for the Symposium, attended by the President of Portugal, was staged in the main square rather than within the closed confines of a conference centre; and the enthusiasm with which the local people joined in the subsequent concert, epitomized the depth of the relationship between the inhabitants of Evora and their cultural heritage. The historic centre of Evora continues to present a remarkable layering of urban spaces, parks and buildings that have been conserved and upgraded to form a large and complex venue for urban tourism.

Hoi An: International Best Practice Applied to Local Requirements

Hoi An was selected to join a major urban tourism project undertaken between 1999 and 2002 by the UNESCO Principal Regional Office for Asia and the Pacific, in Bangkok, with the generous support of the Norwegian World Heritage Office. The project was known as 'Lijiang Models for Cooperation among Stakeholders' (UNESCO Bangkok, 1999). The objective of the project was to open and structure avenues of communication between the tourism industry and those responsible for the conservation and maintenance of cultural heritage properties so as to form mutually beneficial alliances that would be both economically profitable and socially acceptable to local inhabitants and other stakeholders.

The project resulted in the development and implementation of site-specific strategies for historic towns. The model is complex and encompasses five phases: the identification of stakeholders; supporting fiscal management for heritage conservation, maintenance and development at the municipal level; fostering involvement and investment by the tourism industry in the sustainability of the culture, heritage resource base and supporting infrastructure; facilitating community education and skills training leading to employment in the heritage conservation and culture tourism sector, with emphasis on opportunities for women and youth; and encouraging consensus building (conflict resolution) among tourism promoters, Government agencies, property developers, local residents and heritage conservationists (UNESCO Bangkok, 1999) (see Diagram 17.1).

In particular, the models were applied to eight historic towns and cities in Asia, including Bhaktapur, Nepal; Lijiang, China; Levuka, Fiji; Kandy, Sri Lanka; Luang Prabang, Laos; Melaka, Malaysia; Vigan, Philippines; and Hoi An, Vietnam. Many of these towns, including Hoi An, are inscribed on the World Heritage List. The author was a participant in this project.

In the case of Hoi An, two critical issues were identified during the UNESCO project. The first was to spread the income derived from tourism away from the famous riverside marketplace and into other sections of the historic town. Secondly, there was a need to develop long-term sustainable mechanisms to enhance the livelihood of local people while conserving and presenting the unique and multi-layered cultural heritage of the place to the outside world. The project took place at a time when Hoi An, along with much of Vietnam, was just emerging on the international tourism stage. There was a great need expressed within the local community to capture tourism spending and direct it towards economic development.

Three priority areas, of relevance to this case study, were identified: income redistribution, promotion of Hoi An as an historic town and access to external funding.

Income Redistribution

Modern Hoi An reflected its traditional role as a river port. Most of the commercial activity and tourism interest was confined to Tran Phu Street, which runs along the riverfront and contains the local markets. Not only did this cause excessive congestion among both local people and visitors, but also there was a great difference in income between

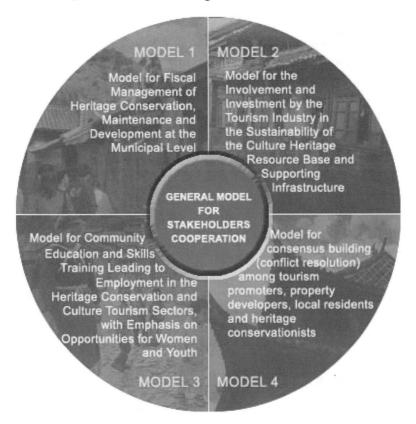

Diagram 17.1 Lijiang Model for Cooperation

those who lived or owned property in this street and those in the streets behind. Tourism-related shops and cafes were tending to locate directly on Tran Phu Street.

The action plan stressed the need to encourage tourism activity on the second and third streets in the historic town, thus spreading activity away from its concentration on the riverfront. A series of proposals was developed including upgrading the condition of the streets, especially Nguyen Thai Hoc Street, improvements in many of the commercial and residential buildings, closing the streets to traffic, conserving the historic community buildings such as temples and meeting halls, encouraging and facilitating commercial re-use of secondary buildings, and the provision of incentives for businesses to move to the additional streets.

Promotion of Hoi An as an Historic Town

Despite its inscription on the World Heritage List, Hoi An was relatively less well known internationally than other places in Vietnam, such as Hanoi, Ha Long Bay, Hue, Da Nang and Ho Chi Minh City (Saigon). For those visitors who did come to Hoi An, there was a strong need for them to be informed of the many sites within the old centre of the town so that they would explore further afield than just the riverside markets.

A combination project was developed including creation of web sites to raise the international profile and a 'Hoi An Passport' system to let visitors know about more places within the township. The 'Passport' provided a common entry ticket system for many of the historic buildings and museums throughout the town. Visitors to any of these attractions would buy a single ticket that gave access to all of the places that were open for inspection. This simple mechanism provided information about other attractions while encouraging visitors to stay longer in the town and consequently spend more money on local goods and tourism services.

Access to external funding

The initial thinking of the local authorities was to approach external aid or cultural heritage agencies to provide grant funding for the conservation of over 1000 somewhat dilapidated historic properties within the town that they had identified as requiring urgent attention. However, through the process of the UNESCO project Hoi An city officials realized that the 'Passport' idea could provide a sustainable local source of funding for conservation projects within the historic town.

As tourism activity in Hoi An rose, so did the income generated by the 'Passport' tickets that visitors were increasingly encouraged to purchase. Income from ticket sales is distributed to provide organizational and promotional support for individual historic attractions within the town, and to fund the actual conservation of additional buildings or historic places, thus expanding the overall heritage and tourism resources of the town. A relatively minor proportion of the income is directed towards administration, which is the responsibility of the local authorities.

The author visited Hoi An in 2003 and again in 2005. Each time there were clear indications of the success of the actions developed by the local authorities in response to the international project initiated by UNESCO in Bangkok. The centre of Hoi An is now a lively historic town, with many local people employed in relatively recently established businesses manufacturing and selling local merchandise to visitors. Tourists move easily through a number of streets that were formerly unattractive, visiting museums and historic houses, shopping and enjoying local cuisine in cafes and restaurants. Virtually all of the historic buildings, including local community buildings such as temples and meeting houses, in these formerly quiet streets have been upgraded and there are active social programmes to enhance the livelihood of local residents.

Lessons for Practice in Precinct Marketing

Inscription on the World Heritage List inevitably raises the international profile of an historic town and results in an increased tourism profile. Evora and Hoi An cleverly exploited the status, recognition and support received from inscription on the World Heritage List to improve urban tourism management, develop a sustainable long-term framework for the conservation of their cultural heritage and enhance the livelihoods of the local inhabitants. Evora has used this status to promote itself as a tourism destination. Hoi An has become a major tourism attraction in central Vietnam.

Through the support of the UNESCO and the Lijiang Models for Cooperation project Hoi An was able to make the necessary improvements to the back streets of the historic area and to identify ways in which to leverage funding that would assist in the marketing of Hoi An.

Conclusion

The case studies presented here have a high degree of relevance to the subject of urban tourism precincts, given that there are some 200 historic towns and cities on the World Heritage List and many hundreds of other historic cities throughout the world that are attractive venues for urban tourism. Evora and Hoi An are uniquely different and required different sets of strategies to conserve their historic centres and districts. What worked in one region may be inappropriate or impractical for the other. Safeguarding these places has relied upon politics, resources, economics, community interest, laws, administrations and the support of international agencies. What is universally important is the need to preserve the everyday culture, as well as the precious physical fabric. *Urban conservation* implies *cultural conservation*, which means that the characteristics of the existing population and its cultures should also be valued and preserved.

Discussion Questions and Exercises

(1) If you were asked to visit a heritage precinct and identify examples of best practice, what would be the key indicators that you would look for as a basis for making your judgements?

(2) Go to the website http://www.unescobkk.org/index.php?id=474 where you will find the World Heritage Centre's Lijiang Models for Cooperation among Stakeholders. Review the four phases of the model and discuss whether the model would be applicable to other urban destinations not just those of an historic focus.

(3) Having reviewed the Lijiang Models for Cooperation among Stakeholders could this model be considered as over-planning? Discuss why or why not.

(4) Evora is a walled city that is distinctive from other modern developments that surround it. Identify and discuss some of the complex planning issues that would confront urban planning agencies as they seek to balance the old with the new.

(5) The author stated that 'What worked in one region may be inappropriate or impractical for the other'. Supplement the information provided in this chapter with an Internet search of both Hoi An and Evora. Identify the key attributes and contextual elements of both historic cities that would require different planning and management strategies.

(6) World Heritage Listing offers a clear and recognizable brand with an international profile. Choose an urban destination in your country or a country of your choice that has World Heritage Listing. Identify the characteristics that make the site unique. How has this city leveraged the 'World Heritage' brand?

References

Fernandes, A.D. (1997). Introduction to the *4th International Symposium of World Heritage Cities*. Paper presented at the *4th International Symposium of World Heritage Cities*, 17–20, 1997 September, Evora, Portugal.

UNESCO Bangkok (1999). *Cultural Heritage Management and Tourism: Models for Co-operation among Stakeholders*. Retrieved 28 August 2007, from http://www.unescobkk.org/index.php?id=474

United Nations Educational Scientific and Cultural Organisation (2007). *World Heritage List*. Retrieved 28 August 2007, from http://whc.unesco.org/en/list/

IV

Lessons for Theory and Practice

18

City Spaces – Tourist Places: A Reprise

Bruce Hayllar, Tony Griffin and Deborah Edwards

Introduction

The framework for this book was designed around a series of questions we raised in Chapter 1. These questions arose from two sources: our observations and experience of cities, and our inquisitiveness as researchers. Like the other contributors, we had questions about tourism and tourists in cities for which we were seeking, if not the answers, then at least some more insights and clarity. It is appropriate therefore to revisit those questions and to examine the extent to which we have effectively engaged with them.

In thinking about our questions, which were somewhat random at the time, they seem to reflect four central themes in the study of urban tourism precincts: the relationships between visitors and their host communities; the interaction and experience of tourists within these developed settings; the complexities of development, design and management processes and challenges; and the benefits and costs of precinct development to the broad community of stakeholders.

While seeking answers to these questions is important, it is equally appropriate to determine the questions that remain unanswered and to consider what research lies ahead. This chapter then is about looking back, to the known, and looking forward, to the unknown, and the subsequent questions that might guide future research.

Tourists and Locals

The relationship between tourists and locals is often portrayed as one bound by mutual antipathy. Accounts of tourists descending on seaside resorts in Spain, the Greek Islands or on the Australian Gold Coast convey images of populations under 'siege' from tourists (Archer et al., 2005). In these scenarios, the local culture is subsumed by the needs of tourists, and another form of serial reproduction of space and experience evolves – primarily to the detriment of the local population. In these resort areas and other 'high impact' tourist sites around the world, the effects of tourism may be quite profound – socially, culturally, environmentally and economically. This is particularly the case where a locality's 'old' economy is replaced – with its concomitant dislocation of work and traditional social networks – by the 'new' economy of tourism.

However, in the context of city spaces, while there are examples of antagonism between tourists and locals, their relationship is typically more symbiotic. Large cities have an economic and social character of their own which is primarily driven by the commercial exigencies of the city and its hinterland. While tourism's role in the local economy will vary depending on the size and scale of tourist activity relative to the city, tourism typically represents just one of many dimensions within a city's multifaceted economic and social fabric. Given this relationship of variable interdependence, what has this book contributed to our understanding of these relationships?

The arguments put forward by Maitland and Newman (Chapter 11) challenges some of the conventional wisdom surrounding tourist–visitor relationships. As city spaces have increasingly become sites for consumption, a type of new urban resident has emerged whose tastes, desires and culture are not too far removed from those of the experience seeking city tourist. Thus, Maitland and Newman argue that many of the services and facilities of consumption developed for the new city dwellers mirror those demanded by tourists.

In a similar fashion, the gentrification of spaces in older areas of a city creates the very aesthetic sought by the tourist. Importantly, however, Maitland and Newman argue beyond the creation of space and the aesthetic, and move our understanding towards the experience of visitors and locals within these settings. Their research revealed that a type of mutual conviviality takes shape where everyday spaces are shared and consumed. Theoretically, this sharing of space and cultural capital fundamentally repositions the traditional visitor–host relationship. Thus, the relationship moves from one being marked as the 'other', towards a form of mutual reconciliation. As Maitland and Newman note: 'If the city is an object of desire for residents and visitors, then non-residents who invest cultural value or support consumption advantages are associated with the prestige of the city and have a stake in its future'. Thus, in some respects the urban precinct becomes a new type of 'commons', a locality for shared and mutual interaction.

Both Griffin, Hayllar and Edwards (Chapter 3) and Maitland and Newman (Chapter 11) highlight the importance of precincts as interactive spaces within a context of 'authentic' engagement with residents of the city. This engagement takes many forms, such as the observation of freshly washed shirts airing on a clothesline in The Rocks, through to watching school children and their teachers negotiating the precinct's pedestrian traffic on their way to the Sydney Opera House; or looking at friendship groups form briefly and then disperse as they move off to work or school on the fringes of Federation Square in Melbourne. The less well-travelled precincts on the fringes of central London, which are discussed by Maitland and Newman, also provide 'authentic' experiences where visitors can momentarily connect with the cultural life and residents of the city. In both these examples, space and relationships are not contested. It is through these parallel engagements that city spaces become imbued with meaning (after Tuan, 1977).

Precincts also have a role in diluting potential visitor–host conflicts. Kelly (Chapter 6) discussed the outcome of poor internal flow patterns within precincts where locals and visitors compete for shared space. While precinct design can assist to ameliorate this congestion, other 'organic' forms of precinct development also contribute by moving visitors away from precinct hubs towards less well-defined areas. If the well-known relatively intensely developed city precinct is the home of the *Sampler* and *Browser*, the organic precinct is the domain of the *Explorer* (Chapter 3). If the developed city precinct is concerned with 'experience compression' – clustering attractions in recognizable and definable spaces – then the organic is concerned with 'experience expansion' where the tourist *gestalt* shapes, connects and makes linkages through and across city spaces. Such diffusion has the potential to draw visitors away from developed sites with its commensurate impact upon congestion and, more importantly, providing for a different form of non-contested interaction.

Taken together, the contributions here provide some fresh insights into conventional perceptions of the relationships between visitors and their host communities – these relationships are not fixed, unidirectional or necessarily adversarial. On the contrary, they are decidedly labile.

Precinct Design and Experience

Krolikowski and Brown (Chapter 7) point out that, 'precincts are defined by their particular patterns of architectural design, layout, attractions, and the overall configuration of the physical elements that help to forge a particular sense of place'.

The extent to which visitors experience the sense of place described by Krolikowski and Brown is problematic. Arguably historic precincts have an advantage. In many cases, they have a unique architectural and social fabric which sets them apart from the rest of the city. In the case of 'cities as precinct', such as Evora in Portugal (Chapter 17), the city as a whole is set apart. Indeed, the act of preservation is in itself a signal to tourists of the historic precinct's intrinsic 'worthiness'. Within these precincts Urry's (1990) 'romantic' gaze is played out.

By way of contrast, festival marketplaces typified by Navy Pier (Chapter 2), Harborplace (Chapter 10) and Darling Harbour (Chapter 14) are often viewed pejoratively because they are perceived as commercial manifestations of global capital and serial reproduction (see Stevenson, 2003). As a logical corollary, they are the counterpoint of the historic or organically developed precinct – they are placeless. In Urry's (1990) dichotomy, these are spaces for the 'collective gaze'.

Somewhere between these two archetypal precincts and their attendant architectural forms are a range of other precincts with their particular legacies of design, configuration, levels of preservation and development strategies. Together these precincts perform a range of functions (Chapter 3) yet probably differ in the extent to which they provide the sense of place noted by Krolikowski and Brown.

What we would argue is that 'place' is more than the bounded physical manifestation of a precinct and its agglomeration of attractions and services. Rather, place is more about how we emotionally engage with the physical dimensions and how we experience and determine the contingent meanings of these spaces. As was noted in Chapter 3, the tourist is not simply seeking connection to the physical place they are in, but rather arriving 'at the mental place where they desire to be! The physical place, the precinct, needs to facilitate that by generating an appropriate atmosphere or providing certain opportunities for the tourist'.

These arguments are not a refutation of the importance of the physical form because it does impact upon us psychologically (Carmona et al., 2003) and might encourage or discourage our engagement with the space. However, what we have argued in Chapter 3 and in Selby, Hayllar and Griffin (Chapter 9) is that our engagement with space is an interpretive, interactive and ultimately dynamic dialectic relationship. This relationship is shaped through our interactions with both the physical and essentially human dimensions of the space.

The physical design of a precinct is therefore one vehicle for this psychological engagement. Through their interactions, visitors seek out and determine their own meanings, irrespective of the given interpretations and expectations of planners and developers. Visitors' responses and interpretations are also occasionally at odds with critical public commentary, including that from academics. Darling Harbour, for example, received ongoing media criticism in respect of its physical design, architecture, attractiveness as a destination and its connection to the surrounding city (see Searle, Chapter 10, and Edwards et al., Chapter 14). Yet, in spite of this critical commentary it is a space with almost universal appeal to visitors and locals (Chapter 14).

The discussion so far has been 'generalized' to all tourists. However, Darcy and Small (Chapter 4) point to debates around the gendered (sexualized) consumption of space and time. Similarly, they demonstrate that urban destination accessibility can be a significant constraint to the travel experiences of people with a disability.

Overall, the contributors confirm the relationship between form and experience. However, more importantly, they draw attention to the interactive and interpretive nature of this relationship.

Development and Management of Urban Precincts

In thinking through the questions we posed about the management and development of precincts, it is apparent from the contributions that there is no one best-practice development, planning or management model. To some extent it would have been a valuable outcome of the book if such a model were to be created! However, what the case studies and examples sprinkled throughout the book reveal is that the world is rarely linear or orderly. Indeed, the conceptual model for precinct development outlined in Chapter 5 unintentionally draws attention to this potential for 'disorder'. While presented in a linear fashion, the model posits a number of internal and external forces and relationships that have the potential to impact upon development and management processes – from the diverse possibilities presented by the urban destination context through to the potentially volatile mixture of competing governance, public policy and needs of political stakeholders.

The evolutionary nature of these various processes is highlighted in Chapter 2. Plaka in Athens exemplifies the impact of the changing social and economic nature of an area and how government intervened in an effort to retain vestiges of its highly valued material quality. Plaka had grown somewhat haphazardly in response to a variety of influences: commercial forces reshaped the population mix, from working class to predominantly middle class; non-regulated construction threatened the area's physical fabric; and new uses (such as nightclubs) fundamentally changed the visitor mix, and indeed its reputation.

In circumstances such as those experienced in Plaka, where apparently unfettered commercial forces overwhelm an area to the perceived detriment of its resident population, and quality of the experience for its visitors, some form of government intervention is perhaps inevitable. In the case of Plaka and precincts with similar qualities, the arguments for public intervention are more compelling when the precinct has physical attributes that are either limited or unique or where they have significance beyond the boundaries of the precinct itself – for example *Cadman's Cottage* in The Rocks (Australia's oldest remaining intact building), the *Tower of the Winds* in Plaka (dating back to 1st century AD) or the historic buildings of *Albert Dock* in Liverpool (containing the world's first hydraulic lift).

Governments also tend to be more interventionist where the development of a precinct is part of a broader economic and/or social strategy. Such intervention, for example, was evident in the *Sheffield City Centre* project (Chapter 16), London's '*South Bank*' development (Chapter 15), Chicago's *Navy Pier* (Chapter 2) and Melbourne's *Southbank* (Chapter 10).

The contributions in this book also highlight the varying forms of government intervention. For example, government instrumentalities may act in the role of a conventional planning authority to determine an appropriate land-use mix, establish development standards and building codes, and regulate private development activity. Alternatively, they may assume the role of an all-powerful developer and override existing local regulations in the interest of a regional or national agenda. Searle (Chapter 10) makes particular note of the wide powers given to city-backed corporations in the development of the tourism precincts in Baltimore and Boston. In a similar way, Edwards, Griffin and Hayllar (Chapter 14) note the all encompassing power of the Darling Harbour Authority in the development of that precinct.

There has also been an increasing trend for government agencies to develop commercial partnerships. For commercial investors, these partnerships are particularly attractive for sites where former public infrastructure has become derelict while the value of the land has continued to grow – particularly in areas adjacent to the water and/or city centre. In these cases, governments control the basic resource while it's 'partners' try to maximize their investment through commercial activities such as high-density housing and/or leisure and tourist infrastructure. The private–public partnership (PPP) discussed by Darcy and Small (Chapter 4) is an exemplar of this form of government/commercial arrangement.

The potential for conflict in commercial and public sector relationships is ever present as their goals are potentially antagonistic – particularly in heritage precincts or where there is strong local identification with an area. In such precincts there is an implicit requirement to both maintain the intrinsic qualities of the site while at the same time sustaining commercial profitability. The contrast drawn by Spirou on the development of the *Albert Dock* and *Navy Pier* (Chapter 2) underline the evolutionary interplay between public and commercial interests.

The management of precincts presents an equally mixed approach to that outlined above in respect of development. In some cases, such as the Sydney Harbour Foreshore Authority, the statutory body has an all-encompassing role as landowner, developer and landlord (Chapter 14). This arrangement is similar to Groningen's *Grote Markt* (Chapter 13) where its management (and development) has been centrally controlled through the city government.

Ashworth (Chapter 13) also draws attention to considerations of the historical context associated with management practices and, in particular, the public acceptance of the interventionist role of the state, particularly in the period since the Second World War.

The above examples notwithstanding, management arrangements are often multi-layered and multi-sectoral as in the case of Sheffield's *Heart of the City* project (Chapter 16) or London's *South Bank* (Chapter 15). Moreover, such complex management arrangements are likely to become increasingly common as new tourism precincts emerge more organically from processes such as gentrification and broader exploration of cities by tourists, as exemplified in Chapter 11.

Taken together, the contributions here emphasize the diverse nature of the planning and management practices associated with precincts. While precincts typically have a strong commercial overlay, the central role of government in creating and managing space (either with a 'light touch' or 'heavy hand') is a common integrating theme of their development and management.

Benefits and Costs of Precinct Development

The final theme concerns the benefits and costs of precinct development. In thinking through these questions we have examined them from three perspectives: the physical and aesthetic, economic, and social. However, it should be noted that while we have separated the discussion on costs and benefits into three groups for the purposes of analysis, in practice they are inherently interconnected, and their relationship dynamic.

Physical and Aesthetic Benefits and Costs

By their very existence in the public domain, urban precincts have some form of physical impact. Some of the impacts that are typically identified as negative include but are not limited to the following:

- destruction of historic buildings and urban landscapes;
- modification of tidal flows through waterfront development;
- reconfiguration of city streetscapes and typical pedestrian flows;
- degraded visual amenity;
- inappropriate and/or overdevelopment of specific sites; and
- loss of architectural identity and integrity.

As a counterpoint to the above, more positive impacts include:

- the conservation of historic buildings and sites;
- the creation of new and innovative public spaces;
- regeneration of derelict buildings and open space;

367

- improved visual amenity;
- the clean-up of contaminated industrial sites;
- displays of contemporary art and sculpture in the public realm; and
- the dismantling or refurbishment of the industrial landscape.

As can be seen, the development of urban precincts has the potential to both improve and diminish the urban environment. The potential for physical or aesthetic impact is typically most marked in those situations where a proposed development will lead to a fundamental shift in the commercial use of a given space. Under these conditions, the need to adapt infrastructure from a purpose-built past to more contemporary roles has the potential to create conflict between competing values as to how an area should 'look' and 'feel'. This is particularly potent where there is a clear 'historic landscape' to preserve such as in *Evora*, *Plaka*, *The Rocks*, *Albert Dock*, *Covent Garden* or the *Grote Markt*.

In other developments, while there may be a fundamental shift in commercial purpose, change to the visual landscape is less contentious. Before its makeover, *Honeysuckle* (Chapter 4) was an eclectic and somewhat claptrap mix of 19th and 20th century port buildings housing maritime support industries, light manufacturing and substantial wool and textile storage areas. The demolition of all but a small number of architecturally meritorious buildings took place with little public dissent.

Nevertheless, public debates around the processes of change are complex and problematic, as Searle has indicated in Chapter 10. As a critical review of the case studies and other examples reveals, decisions to change or modify the urban 'landscape' are not made in the idle vacuum of architectural tradition or idiosyncrasy but rather in the vortex of competing economic and social interests.

Economic Benefits and Costs

The call to develop tourism precincts typically arises as a response to, or a need for, change. These changes might be in response to growing rates of visitation to a destination and the need to manage visitor movements more effectively (e.g. see Chapter 6). The imperative to change is often created by shifts in the economic fortunes of a substantial community, city or region; numerous cases such as Albert Dock in Liverpool (Chapter 2) and Sheffield City Centre (Chapter 16) exemplify this. Similarly, precincts may develop in response to the economics of technological change. Changes in shipping technology and methods of cargo handling have in many urban ports led to the demise of existing waterfront practices and the rise of the festival marketplace.

Ritchie (Chapter 8) identifies key economic drivers and benefits of precinct development including:

■ development of new facilities;
■ increased levels of employment;
■ increased levels of tourist activity;
■ construction and management of flagship attractions;
■ the development of agglomeration economies;
■ spillover effects of aesthetic improvements on neighbouring areas;
■ enhanced urban infrastructure, including transport; and the
■ rejuvenation of economically depressed local economies.

While there is somewhat of an economic aura surrounding the development of precincts, there may also be a substantial downside, with possible negative effects including:

■ the concentration of facilities and services in one site drawing resources away from other parts of the city;
■ the uneven distribution of benefits within a community;
■ increases in prices of products serving both local and tourist markets;
■ increased land and housing prices, contributing to change in the socioeconomic mix of urban communities; and
■ the dislocation of local communities.

A particularly challenging task is to assess and measure the ongoing economic benefits of precincts, especially in instances where substantial amounts of investment are periodically required to rejuvenate them. Ritchie notes that there are very few long-term studies of the economic benefits of precincts and even less on those that have failed! Thus, while we better understand the 'precinct economy', some important questions remain unanswered.

Social Benefits and Costs

Research into understanding the social benefits and costs of precinct development is a relatively recent activity. The focus has predominantly been on understanding the physical structure of precincts (the traditional geographical approach) and the economic consequences of such development. An inference from the latter set of studies was that social benefits would accrue as the 'natural' corollary of increased economic activity. The issue of whether there was a social downside to all this was rarely addressed. Some studies, e.g. Pearce (1998), did consider how the intensification of tourism activities in precincts did cause disruption to local communities and consequently required corrective management action, but rarely have such issues been pursued in depth.

In the course of the discussions and questions raised by authors throughout the book, we have at least made some progress towards better understanding these benefits and costs. Searle (Chapter 10) points to the differential costs and benefits to community groups. Using Brisbane's South Bank and London's Covent Garden as examples, he contrasts the relative impotence of the local Brisbane residents (predominantly low-income migrant groups) with the largely middle-class communities organizing opposition in London. In Brisbane, residents were displaced (with inadequate compensation) and those who remained had to contend with a fractured social fabric and decreased public amenity in terms of traffic and noise. However, further down the development cycle, and with the support of professional architects and planners, the proposed 'international' style was resisted in favour of a more inclusive city and regionally oriented development. As a consequence, residents received community benefit in the long term. In London, residents defeated the initially proposed large-scale development in favour of a more modest development concept which emphasized sensitive renewal and the maintenance of existing communities.

These two cases exemplify the potential benefits and costs to communities. Benefits include:

- increased public amenity;
- employment opportunities;
- new services and facilities;
- new community formations;
- increased diversity in the economic and social mix of a community; and the
- empowerment of local communities.

Some of the social costs of development can be identified as:

- fractured and disenfranchised local communities;
- increased rents which drive out 'old' residents;
- congestion and inconvenience for local residents;
- loss of former community spaces and places; and
- loss of local identification with places that are 'invaded' by tourists, and consequent reduction in the sense of belonging to the community.

Tyler and Morad (Chapter 15) outline a process that evolved in London's South Bank to both overcome the social costs and maximize the benefits to all stakeholders. As occurred in Covent Garden, this process was shaped by a professional coalition. Similarly, Holmes and Beebeejaun's case study (Chapter 16) points to issues of leadership. Brooks (Chapter 17) demonstrated that an international agency can provide much needed guidance and support for historic cities that wish to retain their architectural heritage and culture.

The potential benefits of precinct development to a community are substantial, as are the potential costs. The challenge is to better understand processes of inclusive practice that legitimate both the role of local communities and the engagement of professionals in the planning and development of public spaces. The Lijiang Models for Cooperation among Stakeholders (presented in Chapter 17) was successful in bringing together various stakeholders and agencies in such a way as to create mutually beneficial alliances.

Certainly, precinct planners need to understand that tourism has the potential to threaten local residents' quality of life. Hence, planning must attempt to anticipate and mitigate such undesirable impacts before they arise. However, given the uncertainties of correctly anticipating future outcomes, precinct managers must monitor community reactions to tourism as a precinct develops, and be prepared to respond to emerging problems. More broadly, planners and policy makers must recognize that the development of tourism precincts may not only impact on the existing community but also alter the nature and composition of that community. Judgements need to be made about the social desirability of such changes.

Looking Forward

Predicting the future with any certainty is problematic (see Veal 2002). The best predictor, at least in the medium term, is to plot existing trends and to make judgements on the expectations of them continuing. An examination of urban tourism precincts would suggest a continuing, and probably expanding, role given their centrality to city-based cultures of consumption. The middle class is moving back to the cities (Chapter 11) and tourism of the urbane is growing. Precincts provide 'experience compression' for time-poor tourists: for many they are an experience hypermarket where engagement with a city's culture, architecture, aesthetic and contrived attractions are all possible within the confines of a small area, thereby enabling the visitor to extract maximum value from their constrained time.

On balance, it is likely that the urban tourism precinct is a phenomenon with a future. As researchers of cities it is therefore incumbent upon us to put forward some ideas of where future research might be directed. Based on the discussions within this book, we would argue that this research needs to focus around four essential themes:

(1) The expectations, experience and behaviour of tourists within precincts.
(2) The impacts of tourist activity on key stakeholders, economically, socially and culturally, with an emphasis on the long-term consequences of precinct development.

(3) The design, planning, management and marketing of precincts in response to the above, particularly with regard to reconciling the interests of tourist with those of other stakeholders.

(4) The relationships and interactions between the built environment (design, planning and management) and the expectations, experience and behaviour of visitors (both tourists and locals).

Specific research questions that emerge from this book include:

- How do we determine, and plan for, the specific functions that a precinct performs in shaping the experience of the visitor?
- What strategies might be used to ameliorate conflict between stakeholders in times of change?
- How can local 'voices' and perspectives be more effectively captured in planning and management processes?
- How do we ensure that precincts provide opportunities for experiences that match the needs of tourists and locals?
- In what ways do precincts and other attractions within a city 'work together' to create an overall tourist experience?
- What are the long-term economic benefits (or costs) of tourism precinct development?
- How might we better understand the processes, opportunities or behaviours that stimulate the organic development of precincts?
- What role can urban destination marketers play in stimulating the emergence and growth of new tourism precincts?
- What factors lead to the decline or failure of tourism precincts?
- What are the success factors for sustainable precinct enterprises?

The answers to these questions, and the many others that run through your mind as you apply your own intellectual perspective to the material, have both theoretical and professional resonance. These resonances are not simply about ideas and applications. More importantly they are about the quality of experience in a city – a quality that is shaped and sustained through the interactions of individuals and groups with the physical, economic, cultural and social fabric of the city. If visitors are to engage with a city, and indeed return to a city, then their experiences within precincts must be of consequence. They should not simply enter a space within a city; but a place imbued with meaning.

References

Archer, B., Cooper, C. & Ruhanen, L. (2005). The positive and negative impacts of tourism. In W.F. Theobald (Ed.), *Global Tourism* (3rd edn, pp. 79–102). Burlington, MA: Elsevier.

Carmona, M., Heath, T., Taner, Oc., & Tiesdell, S. (2003). *Public Places, Urban Spaces: The Dimensions of Urban Design.* Oxford: Architectural Press.

Pearce, D.G. (1998). Tourist districts in Paris: structure and functions. *Tourism Management*, 19(1), 49–66.

Stevenson, D. (2003). *Cities and Urban Cultures.* Maidenhead: Open University Press.

Tuan, Y.F. (1977). *Space and Place: The Perspective of Experience.* Minneapolis: University of Minnesota Press.

Urry, J. (1990). *The Tourist Gaze.* London: Sage.

Veal, A.J. (2002). Leisure and Tourism Policy and Planning (2nd edn). Wallingford, Oxon: CABI.

Index